IMAGINING INDIA

Also by Richard Cronin

SHELLEY'S POETIC THOUGHT
COLOUR AND EXPERIENCE IN NINETEENTH-CENTURY
POETRY

Imagining India

Richard Cronin
Lecturer in English
University of Glasgow

St. Martin's Press   New York

First published in the United States of America in 1989

Printed in the People's Republic of China

ISBN 0–312–03539–X

Library of Congress Cataloging-in-Publication Data
Cronin, Richard.
Imagining India/Richard Cronin.
p. cm.
Bibliography: p.
Includes index.
ISBN 0–312–03539–X
1. English fiction—20th century—History and criticism. 2. India
fiction (English)—History and criticism. 3. Anglo-Indian fiction–
–History and criticism. 4. India—Biography—History and criticism.
5. India in literature. I. Title.
PR888.I6C76 1989
823—dc20   89–34298
                                                             CIP

To Arun and Maya

'How can the mind take hold of such a country?'

'Half-closing his eyes he attempted to love India.'

Contents

Note on the Texts

Quotations have been drawn from the following editions.

Nirad Chaudhuri, *The Autobiography of an Unknown Indian* (Macmillan, 1951).

Anita Desai, *Clear Light of Day* (Penguin, 1980).

___ *Fire on the Mountain* (Penguin, 1981).

___ *Games at Twilight and Other Stories* (Penguin, 1982).

___ *In Custody* (Penguin, 1985).

___ *The Village by the Sea* (Penguin, 1985).

E.M. Forster, *A Passage to India* (Penguin, 1979).

___ *The Hill of Devi* (Penguin, 1983).

Mahatama Gandhi, *An Autobiography The Story of My Experiments with Truth*, translated by Mahadev Desai (Phoenix Press, 1949).

Ruth Prawer Jhabvala, *Heat and Dust* (Futura, 1976).

___ *A Backward Place* (Penguin, 1980).

___ *Esmond in India* (Penguin, 1980).

___ *The Householder* (Penguin, 1980).

___ *Get Ready for Battle* (Penguin, 1981).

___ *How I Became a Holy Mother and Other Stories* (Penguin, 1981).

___ *A Stronger Climate* (Granada, 1983).

___ *In Search of Love and Beauty* (Penguin, 1984).

M.M. Kaye, *The Far Pavilions* (Penguin, 1979).

Balraj Khanna, *Nation of Fools* (Penguin, 1985).

Rudyard Kipling, *Kim* (Macmillan, 1927).

Ved Mehta, *Face to Face* (Collins, 1958).

___ *Daddyji and Mamaji* (Pan, 1984).

___ *Vedi* (Pan, 1985).

___ *The Ledge Between the Streams* (Pan, 1986).

___ *Sound-Shadows of the New World* (Pan, 1987).

V.S. Naipaul, *An Area of Darkness* (Andre Deutsch, 1964).

R.K. Narayan, *The Man-Eater of Malgudi* (Heinemann, 1961).

___ *My Days* (Heinemann, 1975).

___ *The Painter of Signs* (Heinemann, 1977).

___ *Waiting for the Mahatma* (Heinemann, 1977).

___ *The Bachelor of Arts* (Heinemann, 1978).

___ *Swami and Friends* (Heinemann, 1978).

___ *Mr Sampath, The Printer of Malgudi* (Heinemann, 1979).

___ *The Guide* (Heinemann, 1980).

_____ *The Vendor of Sweets* (Heinemann, 1980).
Jawaharlal Nehru, *An Autobiography* (John Lane The Bodley Head, 1942).
Salman Rushdie, *Midnight's Children* (Jonathan Cape, 1981).
Paul Scott, *The Raj Quartet* (Heinemann, 1976).
_____ *Staying On* (Granada, 1978).
Paramahansa Yogananda (born Makunda Lal Ghosh): *Autobiography of a Yogi* (The Self-Realization Fellowship, Los Angeles, 1971).

Introduction

I had taken a cycle rickshaw at Agra station. For one rupee it would take me to the Taj Mahal, for two rupees it was mine all day. It was late morning and very hot, but it was more than the heat that made me wretched. The rickshaw wallah's thin, straining calves kept me in mind all the way of the brutal simplicities of my bargain – so many coins for so much sweat. I crouched miserably forwards, intent on making the seat as uncomfortable as posible, humiliated by my inactivity, a victim, and not for the first time, of the disease to which Western visitors to India quickly succumb, liberal squeamishness, a futile complaint suffered by those whose moral qualms are unredeemed by moral courage. We passed an awful painted statue of Gandhi. The rickshaw wallah turned and said, 'That is the statue of one of our great kings long ago.' This was in 1970. The man looked to be in his thirties. He must have been ten at least when Gandhi died. Why was he saying this? Was it possible that he lived in a world in which there was no difference between 1948 and the Ashokan empire, where everything that was past was past, and the past was long ago? Or was he making fun of me? And if so, did he really think that I would not recognise Gandhi? Or was his wit subtler? Indians lack a sense of history, white men believe, and perhaps it amused him to offer so egregious a confirmation of their opinion. Or was his remark just a free gift that he offered to tourists – for one rupee a ride to the Taj Mahal, and at no extra cost an anecdote to take home with you? Perhaps he knew from experience that the remark was worth the trouble of making, that it tended to double his tip?

I could not tell. I did not know whether I was being pedalled through Agra by someone who lacked a Western sense of time, by a truculent nationalist, by a harmless exponent of whimsy, or by an experienced tradesman. I only knew that I was a foreigner, and that India was a strange country.

Although my private circumstances have made India important to me, I do not know the country well. I cannot speak any Indian language. I have visited India just twice – the first visit lasted a year, the second only a few weeks. What I brought back were colours, smells, tastes, a memory rapidly dimming of the disturbing assault that India makes on the senses of those who are

1

habituated to a more muted experience, and a handful of anecdotes, each of which in the telling deadens into opacity.

India was a text that I was unable to unravel, a book that I could
not read, and, ever since, I have read books about India, not
systematically, not as part of any course of study, but as I
happened to come across them. This book is the record of my
reading: what prompted the book was not my knowledge but my
ignorance. I did not overflow onto paper because I was saturated
with learning. It was rather that this book was sucked into me to fill
a mental vacuum, to supply the empty space that India had left in
my imagination. I would not have written it had I not admired
some of those who have written about India. Kipling, Forster,
Nirad Chaudhuri, Ved Mehta, and Ruth Jhabvala, for example, all
seem to me good writers. But with the exception of V.S. Naipaul –
and he is a subsidiary figure in this book – the only writer of those I
will consider whose achievement seems to me of the first order is
R.K. Narayan. In the end, my interest is less in the writers than in
what they are writing about. I am interested in India.

Most of the books that I shall talk about are novels, and that may
seem strange. I was trying to discover a real country, and it seems
an odd way to go about it to read made-up stories. But I was
reading to repair my own ignorance, and that was not at bottom an
ignorance of facts. It would not much have helped me to learn how
many tons of steel were produced in India in 1987, nor what is the
precise population of Bombay. What I was in need of was a way of
imagining India, a way of representing India to myself. It was
natural to turn for help to novelists, and so I read novels about
India, reading humbly, gratefully. But at some point it occurred to
me that I might be able to write about what I was reading, that I
might be able to exchange the humble perspective of the reader for
the powerful position of the critic. I envisioned a book in which my
helplessness, the ignorance of India that kept me gratefully sub-
servient to the novelists that I was reading, became itself the source
of my power.

It was to be a wonderful book, a virtuoso performance. Each
chapter would describe a way of imagining India, each of them
complete, and each of them different. To mark this difference the
more emphatically I would jump throughout the book between
different critical styles. When I had finished I would have written a
book that did justice to the dizzying variety of India, and what is
more a book that would have transformed my failure, my inability

to imagine India, into the ground of my authority – it would have become the perspective that enabled me to summon one after another a dozen different Indias while remaining myself aloof from any of them.

It did not, of course, work out like that. For one thing, my critical style proved less chameleonic than I had hoped. Reading through my manuscript I was reminded from time to time of a book on a nineteenth-century poet written by a distinguished American academic, an experimental book that took the form of a conversation amongst a group of the poet's Edwardian critics, all of whom very quickly began to speak in an eerie anticipation of the style of a distinguished American academic. For another, I was forced to realise that there were not a dozen Indias in my book, there was only one. I had asked questions of novels, and those who question works of art do not get answers: what they get is their own questions returned to them more precisely phrased. I had brought to novels my inability to imagine India, and so what I found when I read was the impossibility of imagining India richly explored. I had brought to novels the uneasy sense that overwhelmed me as I sat on the cycle rickshaw, the sense that I was irremediably separated from India by my Western habits of mind and feeling, and what I found was the difference between East and West subtly articulated. We can never understand more than we have it in us to understand, and what I have it in me to understand of India is my own perplexity.

It was a chastening discovery, but not in the end disabling. It gave me a more properly modest ambition, to explain one quality of books about India, the quality that I could see with particular clarity because it corresponded with my own experience. Such books characteristically express a painful awareness that the writers' imaginations are inadequate to their subject. That is what my book is about.

1
The English Indian Novel: *Kim* and *Midnight's Children*

'Is this an Indian disease, this urge to encapsulate the whole of reality?', asks Salman Rushdie in *Midnight's Children*. The answer is, I think, yes, but it is a disease to which only those like Rushdie, who write about India in English, are vulnerable. To write about India in any of its vernaculars, even in Hindi its national language, is inevitably to divide it. Rushdie knows as much. In 1956 Nehru divided India into six states: 'But the boundaries of these states were not formed by rivers or mountains, or any natural features of the landscape. Language divided us....' Writing in Gujarati, or Tamil, or Bengali confers on the writer a regional identity that unavoidably takes precedence over his identity as an Indian. That is why the Indian novel, the novel that tries to encapsulate the whole of Indian reality can, as yet, only be written in English. And this is odd, because English is the first language only of the smallest of India's racial groups, the Anglo-Indians, and of the tiniest of its classes, the few thousand middle- and upper-class families who speak English in their homes, and educate their children abroad or in India's English-style public schools.[1]

Saleem Sinai, Rushdie's hero, loses control of his bicycle and hurtles downhill, away from the middle-class enclave of British-built houses where he lives, isolated from and superior to the swarming life of Bombay. He crashes into a language march, Marathis demanding that Bombay be ceded to Maharashtra and voicing their contempt of Gujaratis. Marathi is Saleem's 'worst subject' at school, and his Gujarati is as bad as his Marathi. Saleem, in this episode, is the true representative of all English Indian novelists. He mounts his bicycle – so very English a machine – and crashes into India, with its teeming masses who stare into his face, and speak to him in languages that he cannot understand. One thinks of the end of *A Passage to India*; Fielding, Aziz, Stella, and Ralph capsizing their boats, and in doing so disrupting a religious ceremony that they cannot fathom. Saleem is an outsider, a 'little

4

princeling', a 'young nawab', a 'lord', but it is because he is an outsider that India seems one to him, so that he can aspire to encapsulate the whole of it. His English language at once separates him irrevocably from India, and makes the whole of India available to him, just as the exclusive hill on which Saleem lives isolates him from Bombay, but at the same time transforms the city into a panorama spread before him, at his feet.

The paradox of the English Indian novel is that it is the only kind of Indian novel that there is, and that it is scarcely Indian at all: it is rather like the swimming pool of the Breach Candy club in Bombay that Saleem's house overlooks. It was for many years the only swimming pool in the city, patriotically shaped like a map of India, and yet a pool from which all Indians were excluded. The paradox of the English Indian novel is so strong that it overpowers differences of race. English Indian novels have more in common with each other than with novels set in India written in any of India's native languages. Salman Rushdie has more in common with Rudyard Kipling than with Premchand or Bankim Chandra Chatterji. It is an ancestry that he resists as energetically as Saleem resists the notion that his real father is an Englishman. Rushdie looks for some alternative, non-English tradition of novel writing, and finds it in the work of Marquez and of Grass, but, for all his efforts, *Midnight's Children* is better seen as a post-independence version of *Kim*.

The first thing that Kipling and Rushdie have in common is impudence, the impudence of the trespasser. Kipling, an Englishman who spent the first five years of his life in India, and returned for nearly seven years as a young man, sets himself to imagine the whole of a subcontinent. There will be Indians who find Rushdie's temerity in *Midnight's Children* no less extraordinary – the history of India since its independence inscribed in the fantastic autobiography of a man who had much of his education in England, who was born a Muslim, and whose family now lives in Pakistan.[2] Kipling and Rushdie are trespassers. It is interesting that both Kim and Saleem Sinai have a mysterious parentage. Kim is the son of a drunken Irish soldier, but he is brought up by a half-caste woman who pretends to be his aunt. Saleem is born to an Englishman and a low-caste Hindu, but he is brought up in a Muslim family who believe him to be their son. Both Kim and Saleem acquire a series of substitute parents. In *Kim*, Mahbud Ali, the Lama, and Colonel Creighton are all surrogate fathers. In *Midnight's Children*, Saleem finds alternative parents in his uncle and aunt, in a German expert on snake venom, in his mother's first husband, and in the snake-charmer, Picture Singh. It is as if Kipling and Rushdie can claim that their subject is theirs by right only by disguising their origins.

Kipling and Rushdie are outsiders, but because they are outsiders, the whole of India becomes available to them. The tentativeness, the modesty, that ought, it might be felt, to characterise the work of a writer venturing into unfamiliar territory, is over-run by a heady sense of power as they see before them a subcontinent, all of which they can seize on as their domain. *Midnight's Children* is, on one reading, the deranged fantasy of a megalomaniac who believes that he contains within himself a nation. But if this is madness, it is the characteristic madness of the English Indian novelist, and it is a mania that betrays itself within their fictions. Saleem's mother's first husband had a friend who set out to be a painter of miniatures, but he was afflicted by 'gigantism', his pictures got larger as he tried to cram more and more into them. A man who feels himself able to re-create a subcontinent will find no reason why he should stop there. In Delhi there is Lifafa Das, the peepshow man, who stuffs his magic box with more and more pictures, determined to make good the boast with which he appeals to his customers, 'See the whole world come see everything!' It is no surprise when Saleem chooses as his time capsule, as the container to hold the personal bits and pieces that will remind future archaeologists of his existence, a battered tin globe. *Kim*, too, is replete with figures for Kipling's all-inclusive ambition. In Lahore there is the 'Wonder House', the museum in which Kipling's father tried to exhibit the whole of India. In Simla there is Lurgan Sahib's richly cluttered shop – 'the Lahore museum was larger but here were more wonders'. Most wonderful of all there is the Lama's picture of the wheel of life, a picture that includes not just the whole of our world, but all possible worlds.

The English Indian novel is characteristically impudent, and it tries, as both cause and effect of its impudence, to swallow India whole, to vie with Krishna and ingest worlds. It is also characteristically fantastic. For Rushdie India is an 'imaginary country', a 'mass fantasy', a 'collective fiction', a country that could never have existed 'except by the effort of a phenomenal collective will – except in a dream we all agreed to dream'. The same is true, I suppose, of any country, but the truth becomes crucial for the novelist who attempts to represent India in English. His claim to authority rests on the pretence that he is representative, the spokesman of a 'mass fantasy', a 'collective fiction', and the language in which he makes the claim, English, renders it fantastic.

Kim is Kipling's account of his imaginary childhood, the childhood he never had. Locked in his room at Mrs Holloway's house in Southsea, or frowsting in his study at school, Kipling's was an enclosed childhood, spent in cold, damp England. He learned at Southsea what it is to be the victim of sadists, and at Westward Ho! how much pleasanter it is to be their accomplice. Hard lessons these, and they marked Kipling for life, but they are lessons that Kim, his imaginary other self, is spared. If Kim is bullied by a drummer boy at the regimental school, it is not long before Mahbub Ali appears and whisks Kim into his saddle. He is sent to St Xavier's in Lucknow, but the long years of his schooling are magically compressed into a couple of paragraphs, so that his real education can take place not in a musty classroom, but outside, in the warm air, on the open roads of India. India is as big and as full as Kim can desire, a 'great and wonderful land', but it has also the special quality of a den, a secret place in which a child's fantasy life can flourish safely, protected from the destructive realism of adult eyes.[3] The whole of India from Benares to the Himalayas becomes Kim's private playground, and the adults allowed to enter must enter on the child's terms.

In *Midnight's Children* this all becomes explicit. The children born in the first hour of India's independence, the children that Saleem talks with at night as he lies in bed, are every child's imaginary friends. Saleem is rejected by the children he plays with: 'expelled from one gang I decided to form my own, a gang which was spread over the length and breadth of the country, and whose headquarters were behind my eyebrows'. His former friends find out his secret place, the clock tower near his house, and Saleem has to find another, a safer secret place inside his head: 'That was how it was when I was ten: nothing but troubles outside my head, nothing but miracles inside it.' That was how it was for most of us, when we were ten.

Like *Kim*, *Midnight's Children* has its origins in fantasy. This is obvious enough, but my point is that it could not be otherwise, for how else, except fantastically, can a white newspaper man like Kipling, or an English-educated Muslim like Salman Rushdie, seek to accommodate the whole of Indian reality, those millions of babbling voices, so many of them speaking in languages that Kipling and Rushdie cannot understand? The India Kipling knows is Mrs Hauksbee's Simla with its boredom and its adultery, and the regimental cantonment with its boredom and its drunkenness. The India Rushdie knows is the Bombay of the Cricket Club and the Mahalakshmi racecourse, schools built in colonial Gothic, and visits to the Saturday-morning pictures in the family car. Neither can emerge from this limited experience into the great and wonderful life of India except through fantasy. They can write an Indian novel only by taking the secret place of a child's fantasy life, and, in a stupendous effort of the imagination, expanding it, until it becomes coextensive with a subcontinent. Or, to put this less romantically, the English Indian novel can operate only by adulterating the high seriousness of the classical novel with injections of genre fiction, of the kind that supplies what lingers in the adult of the child's craving for fantasy. *Kim* includes a spy story, in the pre-Le Carré mould in which the hero, the arch-spy, is a magician, a conjurer, not some balding, menopausal embodiment of Britain in its post-imperial decline. *Midnight's Children* leans on science fiction. Saleem Sinai is Clark Kent, jealously guarding his secret identity, and the children of midnight are the Midwich Cuckoos, aliens with strange gifts that threaten the limited adult notion of reality. Saleem's uncle, Hanif, has a mission to reform the Hindi cinema, to do away with melodrama in favour of documentary realism. He is working on a script with the seductive working title, 'The Ordinary Life of a Pickle Factory'. But the film is never made. The English Indian novel cannot be written by a simple realist, but only by a writer willing to flirt with fantasy; a writer ready to dally with the Bombay talkie.

Fantasy is vulnerable. It is vulnerable to adult obtuseness and to politicians, who respond to any 'alternative reality' as a threat to the monolothic vision of the way things are on which they base their claim to unchallenged authority. When Saleem announces that he hears voices in his head, his father cuffs him round the ear. Later, when he is a man, Indira Gandhi responds more terribly. Saleem understands the Emergency as the attempt by Indira Gandhi and her son to root out the children of midnight, to root them out with cruel literalness, by castration. In *Kim* fantasy is threatened by Father Bennet, the Church of England priest, who cannot tell the difference between fantasy and lies – 'A phenomenal little liar' is his first thought when Kim gives an account of his fabulous childhood – and who views the world with 'the triple-ringed uninterest of the creed that lumps together nine-tenths of the world under the title of "heathen"'. But Father Bennet's bigotry, unlike Indira Gandhi's in Rushdie's novel, is defeated by the genial tolerance of a Catholic priest, a man appropriately named Father Victor. Kim can embody India only by practising, and by being permitted to practise, a large tolerance, by being variously a low-caste Hindu, a Muslim Pathan, a Buddhist novice, and a young white Christian; and, although such tolerance is threatened by the narrow-minded self-confidence of men like Father Bennet, it can flourish, Kipling believes, only under the protection of a benign and powerful authority.

The novel begins with Kim sitting astride Zam-Zammah, the great cannon that stands outside the museum in Lahore: 'Who holds Zam-Zammah, that "fire-breathing dragon", holds the Punjab, for the great green-bronze piece is always first of the conqueror's loot.' Kim has kicked Abdullah, his Muslim friend, off the cannon – 'All Mussulmans fell off Zam-Zammah long ago' – and he has displaced Chota Lal, the Hindu boy: 'The Hindus fell off Zam-Zammah too.' Kim is white, even though 'a poor white of the very poorest', and he sits astride the gun in self-conscious racial arrogance. But Kim is only playing at being arrogant, only pretending to be a Sahib. He is not taunting little Lal and Abdullah, he is playing with them, playing a game of king-of-the-castle. All the way through *Kim* the stuff of conflict is transformed into the stuff of play. Personal insult becomes a sport: opponents test each other's proficiency. Religious bigotry becomes charming. 'God's curse on all unbelievers', mutters Mahbub Ali, before placing his purse and his strong right arm at the service of Muslim, Hindu, Christian and Buddhist, all alike. Urdu, the chief language of Kipling's India, is a playground of words: to speak Urdu in *Kim* is inevitably to make puns. Most striking of all there is Hurree Chunder Mookerjee, the Bengali Babu.

The literate, educated Bengali was the chief hate object of British India. He was a figure of fun – his pompous, error-ridden English was endlessly imitated – but the mockery was a disguise for hatred and for fear.[4] The English compared the Bengali unfavourably with the Indians of the plains and of the hills; stalwart peasants and good fighting men like the Sikhs and the Jats, or ferocious warriors, like the Pathans and the Gurkhas. They made the satisfactory discovery that education in a native inevitably destroyed his better qualities, fostering cunning and cowardice, and these thoughts found their liveliest expression in the myth of the Bengali Babu, with his irritating pretensions to equality with his rulers, his ridiculous aping of English speech, and, underneath it all, his timorousness, his utter lack of the stout, frank virtues of the fighting man. Hurree is – he is always saying so – a 'fearful man', but he is also one of Colonel Creighton's most trusted and daring secret agents, so that the myth of his timorousness coincides with the fact of his courage. His cunning is joyous, for he places it at the service of the Raj. When he attaches himself to the service of the Russian agents, he allows them to think that they have made him drunk:

> He became thickly treasonous, and spoke in terms of sweeping indecency of a Government which had forced upon him a white man's education and neglected to supply him with a white man's salary. He babbled tales of oppression and wrong till the tears ran down his cheeks for the miseries of his land. Then he staggered off, singing love-songs of lower Bengal, and collapsed upon a wet tree-trunk.

He becomes for a moment exactly the kind of Bengali over whom heads were shaken in clubs and messes all over British India; weak, resentful, his treacherous instincts curbed only by his physical cowardice. He acts out the myth of the Babu, but the point is that it is an act. When he tells the tale to his white superior, Lurgan 'mourned aloud that he had not been in the place of the stubborn, inattentive coolies, who with grass mats over their heads and the raindrops paddling in their footprints, waited on the weather'. He grumbles at not having been a spectator of the game. In *Kim* even sedition is touched by the wand of Kipling's benign magic, and transformed into a joke.

The world of *Kim* is a world of play – or illusion, as the Lama would have it. The Lama's Buddhism teaches him that to live is a torture. It is to be bound like Ixion to the wheel of life, and offers only this consolation, that the pain is illusory. India to him is not Kim's 'great and wonderful' land, it is a 'great and terrible' land. But the Lama is a distant oriental cousin of Fielding's Parson Adams: his humanity is forever breaking through his philosophy. He likes to tell children stories; he writes charms (in which he does not believe) to cure a good-natured old woman's grandson of the colic; and most of all, although he knows human attachments to be an illusion and a hindrance to the progress of the soul, he cannot help but love Kim. When he is with Kim, in despite of his philosophy, the painful wheel of life becomes a carousel. He is a Tibetan monk, out of place in the Indian plains, the follower of a religion that India may have given birth to, but which never took root there. He ought to be an alien in a strange land, but he becomes in his wisdom, his gentleness, his childlike simplicity, an embodiment of all that Kipling found most charming and best worth defending in the religious life of India.

Such a life is worth defending, and it needs to be defended. The Lama sits cross-legged on a high Himalayan hill, drawing a picture of the wheel of life. To the two Russian spies his picture is a curio, and they try to buy it from him. The Lama recoils from these men, who can only understand possession, and for whom India is precious not because of the way people live there, but as a warehouse of desirable exotic commodities. He refuses to sell, they try to snatch the picture from him, and it is torn: 'Before Kim could ward him off, the Russian struck the old man full in the face.' It is the one moment of pure evil in the novel. The hillmen who are escorting the Lama reach for their rifles, but before they can shoot, Kim hurls himself at the Russian, and the two roll downhill. The Lama is a man of peace. 'What profit to kill men?', he asks once of an old soldier, and the soldier replies 'Very little – as I know; but if evil men were not now and then slain it would not be a good world for weaponless dreamers.' There is no killing in Kim. The Russian is repaid for his blow with a kick in the groin delivered by Kim, and a long drawn-out, playful humiliation devised by Hurree Chunder. But all the same the old soldier speaks the truth. The land of play must be defended, if necessary by violence. Kipling's problem is how to defend a pastoral land without compromising its innocence, and his solution is to defend it with a secret service. Spying is a game, 'the great game', so that the right to play is protected by something that is itself a kind of playing.

'The great game' is a neat solution to a technical problem, but for Kipling the problem is only technical: it is not a political difficulty. It seemed obvious to him that freedom – Kim's freedom as he wanders the open roads of India – can exist only so long as it is safeguarded by a benevolent authority, and that no authority can survive unless it is prepared, when need arises, to impose itself by

force of arms. When Hurree Chunder and Mahbub Ali pass the
news to Creighton that two northern princes are about to conclude
a treaty with the Russians, Creighton unleashes against them 8000
armed men. For Kipling, war does not disrupt the pastoral, it
secures it. The novel begins with Kim playing on a cannon. It is in
the shadow of the cannon that he first meets the Lama. What this
signifies is that play, whether it be a game of king-of-the-castle or
the Lama's lofty spiritual recreation, can be carefree and secure
only when it is protected, only in the shadow of a gun.

The Lama pursues enlightenment, knowledge. Kim's sign, as
the Brahmin astrologer tells him, is the sign of war. But in *Kim*
enlightenment and war, knowledge and power, are mutually
supporting. Kim is at once the Lama's disciple and his protector,
and the two love each other. At the beginning of *Midnight's
Children* Aadam Aziz, Saleem's grandfather, kneels to pray, hits his
nose on a tussock of hard earth, and resolves 'never again to kiss
earth for any god or man.' Authority for Kipling is embodied in the
Raj, in the British rule of India. For Rushdie it is embodied in Islam,
in the faith into which he was born. But whereas *Kim* begins with a
symbolic acceptance of the authority of the Raj, with Kim playing
in the shadow of a gun, *Midnight's Children* begins with its hero's
grandfather rejecting the authority of his religion. In Karachi, and
again when he stays in the magician's colony in Delhi, Saleem
Sinai lives in the shadow of a mosque. In Pakistan, where the
spiritual power of Islam is identical with the temporal power of the
state, he finds the shadow of the minaret oppressive, an 'accusing
finger'. In Delhi it is a comforting shadow, offering relief from the
heat of the sun, but this is because in post-Independence India
Islam is powerless. The forts, once the visible signs of Muslim
power, are now only tourist attractions, a convenient site where
Saleem's father can pay off the gang of extreme Hindu hooligans
who operate a protection racket aimed at Muslim businessmen.
Aadam Aziz is a doctor, a lover of knowledge, and in order to
pursue knowledge, it seems to him, he must reject the authority of
his faith: he carries his medical equipment in a pigskin briefcase.
He will not allow his wife to live in purdah, he throws the religious
tutor out of his house when he overhears his children being given
lessons in religious intolerance, and the consequence of his brave
attempt to live outside the law in which he was born is to make 'a
hole in him, a vacancy in a vital inner chamber'. *Kim* is a full novel,
Midnight's Children leaks: it has holes in it. It has holes in its story –

the hole in a sheet through which Aadam Aziz sees, bit by bit, the girl he will marry, the hole through which the children gaze at Lifafa Das's peep-show, the hole through which Saleem's sister, Jamila, sings, so that she can become a star without compromising her maidenly modesty – and it has holes in its plot – the failure of Saleem's telepathic powers whenever the plot demands it; chronology tampered with to preserve the correspondence between the life of Saleem and the history of India. The holes in the novel are all of them versions of the hole that appears in Aadam Aziz when he resolves never again to pray: they are the inevitable consequence of separating knowledge and power.

This is the crucial difference between *Kim* and *Midnight's Children*. In *Kim* knowledge and power support each other, like Kim and the Lama. *Midnight's Children* imagines a world where knowledge and power are forever opposed, and where to dream that it might be otherwise, as Aadam Aziz dreams when he becomes a follower of the Hummingbird, or as Saleem dreams when he falls under the spell of Picture Singh, the Marxist snake-charmer, is to suffer from the 'optimism disease', for which the only cure is violent disillusionment. Two children are born on the stroke of midnight, Saleem and Shiva. Saleem has knowledge without power, Shiva has power without knowledge. From the first the two are enemies. Without Shiva Saleem's knowledge is helpless, but Shiva's position is scarcely better, for without Saleem his power is pointless. By separating the two, Rushdie transforms Kipling's version of imperialist India as a pastoral comedy into a vision of India since its independence in which history becomes a savage farce.

It would be possible to understand the contrast as signalling the difference between India before and after 1947. It is, after all, the transformation that Kipling himself predicted in one of the best and oddest of his Indian stories, 'The Strange Ride of Morrowbie Jukes'. Jukes' horse bolts. He careers for miles across the Indian landscape until he is thrown, and falls into the pit where those are imprisoned who have been pronounced dead only to regain consciousness during their funeral obsequies. There is no escape. The pit is surrounded on three sides by high walls of steeply sloping, crumbling sand. On the fourth it is open to the river, but there are quicksands, and during daylight hours marksmen wait in a moored boat, ready to shoot escapers. The community inside the pit is a 'republic', Kipling's baleful vision of an India set loose from

British rule. What remains is a state of anarchy; without law, without traditional authority, or moral conventions, or kindness: a society in which the only virtues are violence and cunning. Jukes is saved by an Indian servant, who tracks his master to the pit, lets down a rope, and helps him to scramble up the sand walls. By his fidelity, by acting out those virtues which, for Kipling, are permitted by an authority that, in their turn, they sustain, the bad dream is broken, and Jukes emerges once more into the security and order of British India. We shall never know how much of its popularity in Britain *Midnight's Children* owes to its capacity for generating the kind of indignant satisfaction with which, even now, too many of the British like to contemplate the political difficulties of their former colonies. But their view is unconvincing. The version of empire offered in *Kim*, – in which India is ruled by gruff, good-natured Englishmen who delight in nothing more than swapping banter with the native population – and Rushdie's version of India since 1947 – in which the nation is ruled by a widow, one half of her hair black, one half white, so that she not only acts but looks surprisingly like Cruella de Ville – are both of them children's histories of India, the products of fantasy rather than historical research.

The contrast is most easily explained by the political differences between the two men – most easily but not most interestingly, for neither Kipling nor Rushdie strikes me as a political thinker worth taking seriously. Kipling's imperialism now has a certain spurious charm, because the once-fashionable sentiments it encourages have become quaint. But it is not a serious defence of empire. Kipling's admiration for the men who maintained the Raj always had in it too much of the bespectacled bookish Beetle's infatuation with more robust boys like Stalky and with the kind of loutish behaviour that English public schools honour as high jinks. In *Kim* the hillmen have a lively admiration for Yankling Sahib, who is a 'merry man', and who never wearies of shooting wild animals, and Kipling is too often given to speaking as though these are the only virtues that a ruler of India needs. In place of Kipling's imperialism Salman Rushdie offers his own, somewhat vague liberal prejudices, which he sometimes – mistakenly – imagines to be consistent with Marxism. It is the defining characteristic of this kind of liberalism that it cannot reconcile its values with any political machinery that would enforce them, so that its exponents are condemned to choose their heroes only from the ranks of political failures, such as the Hummingbird and Picture Singh. Power and knowledge are as necessarily united in Kipling as they are divided in Rushdie, but what is most striking is not the difference of ideology, but the absence of intelligent political thinking, and this is common to them both.

The more interesting difference between *Kim* and *Midnight's Children* has to do with the status of fantasy. The English Indian novel is committed to fantasy, because its premise is the fantastic claim of one individual to embody the impossible diversity of India. But if it were purely fantastic, India would dissolve into a Never Never Land. The characteristic mode of the English Indian novel is fantastic realism. The term is is common enough, but its familiarity should not blunt our recognition that it is a paradox. The fantasist looks inwards at the ordered world of his dreams: the realist looks outwards at the chaotic clutter of the world around him. As Kim walks with the Lama his eyes dart here and there, and he delights in everything he sees. Beside him, the Lama tells his beads, not seeing and not hearing, lost in inward meditation. It is an unlikely alliance, and it can serve as a symbol of the precarious reconciliation on which the English Indian novel depends.

When Kim is fifteen the novel ends. Kipling can take Kim only to the frontier of adulthood. He cannot follow him into his life as a man, because Kim can be the hero of an Indian novel only for so long as he lives in a world where fantasy and reality are equal rulers, only for so long as he is a child. Several times in the novel Kim broods upon his name, upon himself:

> A very few white people, but many Asiatics, can throw themselves into a mazement as it were by repeating their own names over and over again to themselves, letting the mind go free upon speculation as to what is called personal identity. When one grows older, the power, usually, departs, but while it lasts it may descend upon a man at any moment.
> 'Who is Kim – Kim – Kim?'
> He squatted in a corner of the clanging waiting-room, rapt from all other thoughts; hands folded in lap, and pupils contracted to pin-points. In a minute – in another half second – he felt he would arrive at a solution of the tremendous puzzle; but here, as always happens, his mind dropped away from those heights with the rush of a wounded bird, and passing his hand before his eyes, he shook his head.

'A very few white people' and 'many Asiatics', perhaps, but almost all children. Kim is a child, indistinctly related to the world, and indistinctly divided from it. Like all very charming children he is sexually indefinite, and flirts with men and women alike. It is because he is, as yet, unfixed that his name, and the personal identity that it denotes, are mysteries to him. When he is a man, he will stop asking, 'Who is Kim?', and his failure to ask the question will be the sure sign that he has found the answer. He will have become an adult, with an adult's fixed and limited sense of himself. He will no longer say, 'What am I? Mussulman, Hindu, Jain, or Buddhist? That is a hard nut.' And as soon as he no longer asks that question he will have become a British resident of India, and will have lost his claim to be the hero of an Indian novel.

After the assault on him by the Russian, the Lama sickens. Kim nurses him unstintingly as the two make their way down from the mountains to the plains, and the Lama wonders at his capacity for loving care: 'And thou art a Sahib? When I was a man – a long time ago – I forgot that. Now I look upon thee often, and every time I remember that thou art a Sahib. It is strange.' It is an indication that Kim is about to become a man, and a sign, too, that the novel is within a few pages of its end. Kim's India is threatened by two enemies: one of them, Russia, can be met with and confounded, but the other is adulthood, and it can only be evaded, by bringing the novel to its close.

Unlike Kim, Saleem Sinai grows up. *Midnight's Children* does not end until he is thirty. He maintains in adulthood a free commerce between fantasy and reality, but in children this is normal, whereas in adults it is madness. Unlike Kim Saleem Sinai loses his innocence, which is the sign, the somewhat self-conscious sign, that Salman Rushdie has outlived the innocence of the novel. There are 1001 midnight children, because 1001 is the number of 'alternative realities', and because it is 'the largest imaginable number'. It is the richest alternative to reality that the novelist can devise, and it is mocked by the number of the population of India, a number that increases by millions even as Rushdie writes. 1001 is a magical number, a fantastic number, and the difference between it and the 650 million of India's population expresses Rushdie's sense of the impossible, irreconcilable discrepancy between the power of human fantasy and our knowledge of reality. In *Kim* it is a gap that a child can cross without even noticing it. In *Midnight's Children* it is a gulf that only a madman would attempt to leap.

Saleem Sinai writes his memoirs in a pickle factory, his chapters are for him so many jars of pickles. The secret of pickling, he knows, is to preserve the fruit whilst retaining its taste, and this culinary miracle keeps alive in him his ambition to write down the reality of India without losing its savour. But Salman Rushdie is resigned to the knowledge that Saleem's is the ambition of a madman, for only in the dreams of a madman could the experiences of one, middle-class, Bombay-born Muslim be made to accommodate the experiences of the more than 600 million of his fellow countrymen. Kipling must end his novel before Kim becomes a man. Rushdie must end his before Saleem Sinai goes stark mad. Already he is beginning to crack, as his grandfather had cracked before him, under the pressure of being 'so-many-too-many persons', and it will not be long before he shatters into 600 million voiceless fragments. Kim is about to find himself: Kipling is silenced. Saleem is about to lose himself: Rushdie is silenced. Between these two silences there is no logical space, but there is also all the territory that the English Indian novel inhabits.

2

The Indian English Novel: *Nation of Fools* and *The Man-Eater of Malgudi*

Kim and *Midnight's Children* are attempts at the great Indian novel, the novel that aspires to accommodate the whole of Indian reality, and what allows such aspirations is their Englishness. When Saleem Sinai first contacts the children of midnight, he finds that they think in languages he cannot understand: the radio in his head receives only a babble of alien tongues. He must learn to penetrate beneath Pushtu, Tamil, Gujarati, Hindi, Bengali, Telugu, all the languages of India, to an area of the brain where thought exists unclothed in words. It is the central fiction of the novel, the necessary fiction of the great Indian novel, that this language beyond language, this metalanguage, is identical with English. But most novelists are less overweening in their ambitions than the Kipling of *Kim*, or the Rushdie of *Midnight's Children*. In *Midnight's Children* the action extends from Bombay to Karachi, from Dacca to Delhi. In *Kim* the action wanders between Lahore and Benares and high up into the Himalayas. The events of Balraj Khanna's *Nation of Fools* are confined to one small triangle of the Punjab, about 50 square miles.

Nation of Fools tells the story of Paro, Khatri and their son Omi, of how the family establishes itself in Chandigarh, the new capital of the Punjab. The novel begins at a moment of crisis for both father and son. Khatri lives at Camp Baldev Nagar, a temporary settlement for refugees of the partition that has become, as such places tend to do, a semi-permanent small town. But it is only on weekends that Khatri is at home. His work is in Panchkoola, 'a bus stand in the middle of nowhere', seven miles from Chandigarh. A cluster of shops and stalls has grown up around the bus stand, providing for the wants of travellers between Chandigarh and Delhi, and Khatri owns a sweet-shop there. But a bridge has been built across the river Jhajjar, and as soon as it is opened the buses

18

will no longer pass by Panchkoola. Khatri is threatened with the loss of his business. The threat facing Omi is just as serious. He has failed his matric, and is repeating his final year at school. If he fails again, there will be no place for him at university. Both father and son are threatened with exclusion from 'Nehru's Ram Raj', the golden age of opportunity that Nehru promised his countrymen. *Nation of Fools* tells how the threats are circumvented: it is a success story. Khatri moves to Chandigarh and becomes the most successful purveyor of sweets in the capital, and the owner of a luxurious restaurant. Omi learns English, wins a place at Chandigarh University, and then wins social, and – what is just as important to him – sexual acceptance by the student elite, Chandigarh's *jeunesse dorée*, the 'Simla pinks', the 'imported shirts', the young people who came to university from one of the expensive public schools dotted around India's hill stations, and are distinguished from the rest of the student body by their privileged good looks, their social freedom, and above all by their accent, their easy command of English, the language in which they were educated and the only language in which many of them are comfortable.

Khatri's victory is economic, Omi's is linguistic. Khatri manages to persuade a politician suffering from the sudden gush of sympathy for the problems of his constituents that impending elections bring on to compensate him for the loss of his business at Panchkoola by giving him the franchise on two shops in Chandigarh. Omi learns to speak in a passable imitation of the English of Professor Raj Kumar, the only 'Cambridge-Returned' on the staff of Chandigarh University, who 'speaks English like an English lord. You can hardly understand what he says.' Khatri conquers the business world of Chandigarh by making money: Omi conquers Chandigarh society by learning English. Between them, father and son make Chandigarh their own.

Chandigarh is Le Corbusier's town, a monument to the planner's arbitrary will, a city built on the northernmost edge of the great Punjab plain where nothing existed before, to the south 200 flat miles to Delhi, to the north a road twisting upwards to Simla. Simla is the creation of English nostalgia, an English country town in the foothills of the Himalayas, but now that the English have left, Indians have taken over the town. Its sentimentality made it easily available to a people who are connoisseurs of nostalgia. Chandigarh is rigorously unsentimental, the dream it expresses is the dream of the planner in which buildings are modules and people are units. Simla is vernacular architecture, a foreign vernacular, English. Chandigarh is foreign architecture, too, and no one in *Nation of Fools* doubts that it was designed by an Englishman. 'Best and beautiful this is,' says Omi when he sees Chandigarh for the first time, 'Fucking intelligent they are, Englishmen.' Omi is right. The difference between Simla and Chandigarh has nothing to do with the differences between the English and Swiss imaginations. What it expresses is the difference between English in the second half of the nineteenth century and English a hundred years later. When Simla was built English was still a vernacular language, the language spoken by an island people. By the time Chandigarh was built English had become the property of the world, the linguistic equivalent of modernist architecture. Le Corbusier designed Chandigarh, but Nehru permitted it. The new city was the kind of dramatic gesture he loved, a symbol in concrete of all that India must accept if ever it was to find a place in the modern world.

'What sort of houses are these cement boxes? Are they for people or pigeons?' asks Paro as she is driven through Chandigarh, staring in amazement out of the cab of Bola Ram's lorry at the city that will be her new home. The harsh linearity of Le Corbusier's buildings is at first as uncomfortable to her eyes as English diphthongs and drawling English intonation are to Omi's tongue. She and Khatri must make themselves at home in a foreign city, Omi must learn to be at ease in a foreign language. The two tasks are not that different, and the reward is the same, a share in the 'milk and honey Ram Raj' that Nehru promised to India.

Omi and Khatri set about their tasks with unreflecting energy. It is Paro who is aware of the risk that they are running. She is worried about her son: 'Waste of time and money teaching him English ways. He will slip out of our hands. He won't recognize us.' And she is worried about her husband, fearing that as his business grows, as he adjusts himself to the business world of Chandigarh and becomes more and more prosperous, she will lose the man she married. Every weekend Khatri used to come home from Panchkoola feeling 'double hungry, big double hungry', and guide her hand as he ate to the tent peg rising in the middle of his sutthan. In Chandigarh they live above the shop, but somehow Khatri does not come home feeling double hungry so often. 'You don't look at us any more. It is always money, money, money', says Paro. Paro is an instinctive conservative. Her idea was for

Khatri to sublet the shops in Chandigarh, and for the family to remain in Camp Baldev Nagar. It is Omi who goads Khatri into the ways of the modern city, persuades him to sell his sweets in pink and blue boxes stamped with his own name, and then to open a restaurant. Each new project fills Paro with gloom, but her pessimism is born out of a real worry: that the shock of moving to Chandigarh with its new ways will split the family apart; that Khatri, as his business interests expand, will lose his interest in her; and that Omi will be so caught up in the new world to which he has gained entry, a world of parties, dancing and exciting sexual freedom, that he will drift away from his family. She is frightened that Khatri and Omi will win a place in Chandigarh, but only at a cost of losing themselves, and Paro's fears threaten to come true.

Omi is at last invited on a picnic with his Simla pink friends, a picnic with beer, dancing, and girls, and he ends up sitting by the river throwing pebbles into the water, 'a solitary figure with his chin cupped in a hand and his elbow resting on a knee', while his girlfriend couples in the grass with a hairy-chested young army lieutenant. Khatri opens his new restaurant, its success exceeds his dreams, and it leaves him feeling 'a strange kind of loneliness that he had never felt before', as if there was 'a hole in his heart'.

It is Balraj Khanna's version of the central dilemma of modern India, the dilemma that I will return to again and again. Khatri and Omi must either stay in Panchkoola, and grow older and poorer as the traffic of modern India passes them by, or they must go to Chandigarh, inhabit foreign buildings, learn a foreign language, and find a place in the modern world only by losing their place in India. The only way they can find a house is by losing their home. They risk alienation, a disease still fashionable amongst second-rate novelists. It is a danger that they triumphantly overcome. That is their victory, and it is Balraj Khanna's, too. Khatri and Omi find happiness, and Khanna remains true to his comic vision, bravely refusing to allow his novel to collapse into cheap pathos or glib despair.

Khatri's heart lifts as he decides to give the restaurant over to his brother-in-law to manage, and become once again a maker of sweets. Making sweets for Khatri is not just a trade, it is an art. It is work that he loves for itself as well as for the rewards it brings, and to go back to such work will, he knows, fill the hole in his heart and cure his loneliness. Omi submits to his parents' pressure, and agrees to the arranged marriage that he has resisted for so long, and as soon as he sees his bride he realises that his Aunt Vidya was right after all: 'the girl is so beautiful that you would faint if you saw her'. Omi, Khatri and Paro still live in Chandigarh, but the wedding is held in Camp Baldev Nagar, their old home town. It is an emblem of the truth that the whole novel insists on: that you can have the best of both worlds.

Nation of Fools tells the story of how Khatri and Omi escape from a backwater into the mainstream of the modern world, but the novel ends in gestures of retraction: Khatri retreats to his original profession, and Omi agrees to a traditional arranged marriage. Father and son both make an act of accommodation: they acknowledge their origins, and in doing so they secure the comic harmony of the novel's conclusion. Khatri mends the rent that had appeared in his marriage, and Omi reconciles himself with his parents. Both men rid themselves of the hole in their hearts, they make themselves whole. Nothing could be more different from the conclusion of *Midnight's Children* which ends as Saleem cracks up, shatters into six hundred million fragments. It is a difference that marks *Nation of Fools* as a quite different kind of novel, a kind I call the Indian English novel. This kind of novel begins from a small place within India, a place cut off from national events, cut off from the outside world. From this small place, from Panchkoola and Camp Baldev Nagar, the novel reaches out towards the modern world, but it reaches cautiously. The novel searches for the point at which Khatri and Omi can accept the new world without severing themselves from their origins. New ways must be learned but only so far as they can be assimilated with the old ways. Chandigarh and the English language can both be accepted, but only because the novel shows how they can both be made Indian.

English and Chandigarh may both have been imposed on India from abroad, but neither remains foreign. The bus to Chandigarh leaves from Old Delhi with its temples and twisting lanes, and to get off the bus in Chandigarh is to be shocked by the contrast between the rich confusion of an Indian city and the geometrical simplicities of a planned town. But the shock soon wears off. Omi, when he first sees Chandigarh, is stunned. 'Are we still in India, are we?' he asks. His father expects him to spend the day sightseeing, but he and a friend choose instead to go to a restaurant, where Omi eats his first plate of dhosa, and then to the cinema, where Vijayanti Mala is appearing in 'the all-time box-office record-breaker' Nagin. Omi's friend schools him in the distinctive characteristics of Chandigarh's architecture – 'Say the Secretariat looks like a huge American hotel, the water of the lake is too muddy and the High Court looks like the grandstand of a racecourse' – and believing that this will convince his father that he has spent his time improvingly Omi feels free to pass the afternoon in rapt contemplation of Vijayanti Mala's breasts – 'Those tits. Ummm . . . ' Chandigarh becomes for him only an exotic frame for a plateful of dhosa and Vijayanti Mala's cleavage. The city may be a remarkable example of the modern architect's capacity to impose his vision on a landscape without being deflected a hairsbreadth by any concern for the traditions and the tastes of the people to whom the landscape belongs, but it has become a monument to the Indian ability to accommodate the alien. Its strangeness is as much a part of India as Cleopatra's Needle is a part of London, it is now as naturally situated in the Punjab as the Egyptian obelisk is on the Thames embankment.

What is true of Chandigarh is also true, Khanna implies, of the English language. Khanna's own prose is elegantly neutral, as international as airport buildings, though a good deal more agreeable than they tend to be. But his prose is only a frame for his characters' speech. Narrative is subordinated to dialogue – it is a mark of the kind I have called the Indian English novel that this should be so – and the English of the novel's dialogue is not at all an international language. Volatile Sikhs are forever threatening to 'strike their twelve o'clock', irascible schoolmasters threaten to make chutney of their pupils, 'best chutney ever'. Boys given a beating are likely to end up looking 'like a peacock's arse'. Adolescent boys boast of how easily they are aroused,'ninety degrees, man, pukka ninety degrees'. In the dialogue of *Nation of Fools* English is re-created as a dialect of Punjabi. *Midnight's Children* must be written in English, because only in a foreign language, in a language that looks at India from the outside, can India appear whole. But *Nation of Fools* is written in English only by chance, and it is only possible to write it in English at all if, somehow, English can be made into an Indian language, if it can be transformed from the language of the world into a vernacular, a dialect.

Balraj Khanna celebrates India's capacity to assimilate, its comic inclusiveness. He celebrates what he calls India's foolishness, the Indian capacity to dissolve conflict into comedy. 'What sort of houses are these cement boxes?' asks Paro when she first

sees Chandigarh. 'They got an Angrez to design them', she is
told.

 'Couldn't they get hold of an Indian?'
 'The contractors were Indian.'
 'Then these buildings won't stay up for very long. I can tell you
 that.'

The self-contradictoriness is nonsensical, but it is playfully,
self-mockingly nonsensical. It is nonsense as a social grace, and
it dissolves racial tensions into laughter. Omi, Khatri and Paro go
to watch two processions marching through Chandigarh, two
language marches, one of Sikhs demanding that Punjabi be made
the official state language, one of Hindus asserting the claims of
Hindi. Neither Omi, nor Khatri, nor Paro knew that they had an
official state language, and they have no notion what it might be.
They ask one of the Sikh protestors. 'Hindi', he replies, but he is
wrong. One of Omi's fellow students knows the answer, 'English'.
'"Doesn't make sense," everybody said. "Right. Let's join the
march then," Omi said. Everybody laughed.' It is nonsense for
English to be an Indian language, absurd, and absurdities can be
resented, but they can also be enjoyed. *Midnight's Children* suffers
the paradox of its Englishness. Rushdie suffers because he is
forced, absurdly, to write his Indian novel in a language that is not
Indian at all. Khanna laughs because he chooses to write his novel
in the most absurd of Indian languages.
 Balraj Khanna's is hearty Punjabi laughter, not much like R. K.
Narayan's wry chuckle. The 'nation of fools' that Khanna represents is quite different from Malgudi, the small South Indian town
that in Narayan's novels stands for the whole of India. All the
same, Narayan is Khanna's master, for it was Narayan who
invented what I have called the Indian English novel, the novel
that can be written in English because it makes of English an
Indian language. Even the differences between the two writers are
secret signs of their kinship, because the differences derive from
the central strategy of the Indian English novel. Khanna re-creates
English as a dialect of Punjabi, Narayan as a dialect of Tamil. In
Narayan's hands English becomes a gentler, more fastidious
language, a language of delicate, easily bruised politeness. The two
writers are different from one another because they both write local
novels. What distinguishes them is what distinguishes the Punjab

rom Tamil Nadu. 'Whatever happens, India will go on,' Narayan
)nce told V. S. Naipaul.[1] Both Khanna and Narayan celebrate the
'esilience of India, and if Narayan is more concerned to celebrate
1ow successfully India can resist alien attempts to infiltrate its
:ulture, and Khanna is intrigued by how successfully India can
mpose itself on any alien intruder, then this, too, is perhaps as
nuch a regional as a temperamental difference, between the
•ggressive initiative and ebullience of the Punjab and the quieter,
nore conservative manners of the South.

   The alien presence in Narayan's *The Man-Eater of Malgudi* is not a
•anguage or a city but a taxidermist called Vasu. Vasu has a South
ndian name, and he claims to have attended Madras University,
)ut he is a foreign presence in Malgudi, a rootless man with an
:xotic history. In his early manhood Vasu was a circus strong man
•fter which he trained under the suspiciously foreign sounding
;uleiman, and became a hunter and taxidermist. He comes to
Vlalgudi because of the nearby Mempi forests which are well
•tocked with game, and quarters himself on Nataraj, the gentle
)rinter of Malgudi. Nataraj was brought up in a house where each
lay his grandfather gave him a coin to buy sugar for the ants,
vhere crows and sparrows were allowed their share of the crops,
•nd squirrels and mice were allowed to deplete the granary
indisturbed. Vasu's profession is an abomination to him. But
Nataraj is a mild man, unused to aggressive behaviour, and he
•eems helpless against Vasu's enormous physical strength and
)lustering egotism. The junk room above Nataraj's shop is turned
nto a charnel house in which Vasu pursues his frightful trade, and
•ll Nataraj's remonstrances are coolly brushed aside. Then Nataraj
•earns that Vasu is not content with despoiling the forests. He
)lans to shoot a temple elephant, to sell its tusks, its four feet
nounted as umbrella stands, and even its eyelashes. Nataraj
•ummons all his resources in a desperate attempt to foil Vasu's
)lan, but his resources are not many, and Vasu must have
•ucceeded had he not been prevented at the last by a miracle. As
1e waited, his gun beside him for the elephant to pass in
)rocession before Nataraj's shop, a mosquito settled on Vasu's
•orehead. Vasu had a horror of mosquitoes, and brought his iron
ist crashing down onto his skull, killing the mosquito and himself
vith one blow.

   It is a miracle, but Nataraj dimly understands that it was an
nevitable miracle, inevitable because Vasu was not a man but a

rakshasha, a demon, and it is in the nature of things that demons,
however powerful they may appear, should in the end destroy
themselves.[2] 'Whatever happens, India will go on', Narayan told
Naipaul, and he said it so casually that Naipaul recognised at once
that this was a conviction beyond argument. It is a religious
conviction, and in *The Man-Eater of Malgudi* Narayan lays it bare.
Vasu threatens the pieties through which Malgudi, Narayan's
India, subsists, and in doing so he loses his humanity, is revealed
as a rakshasha, and falls victim to his inevitable self-destruction.
This is the myth that Narayan elaborates in almost all his novels,
and it becomes in his hands the most powerful myth of nationhood
that India has yet created. Indian history is a sequence of invasions
– Moghul, British, Chinese. In the face of every invader India
seems helpless, and yet it is India, apparently so disorganised and
so passive, that survives, and the invader that somehow or other
destroys himself. As national myths go this is modest and
eccentric. Indians are the chosen people, and they reveal their
special status not by any glorious achievements, indeed not by
doing anything at all, but simply by going on. Narayan's novels are
religious ceremonies in which he invites his countrymen to join
him in rapt contemplation of their own survival. Or rather this
would be the case if the novels could be reduced to the fables that
they contain. As a fabulist Narayan preaches a sentimental,
religious nationalism that can be admired in the West only because
it is protected by its exoticism from uncondescending critical
interest. But Narayan is never quite the maker of fables that he
seems.

Nataraj works as a printer, if he can be said to work at all. In fact,
the business is carried on by his employee, Sastri, who only
demands Nataraj's assistance when he is pressed for time. Nataraj
spends his day talking with his friends. His old-fashioned printing
press is set up in the back room of his shop. The front room,
looking onto Market Road with a view of the fountain, would be a
valuable property were he to let it, but Nataraj prefers to keep it as
a kind of parlour. Any of his acquaintances is free to drop in, draw
up a chair, and pass the time of day. The two most frequent visitors
are a poet, who is 'writing the life of God Krishna in monosyllabic
verse', and Sen, an unemployed journalist very critical of Nehru
and his five-year plans. Nataraj seems able to support his wife and
small son effortlessly, without ever compromising his rule that the
business of making money should always be subordinated to the

pleasures of society; that work must always defer to conversation.
The talk that Nataraj loves, that occupies most of his day, is neither
informative, nor exploratory, but simply an expression of
sociability – phatic communion. It establishes his front parlour as a
community that imposes on its members one duty, and confers on
them one pleasure, an ideal community because the duty and the
pleasure of membership are one and the same – sociableness.
Nataraj's front parlour is a miniature realisation of Narayan's ideal
India. But it is secured by a fiction: that there is no distinction
between work and play.

Between the parlour and the inner room hangs a blue curtain,
through which Nataraj shouts instructions to 'the foreman, com-
positor, office-boy, binder or accountant', an impressive list of
imaginary staff with which he supplements the services of Sastri,
his one employee. The curtain protects the illusion that the work of
the press is done by magic. Nataraj's friends all obey the unspoken
tradition that none of them should look beyond the curtain, so that
Nataraj's fiction is maintained by the tender complicity of his
friends. But then Vasu arrives in Malgudi, comes to Nataraj's shop,
and enters the inner room, 'practically tearing aside the curtain, an
act which violated the sacred traditions of my press'. That is a joke,
of course, but, like so many of Narayan's jokes, it is serious, too.
Vasu comes to Malgudi to pursue his business, but he brings with
him a vision of a new India, a vision that violates traditions that
Narayan holds sacred.

'You know nothing, you have not seen the world', Vasu tells
Nataraj. Vasu's speech is sprinkled with comic-book Americanisms
like 'wise guy'. His stuffed animals are despatched to the four
corners of the globe. He brings the outside world and its ways to
Malgudi. He believes in only one thing, work and its rewards. He
is prepared to cut through any tradition and sacrifice any friendship in pursuit of profit, and he does so not apologetically but on
principle. Nataraj's insistence on subordinating economics to
friendship does not strike him as charming, but as the expression
of a national disease. Vasu's aggressive social manner, even his
profession, taxidermy, are selected as a calculated affront to the
prejudices of men like Nataraj. He lives as he drives, grazing past
pedestrians and enjoying their fright: 'More people will have to die
on the roads, if our nation is to develop any road sense at all.' Vasu
is utterly self-centred, and he is also a kind of missionary with the
goal of shocking India into the twentieth century. Self-centredness,

the cultivation of a dynamic, asocial ego, is his recipe for national regeneration. It is his notion of democracy. When Nataraj complains of the smell emanating from the hides he cures in his room, Vasu becomes self-righteously indignant:

> Oh, come on, don't be a fussy prude, don't imagine that you are endowed with more sensitive nostrils than others. Don't make yourself so superior to the rest of us. These are days of democracy, remember.

Nataraj is appalled at the 'notion of democracy as being a common acceptance of bad odours'. He offers instead the apolitical democracy of his front parlour, where the equality of all who enter is secured not by act of parliament but by politeness. Vasu counters this with a vision of India in which each individual is an isolated ego, knowing only its own desires and with an inalienable right to seek to satisfy them. He does not drink, but sees no objection to it: 'If people like it, it's their business and nobody else's.' Sexual appetites are exactly the same: 'If you like a woman, have her by all means.' For Nataraj humanity is defined by its sociability, for Vasu by its will to power. It is right and natural for an individual to seek to dominate his fellows, as it is for man to seek power over nature: 'After all we are civilized human beings, educated and cultured, and it is up to us to prove our superiority to nature. Science conquers nature in a new way every day . . .'.

It is not hard to say where Vasu's vision of India comes from. The journalist alerts us to it. When Vasu first comes to Nataraj's shop, the journalist is fulminating against one of Nehru's five-year plans: 'Anyway, in ten years time what are we going to do with all that steel?' Vasu retorts, 'If you feel superior to Nehru, why don't you go to Delhi and take charge of the cabinet?' Vasu is an embodiment of a new order that Narayan associates with Nehru. With his energy, his disregard for traditional restraints, and his capacity for hard work he builds up his taxidermy business into a thriving international concern. Just as much as Balraj Khanna's Khatri and Omi, Vasu is the beneficiary of Nehru's Ram Raj, of the new India that Nehru envisaged. But Nehru's India is now presented to us filtered through a deeply conservative South Indian sensibility. Its representative is Vasu, who is less a man than a tiger run wild, the man-eater of Malgudi. Narayan's novel is a satire on Nehru's politics so virulent that it has passed unnoticed – it fits too uncomfortably with Narayan's reputation for genial quaintness.

In the climax of the novel, the two Indias, old and new, confront each other. The poet has completed his verse life of Krishna, and Nataraj has arranged a ceremony in which the first copy of the work will be presented to the temple. The procession led by an elephant becomes a ritual through which Malgudi celebrates its own cohesiveness. But Vasu sits at the window with his rifle beside him. He would 'prohibit celebrations of this kind as a waste of national energy'. He plans to sell the elephant for profit; 'eight hundred rupees' for the tusks, 'twelve annas' for each hair on the elephant's tail when made up into a ring or a bangle. He already has an order for the legs 'mounted as umbrella stands', and there have been 'several inquiries from France and Germany and from Hong Kong'. For Vasu profit is a principle. If money was his sole objective, his scheme – to shoot the elephant before a thousand witnesses – would be irrational. He is fired by a missionary zeal to shock Malgudi out of its traditional pieties, to divert their energies from unproductive celebrations of their own sociability. He plans to shoot the elephant for the same reason that Nehru allowed Chandigarh. Confronted with this threat, all that Nataraj can do is to flap helplessly. And there is no need for him to do anything else. The Gods do not permit such blasphemy. Vasu kills himself. The elephant, and Narayan's India, are preserved intact. In spite of all Vasu's plans, or Nehru's, India goes on.

So it might seem, and if we read *The Man-Eater of Malgudi* as a fable, so it is. But Narayan is a novelist as well as a fabulist, and as a novelist he subjects the values that inform his fable to a bleak commentary. Nataraj is not quite the simple representative of traditional Indian ways that he pretends to be. He lives with his wife and child in the house his grandfather built, but it is not the household that his grandfather had planned. Nataraj's father and his brothers had fallen out, the extended family had disintegrated after the grandfather's death, and Nataraj finds himself living in a house absurdly large for his small, nuclear family. India is changing, whether Nataraj likes it or not, and he is himself the product of that change. That is why, for all that he recognises Vasu as a rakshasha, he finds Vasu's company fascinating. When Vasu keeps aloof for a while, Nataraj begins to 'miss his rough company'. Talking with Vasu, responding to his forceful egotism, Nataraj feels a strange exhilaration: 'I enjoyed taunting him.'

Habits of feeling so engrained in him that he no longer examines them begin to yield to Vasu's disturbing influence. When he speaks to Vasu's woman, Rangi, the dancing girl, he finds himself responding to her coarse physical magnetism:

> My blood tingled with an unholy thrill. I was no longer a married man with a child and home, I was an adolescent lost in dreams over a nude photograph.

He is saved only by the metal grille through which they speak. After Vasu's death, Nataraj returns to his old friendships, and retreats into safe, unexciting monogamy. His world is secure, but without Vasu it seems flatter. He may end the novel printing once again the labels for K.J.'s soft drinks, but the fizz has gone. And in any case there is no returning completely to his old self. Nataraj could think of nothing to frustrate Vasu's plan until it was almost too late. Then he climbed the stairs to Vasu's room, pushed the door open, and saw Vasu sitting in his chair apparently asleep, his rifle beside him. Nataraj crawled slowly across the floor, and seized the gun:

> As my fingers reached the cold butt of his gun, I could have swooned with excitement. I had never touched a gun before and felt scared. Below the window the procession was passing rather quickly, as I thought. I wished I could go up and take a look at it, but he was between me and the window, and if he slept through it that would be the best arrangement possible. If he woke up, well, I had the gun with me at point-blank range. I would follow the method they used in films and command him not to stir until the procession passed. If he made the slightest movement I would pull the trigger.

Vasu was already dead, but Nataraj had taken the decision, if the need arose, to kill him. As he stands there holding the gun, he feels something of the lonely power of the hunter. He becomes in his own person evidence that Vasu's mission has not failed. Vasu survives his death, because his vision has infected Nataraj. The man-eater lives on within the gentle printer.

After the body is found, Nataraj is suspected of murder. There is no evidence against him, but the whole town thinks him a murderer, and there are even times when Nataraj thinks it of himself. Perhaps, Nataraj thinks, I 'rammed the butt of the gun into his skull, and then erased the crime from my mind'. His friends, the poet and journalist, keep away from him. Even Sastri leaves to go on pilgrimage, returning only when Rangi tells him the true story of how Vasu died. Without his friends Nataraj feels bereft, lonely, but also imbued with a new power. He accosts the lawyer, a man he has previously held in awe, and roughly demands settlement of his bill:

> A touch of aggression was creeping into my speech nowadays. My line of thinking was, 'So be it. If I have rid the world of Vasu, I have achieved something. If people want to be squeamish, they are welcome to be so, but let no one expect me to be apologetic for what I have done.'

Nataraj believes himself to be a murderer, and murderers, it seems, are condemned not only to live their own lives, but to live out the life that they have taken. 'Everyone thinks that this is a murderer's press', Nataraj tells Sastri when Sastri returns. Sastri reassures him, 'They are fools who think so, but sooner or later they will know the truth.' Perhaps, but the novel ends before we learn whether Sastri's confidence is justified.

The Man-Eater of Malgudi includes among its cast of characters two artists. There is the poet who writes the life of Lord Krishna in monosyllabic verse, occasionally lapsing into obscurity when 'he totally failed to find a monosyllable and achieved his end by ruthlessly carving up a polysyllable'. And there is Vasu, who insists that taxidermy is 'an art': 'We have constantly to be rivalling Nature at her own game. Posture, look, the total personality, everything has to be created.'

Vasu's is an art that destroys life, the poet's is an art that is subsumed within the life of the community. There seems no doubt as to which kind of art Narayan compares with his own. It has been argued, after all, that India as Narayan represents it is a land in which all polysyllabic complexities have been ruthlessly carved up into the simple, monosyllabic pieties of Malgudi life. But, for all that he has produced a translation of the *Ramayana* of a determined simplicity that the unkind might compare with the poet's verse life of Krishna, Narayan is too self-aware to compare his own achievement with the work of a small town poet.

The Man-Eater of Malgudi was first published in 1961, by which time Narayan was internationally famous. He had already become the first Indian writer since Tagore to achieve an international reputation. His novels do not find their proper home in a Malgudi temple, but are despatched, like Vasu's stuffed animals, to France, Germany, and Hong Kong, to the four corners of the globe. Vasu 'had set himself as a rival to Nature and was carrying on a relentless fight'. It seems a blasphemous project, quite unlike Narayan's gentle art. But for many readers throughout the world Malgudi, Narayan's fictional world, has ousted India; his characters have proved so lifelike, such striking examples of a taxidermal skill, that they are accepted as adequate substitutes for 600 million Indians. Thousands might say with Graham Greene: 'Without him I would never have known what it is like to be an Indian.'[3] Narayan's art is a distillation of native Indian traditions of story-telling, but it is more than a homespun art. Like Vasu, Narayan has masters with foreign-sounding names, not Suleiman, but Firbank, perhaps, and Wodehouse. Vasu is particularly proud of the eyes of his stuffed animals: 'All these are from Germany. We used to get them before the war. Now you cannot get them for love or money. Just lenses! I paint an extra shade at the back for effect.' One suspects in Narayan a matching confidence that his own easy and confident borrowings from a foreign literary tradition are unlikely ever to be possible for Indian writers who learned their English after the war, after independence and the snapping of the continuity between India and the English language.

Nataraj sees in Vasu's room a stuffed tiger-cub. He 'shivered slightly at the thought of anyone taking so young a life', but he is anxious to humour Vasu, and so he says, 'A pretty cub that!' Vasu asks him to estimate how much it would cost. Nataraj guesses two thousand rupees: 'You are right. It's slightly less. I never charge a round sum. My bill for it would be eighteen hundred and twenty-five, packing extra.' Vasu thinks of the cub as 'his masterpiece'. After Vasu's death Nataraj searches his room, looking for the donations to the ceremony for the poet that Vasu has collected, but all he finds is the tiger-cub. He takes it, and hides it in his roll-top desk. Later, he tries to present it to the poet.

> He gazed back at me as if noticing for the first time unplumbed depths of lunacy. He pleaded desperately, 'No, I don't want it. I don't need it. I do not want anything. Thanks.' He suddenly

shot out of the Queen Anne chair, dashed out, and was soon lost in the crowd on Market Road.

Nataraj is left with this odd, charming, unholy trophy hidden away in his desk. It is a badge of the little bit of Vasu that has become a part of him. But it is a sign too of Narayan's uneasy sense that his own art includes aptitudes at odds with the traditional sanctities that his novels seem to celebrate. A stuffed tiger-cub hidden in a roll-top desk – it is a strange image, but characteristic.

The English Indian novel begins from a vantage point outside India. Its English language is the tool it needs to swallow India whole. It ingests a subcontinent, and must end before internal pressure shatters the novel that has sought to accommodate too much. The Indian English novel begins from some small place within India, and moves cautiously outwards to accommodate the alien. It ends in a moment of retraction: Khatri resuming his profession as a maker of sweets; Omi marrying the bride his parents have chosen for him; Vasu dead and Nataraj getting on with his old life. Such novels accommodate, but only up to a point – and the whole novel is a search for that point – at which one can become a citizen of India without ceasing to be someone from Panchkoola or Malgudi. Between them the two kinds of novels establish the patterns that dominate all novels about India. Indian novels begin from a point cut off from the life of the nation, cut off by the writer's foreignness, or his exclusiveness, or his parochialism. From this point the novel moves expansively outwards, until it reaches a point at which the imagination recoils, a point beyond which the writer can absorb no more. In the three chapters that follow I will trace different versions of this same pattern in the fiction of Ruth Prawer Jhabvala and Anita Desai, before returning to R. K. Narayan.

3

Riding the Beast: Ruth Prawer Jhabvala in India

'The most salient fact about India is that it is very poor',[1] writes Ruth Jhabvala, doggedly pointing out the obvious to the Western reader, and knowing all the time that she cannot make that reader understand what she means. She cannot, because the poverty of India is strictly unimaginable. To live in India is to be confronted many times a day – in the face of a hungry child, in the blunted fingers of a leper, in legs grotesquely twisted out of shape by a thoughtful parent anxious that his child acquire the professional qualifications for a life of beggary – with a human misery that one seizes on as absolute, only to be reminded just as often that there is no worst: that there is someone in India living a life more degraded than this, and someone else living a life more degraded still, and so on, and so on, in what seems an infinite recession of misery that plunges away into a darkness that the imagination cannot begin to penetrate. To live in India, to live with this knowledge, is what Ruth Jhabvala thinks of as 'riding the beast'. It is a useless knowledge: 'there is no point in making a catalogue of the horrors with which one lives, *on* which one lives, as on the back of an animal'. No point, because it would only be a catalogue, a dry listing of facts that the brain accepts, but that the imagination cannot comprehend. All the same, it is a knowledge on which Ruth Jhabvala's achievement as a writer of fiction depends.

Jhabvala's narrative skills are nowhere better displayed than in the shifting, fluid chronology of her American novel, *In Search of Love and Beauty*. And in that novel, too, we find her familiar cast of characters; the exiled looking for a home, and the spiritually wounded looking for a cure. There is Mark – separated from the German Jewish mother he loves by the unspoken fact of his homosexuality; separated, too, from the Anglo-Saxon father he never knew – laying claim, in the fair-haired boys he falls in love with, and in the New England property he buys, to 'a landscape, a country, a way of being, that he longed for but only half

34

possessed'. And at the centre of the novel there is Leo Kellerman, who begins as a drama teacher, becomes a psychotherapist, and emerges at last as the prophet of a thoroughly American, utterly ersatz religion, promising his disciples to lead them to 'the point', the place where spiritual and physical orgasm coincide, and the sick will all at once be made whole. The novel is assured, the work of a craftsman at the peak of her powers. But for all that, it is, in the end, a bit limp. 'I am irritable and have weak nerves', Ruth Jhabvala writes in India. In America, it seems, she has lost her irritability, her writing becomes, in both senses of the word, less nervous. I believe that this is because in America she is freed from the guilty knowledge that 'the most salient fact' about the country is a fact that she cannot get into her fiction.

Natasha, Mark's adopted sister, is found by her grandmother, lying face down on her bed, sobbing. She has seen a man sitting on a dustbin.

> He sat enthroned on the dustbin, like a god wafted up from the depths. He was enormous and red in the face and wore a hat without a crown on his wild hair; a pair of stiff black trousers encased one massive leg, exposing a surprisingly soft, lily-white expanse of thigh. His trident, or escutcheon, was an empty bottle held aloft in one hand, and he was alternately shouting and singing to passers-by.

This is the poverty that America has to offer, and Ruth Jhabvala can look at it. She can even find there a certain jaunty flamboyance – her prose is not all mock heroic. It is not like Indian poverty.

In *Heat and Dust*, the young English girl who is visiting India in quest of her family history passes a fourteenth-century tomb. She hears a groan from inside it, and, ignoring the protests of her Indian companion, turns back to investigate:

> At first all I could make out was the vague mass of the sarcophagi in the centre; but when the groaning noise was repeated, I noticed that it came from another shape huddled in one corner. This was human and dressed in something orange. I went up close – Inder Lal had given a warning shout from outside – and got down to peer at the groaner. I recognized him as the white sadhu, Chid, whom I had once met outside the travellers' rest-house.

It is an incident, but it is also an allegory. The girl stoops to
examine Indian poverty, a poverty that has receded from her so far
that she can recognise only its shape as human, and what she sees –
all that she *can* see – is a white sadhu, a boy who may have taken the
name Chidananda as a sign that he has abandoned his previous
life, but who still speaks, reassuringly, in 'a flat Midlands accent'.

There is another episode in *Heat and Dust* where Ruth Jhabvala
tries to imagine the unimaginably poor. In Satipur there is a concrete refuse dump, but most people drop their rubbish outside the
enclosure. The English girl sees a beggar stretched out in the refuse,
dying, ignored by the passers-by, ignored even by the animals:
'Only the flies hovered over her in a cone.' The girl goes home,
but cannot get the dying woman out of her mind. She returns:

> I went up to the refuse dump. I stood over the beggar woman:
> her eyes were open, she was groaning, she was alive. There was
> a terrible smell and a cluster of flies. I looked down and saw a
> thin stream of excrement trickling out of her.

She goes home, and washes herself. Later, she goes to the
hospital, but the doctor there either will not, or cannot, help. On
her way home she passes the hut where the town's holy woman,
Maji, lives. She tells her story, and Maji's reaction is 'not at all like
everyone else's': ' "What?" she cried. "Leelavati? Her time has
come?" Leelavati. The beggar woman had a name!' The two hurry
to the garbage heap, but the beggar woman has gone. She has
managed to crawl all the way to the town reservoir. There, Maji
and the girl find her, and there she dies, in the last hour of
daylight, when 'everything was luminous', and the still, pure
water of the reservoir 'was disturbed only by the reflection of
swooping kingfishers or of trees momentarily nodding their leaves
into its silence'. She dies smiling:

> Suddenly the old woman smiled, her toothless mouth opened
> with the same bliss of recognition as a baby's. Were her eyes not
> yet sightless – could she see Maji looking down at her? Or did
> she only feel her love and tenderness? Whatever it was that
> smile seemed like a miracle to me.

The miracle is expensive. Ruth Jhabvala makes an unexpected
appearance in fancy dress, got up like a contemporary of Dickens:

the death of Leelavati is not much different from the death of Jo in
Bleak House. It is as if, whenever Jhabvala tries to reach out to what
she knows is the great fact of her Indian experience, to comprehend it within her kind of fiction, she recoils. Her cool, realist's eye
mists over, and she becomes sentimental, or the thing recognisable
as a human being only by its shape turns out to be only a pretend
pauper, a white sadhu. At the end of the novel Chid can cast aside
his saffron robes, put on a shirt and khaki shorts, and fly home to
England.

British novelists, when they go to India, are obsessed by the
pathos of lost Empire, by the dust they disturb when they pat the
seat of the viceregal throne in Simla, or the statue of Queen
Victoria 30 feet high, that was pulled down by nationalists, and
now, because someone took a fancy to it – who knows why? –
stands in the small garden of a little bungalow in Bombay. They
produce a weak fiction in which proper liberal principle jostles
uneasily against a damp-eyed nostalgia for departed glory. Paul
Scott is their type. But Ruth Jhabvala was not born British. The lost
empire that obsesses her is the lost empire of the imagination, the
bleak knowledge that India has robbed her of her right to claim that
she can comprehend within her fiction the whole of human life.
When she married an Indian, and went to live in Delhi, she found
herself in a country that offered her one great fact, the fact of
unimaginable poverty, and because it was unimaginable, she could
not write about it. Her odd achievement is to turn this block into
the foundation stone of her talent.

There comes a point, she writes of her experience in India,
where one must escape, and if one cannot escape like Chid, by
taking a westward-bound plane, then one must escape 'some other
way': 'I shut all my windows. I let down the blinds, I turn on the
air-conditioner; I read a lot of books with a special preference for
the great masters of the novel.' In turning away from the unbearable reality of India, Ruth Jhabvala finds the connection she needs
with Indian people: 'I think it is not only Europeans but Indians too
who feel themselves compelled to seek refuge from their often
intolerable environment.' She does not, of course, find a connection with Leelavati, dying on a heap of municipal rubbish – her
she can only transport, fictively, to a more consoling landscape –
but with urban India, the India of prosperous businessmen and
rising young executives with smart wives and American records
not outrageously out of date. In them she recognises herself. Like

her they are dispossessed, surviving only by a practised inattention to what goes on around them, adept in the art of not noticing. The car of a government minister is stopped by policemen. They apologise, they ask if the minister would please take another route. Slum houses are being demolished. Hovels made of 'old tins and sticks and rags' are being pushed over by a bulldozer. Those who lived there are picking through the debris, rescuing what they can – for rubbish in India is not like rubbish in the West; there is no piece of rag so worn out, so filthy, that someone will not find it worthwhile to pick it up. The slum-dwellers are passively wretched. Only one woman shakes her fist, and shouts:

> She ran around and got in the way of the workers till someone gave her a push and she fell over. When she got up, she was holding her knee and limping but she had stopped shouting and she too began to dig among the debris. The Minister was getting very impatient with the car not starting, and he was busy giving instructions to the chauffeur. When at last we managed to get going, he talked all the time about the car and that it was a faulty model – all the models of that year were – cars were like vintages, he said, some years were good, some not so good.
>
> ('Rose Petals')

Ruth Jhabvala hates that Minister, but it is a guilty hatred. There are places where talking about cars and reading Flaubert are morally equivalent activities.

Jhabvala finds India through people like Har Dayal of *Esmond in India*, the nationalist who never went to prison, who lives in independent India in the cool luxury of his Delhi house, serves on cultural committees, and quotes Wordsworth to his gardener. Whenever contact with Ram Nath – the old freedom fighter who now lives a life of simple poverty, having turned his back on a public life that must seem to him a mockery of all that he fought for – guiltily reminds him of his own good fortune, he is quickly able to reassure himself: 'For him the life of action, for me the life of the spirit . . . Who is to say which is the better?'. Or through Ushi Saxena in *Get Ready for Battle*, whose husband, Toto, is a promising young executive in an oil company. Ushi has

> a lot of conversation, for she kept up on things: she read a lot – the *Illustrated Weekly* and *Femina* and *Time* magazine (which kept

her up on international affairs) – and she went to the local art exhibitions, and she and Toto always bought tickets for the productions of the U.K. High Commission or the Army Head-quarters Dramatic Groups.

In *Heat and Dust* there is the heir to the Nawab, Karim, and his wife Kitty, who invites guests to 'take a pew'. They and their friends are all of them 'eager to serve India', but have found difficulty in cutting through bureaucratic red tape. Meanwhile, they stay in London, and discuss how their family art treasures can be got out of the country. Mrs. Kaul in *A Backward Place*, Honorary Secretary of the Cultural Dais, has two ambitions: 'to draw in the cultural threads of all nations'; and to persuade the prime minister to attend one of her meetings. These are Ruth Jhabvala's kind of people, spending their lives not noticing the country that they live in, but do not belong to. Sometimes, a character, often a Westerner, will be allowed to voice her opinion of them. Georgia, a modern young English girl of stunning banality, has followed her boyfriend, Ranjit, to India. She goes with him to the restaurants where he meets his friends to smoke, drink milkshakes, and feel melancholy at the thought of the life awaiting him when he at last agrees to accept the well-paid, undemanding job that his parents' influence will secure him. Georgia tells Ranjit 'all the things he should be doing – building dams, teaching peasants to read and write, defending the frontier'. Occasionally, she explodes:

"What about you?" she suddenly turned on them. "I never see *you* do anything. What's wrong with you? There's the whole of India, bursting with problems, screaming for help, and all you do is sit around here drinking, God help us, milkshakes."

('A Young Man of Good Family')

But Georgia is no moral authority. Her one discovery is that the pop culture she is heir to is so undistinguished that it has made her a citizen of the world. When it becomes obvious that Ranjit is growing tired of her, she and her friend Suzanne plan a trip to Ceylon: 'From there we may go on somewhere else – what do you think of Japan? We might get jobs there, or push on to California.'

Ruth Jhabvala likes Indian music: Indian devotional songs are 'pure like water drawn from a well'. For a while, as she listens to them, she feels reconciled to the place where she lives. Musicians, when they appear in her stories consistently command her respect; Ahmed the sarod player, and Sujata the singer of *In Search of Love and Beauty*; Shakuntala and her singing teacher in the story 'The Housewife'. Even the great singer, Khan Sahib, of 'In a Great Man's House', who is an odious, self-obsessed domestic tyrant, can make his wife fall in love with him all over again just by singing a song: 'What things he could make her feel, that fat selfish husband of hers.' Jhabvala admires the concentrated discipline of Indian musicians, and their practice of an art that transcends rather than weakly escapes the poverty, the filth, the degradation of the country they live in. There are, then, the musicians, but alongside them there are the devotees of culture – Mrs Kaul of the Cultural Dais, Ushi and Toto Saxena patronising amateur dramatics, Har Dayal, a regular member of the government's cultural committees, and his artistic daughter, Shakuntala, who would be a painter if she could paint, or a writer if she could only write. Their championing of culture is just one more expression of the bad faith that they cultivate so assiduously in order to survive. We might ask which group Ruth Jhabvala belongs to, sitting in her air-conditioned room, all the blinds drawn, reading 'the great masters of the novel' or practising her own sullen art, but she belongs to both. For the craft of fiction requires no less discipline and no less concentration than the art of music, but, unlike music, it is necessarily an impure art: it cannot transcend, it can only escape the social realities out of which it is born. Ruth Jhabvala shares an irritable intimacy with characters like Har Dayal and his daughter. They grate on her – 'my teeth are set on edge' – but, equally, she grates on herself. She has an uneasy sense that, in India, her own exercise of the craft of fiction is inevitably an exercise of bad faith.

The best response to India is to be 'a strong person who slogs on and does what he can as a doctor or social worker', but she is not a strong person; she is 'irritable' and has 'weak nerves': 'All right, so I am not a doctor nor a social worker nor a saint nor at all a good person; then the only thing to do is to try and push that aspect of India out of sight and turn to others.' The only thing to do is not to notice the animal you are riding on, not to attend to 'the most salient fact about India'. And so it is that to look at Mrs. Kaul and her like is to be forced to recognise a grotesque reflection of yourself.

Some manage to escape their country without maiming themselves. They do so by retreating to their homes, and finding in the love of wife or husband a reality strong enough to occlude the terrible facts of life outside. Judy in *A Backward Place* has that kind of love for her husband Bal, and Prem in *The Householder* learns to feel it for his wife Indu. But, for the most part, it is not so. 'A very great number of Indians never get enough to eat . . . *Can* one lose sight of that fact? God knows I've tried.' Jhabvala has tried, and she has failed, and her failure is the one, subdued and ironical, claim she makes for her own humanity. The heroes of her novels are those, like her, who have failed to go blind. In *Esmond in India* there is Ram Nath, the ageing nationalist who has held true to his values through all the disillusioning years of independence. He is a tarnished hero. He has retreated from his wife, who does not share his principled contempt for material comfort, into a silence which he breaks only with ugly, cackling laughter when his wife once again shows herself uncomprehending of the values he lives by. Their relationship is like a bitter parody of Gandhi's with Kasturbai. As well as being cruel Ram Nath's heroism is futile. He tries through his simple, graceless way of life to cling to the sense that once inspired him, that he was at one with the Indian people he fought for. But at the end of the novel he confesses that he feels more and more alone:

> He had travelled in third-class railway carriages, with peasants and priests and prostitutes; had tramped through the jungles in his journey from one village to the other, and seen eggshell dawns breaking over a landscape of dust and dry thorns. He had penetrated into the narrowest lanes in overcrowded cities, stepped absent-mindedly over naked children in silver anklets and haggled with fat money-lenders who sat cross-legged on their stringbeds and scratched their testicles. He had known all the smells and sounds and sights of the day and the night: and he had always promised himself that one day, when he grew old, he would sit and think about that deep thrill which they gave him and would ferret out their meaning. Well, he had grown old: and up to now he had not even noticed that he had ceased to notice them.

In *Get Ready for Battle* Sarla Devi has parted from her property-speculator husband, and lives a life of austere simplicity devoted to serving the poor. She takes up the cause of the inhabitants of a shanty town who are to be evicted to make way for industrial development. Her campaign comes to nothing. The leader of the shanty town residents sells out to the developers, the rest accept their eviction passively. Only for a moment, sitting by the river, acknowledging her defeat, does she give way to lassitude:

> All her life she had wanted to be free and alone, like this, thinking nothing and being nothing, only a disembodied state of acceptance; and all her life she had been tugged back by her compassion into a world where nothing could be accepted and everything had to be fought against.

We admire her heroism but we are forced to acknowledge that it is neurotic. She needs to make of her existence a lifelong exercise in self-mortification, because only in this way is she able to tolerate the guilt and the shame of having enough to eat while people around her starve. She gives her life to others, but her attention is always on herself. All her doings are 'sops to a conscience which nevertheless hardly ever ceased to trouble her'. That is why she finds it hard to understand other people, why she believes her son to be in rebellion against his father's materialism, when all he really wants is to set up a factory manufacturing fountain pens.

In *A Backward Place* Sudhir, an idealistic Bengali works for Mrs Kaul at the Cultural Dais, but leaves to teach in a Literacy Institute in a backward province. He leaves not in any glow of enthusiasm, but because he is bored and irritated. His heart sinks when he sees a photograph of the Institute, an ugly brick building in which 'a few unintelligent-looking peasants' are sitting, set in a landscape that is 'flat, stony and empty'. He goes sullenly, but he goes, and, as his train cuts through India, he is blessed. It is night. His fellow passengers are sleeping, but he recalls the conversations that he has overheard, and he no longer feels any distaste for their 'obvious sentiments' and 'obvious phrases'. Instead, he recognises in them

> a manifestation of all the variety and unexpectedness of the fertile lives that sprang out of this soil, which was in itself so various and unexpected and was now desert and now flourishing fields and now the flattest plains and now the highest and most holy of mountains.

He becomes an Indian, the landscape of his country and its people linked to him as a part of his being. There the novel leaves him. We wish him well, but have no confidence that his vision will survive when his fellow passengers emerge from the darkness and thrust themselves more importunately on his attention. We may doubt whether it will sustain him in the months ahead, when he will have to look for fellowship, not to the dispossessed intellectuals of urban India, but to a few unintelligent-looking peasants.

These flawed and fragile heroes are the best that Ruth Jhabvala has to offer. They are not the best there is. Ram Nath's son, Narayan, was a brilliant medical student, but turned his back on the chance of a lucrative Delhi practice and went to serve as a doctor in the isolated villages of rural India. He does not appear in the novel. We learn of him only through a letter that he writes to his father. This is no accident. Jhabvala can recognise his kind of heroism, but she can do nothing with it. She once met such a person, an expatriate doctor returning to India after her first home leave for twelve years:

> I asked her: but what does it feel like to go back after such a long time? How do you manage to adapt yourself? She didn't understand. This question which was of such tremendous import to me – how to adapt oneself to the differences between Europe and India – didn't mean a thing to her. It simply didn't matter. And she was right, for in view of the things she sees and does every day, the delicate nuances of one's own sensibilities are best forgotten.

She was right, and in being right, in refusing to attend to her own sensibilities, she disqualifies herself as a possible character in a novel by Ruth Jhabvala. Jhabvala cannot get into her fiction the unutterable misery of India, nor its true heroism. Her people are not those who, self-forgetfully, devote their lives to the service of the beast, but those who look at it, if they look at all, only out of the corner of the eye.

In the story 'Suffering Women', Anjuna, a retired film actress, a loving mother, a good friend, and a kindly mistress, watches from the window her daughter drive off with her boyfriend, Rahul:

> Crowds had come out to enjoy a promenade by the sea, and with the crowds came the beggars lucky enough to have the sea-front for their beat: the man with the twisted limbs who wound himself like a creeper round the long pole he carried, the very

respectable woman who wore shoes and spoke English and hadn't eaten for three days. Anjuna saw a few crippled children clinging to Rahul's car and tapping on the windows, but Rahul swiftly drove off so that the children fell back and hobbled as fast as they could to surround some other car. The woman in the nursing-home opposite was at her post, her blank face gazing over the iron bars.

On one side of the street Anjuna looks with her busy, attentive gaze. On the other a madwoman stares with blank, unseeing eyes. It is the tense opposition between those two pairs of eyes that lends Ruth Jhabvala's fiction its strange, nervous power.

4

The Quiet and the Loud: Anita Desai's India

'Quiet writing, like Anita Desai's, can be more impressive than stylistic fireworks', wrote Victoria Glendinning in *The Sunday Times*.[1] Anita Desai may let fireworks into her stories, but not into her style. At the end of *The Village by the Sea*, Hari and his sisters celebrate Diwali: 'Hari carried the basket of fireworks onto the grassy knoll in the coconut grove, and, to the sound of Bela's and Kamal's excited shrieks, he set off a rocket into the sky where it exploded with a bang into a shower of coloured sparks.' The rocket bangs, the girls shriek, but the prose stays quiet. In *Midnight's Children* the 'saffron minutes and green seconds' that separate India from its moment of independence tick by. Crowds – 'the men in shirts of zafaran hue, the women in saris of lime' – watch a celebratory firework display, 'saffron rockets, green sparkling rain'. There is a part of most English readers that distrusts such flamboyance, and recoils from it with relief to the sober, guilt-free pleasures of Anita Desai's quiet prose. But there remains a nagging worry that it may not be easy at once to conform to English standards of good taste, and be true to the place Anita Desai writes about. India, after all, is not a quiet country.

In *The Village by the Sea* Anita Desai dispenses with her usual cast of characters. It is Hari's story, and his sister, Lila's. With their drunken father, their sick mother, and two younger sisters, they live a life of wretched poverty in the little fishing village of Thul, not far from Bombay, the full weight of family responsibility thrust prematurely on their young shoulders. As the novel begins Lila performs her morning puja to the sacred rock in the sea. Then she walks home through 'dew that still lay on the rough grass, and made the spider webs glitter'. She sees butterflies, and she sees birds; 'flute-voiced drongoes that cut the air like dazzling knives', and 'pert little magpie robins':

A single cock-pheasant, invisible, called out 'coop-coop-coop' in

45

its deep, bogey-man voice from under a bush and a pigeon's
voice gurgled on and on. It was the voice of the village Thul as
much as the roar of the waves and the wind in the palms.

Like her friend, Ruth Jhabvala, and like Forster before her, Anita
Desai loves Indian birds. Their easy grace in a climate that can be
so pitiless to human beings rarely fails to move her. In one of her
best short stories, a querulous, asthmatic old man finds his
irritability disappear, and his heart lift as dawn brings a cool
breeze, and pigeons rise into the sky:

> Then, with a swirl and flutter of feathers, a flock of pigeons
> hurtled upwards and spread out against the dome of the sky –
> opalescent, sunlit, like small pearls. They caught the light as
> they rose, turned brighter till they turned at last into crystals,
> into prisms of light. Then they disappeared in the soft, deep blue
> of the morning.
>
> ('Pigeons at Daybreak', *Games at Twilight*)

A city-bred, middle-class old man might see such a thing and find
peace, but would a girl like Lila, a girl born in a village, who is
troubled not by asthma but by how to find the wherewithal to keep
her family alive, be quite so tremblingly sensitive to a cock-
pheasant and a pigeon? Anita Desai insists that *The Village by the
Sea* tells a true story, a story 'based entirely on fact'. But truth in
stories cannot be won just by sticking to facts, it must be an
achievement of language. Anita Desai recalls in her dedication the
'many holidays' she has spent in Thul, and it is hard not to feel that
the cock-pheasant and the pigeon are being looked at by a writer
on holiday, not by a peasant girl in debt. All through *The Village
by the Sea* Anita Desai's prose places a barrier between the reader
and the characters. Its quietness, its transparency, separates us
from them as effectively as the scenic windows in Bombay's
modern apartment blocks separate those inside from the squatter's
colonies just a hundred yards away – so near and yet so far.

Near the hut where Hari and Lila live is a holiday home owned
by a rich Bombay businessman. It is here that Sayyid Ali stays
when he comes to Thul to study the nesting habits of baya birds.
When Hari's sisters learn what he is up to, they 'burst into
uncontrollable giggles'. It is as if Anita Desai has realised that
crediting a village girl with a lively interest in bird-song was
incongruous, and feels the need to correct her mistake. But it is

more than that. The novel assumes as its premise a complicity between Anita Desai's own educated, aesthetic feeling for Thul, and the feeling of those like Hari and Lila, for whom Thul is home, and whose pressing realities are the shortage of food; the high price of medicine; and the cheapness and easy supply of toddy, the fermented coconut milk on which their father drinks himself into a stupor every night. But the story works to show that such complicity is only, can only be, an illusion.

The government plans to make Thul the site of a large industrial complex producing chemical fertiliser. The villagers see the plan as a threat to their livelihood. They sail to Bombay to protest against the decision, and Hari goes with them, fired with indignation against the government, but also intent on staying in Bombay to find work. In Bombay the villagers are addressed by Sayyid Ali. Hari finds it odd that a 'city man – neat, clean, and educated – ' should take up their cause: 'Yet he spoke of fish and cattle and trees with feeling and concern.' Hari is impressed: 'He speaks well,' Hari said, 'Very well.' So well that he successfully disguises the fact that his own interest in Thul and the interests of those who live there are poles apart. He is worried about pollution, they are worried about their jobs.

When Sayyid Ali comes to Thul, he scarcely notices the villagers. Instead, he looks at birds, through binoculars. It is Anita Desai's way of recognising that when she looks at Hari, Lila, and their family, she can look at them only as if they were birds – charming, interesting, and of a different species from the observer. She can look at them so nearly only by using a prose that works like a pair of binoculars, allowing her to show in close-up people who would be too shy of her presence ever to let her approach their lives too closely.

In Bombay Hari learns how to mend watches. When he returns to Thul his new skill soon finds a use. Sayyid Ali has dropped his watch into water, and it has stopped. The incident exposes the insecurity of the alliance between the villagers, fearful of a change that they cannot understand, and those like Sayyid Ali who resent change because it threatens their taste for the picturesque, their hobbies of bird-watching – or villager-watching. Hari has learned how to mend watches, how to make the most of time. His new skill will be useful when watch-wearing engineers come to Thul, and he thinks of starting a poultry farm and selling the produce to the newcomers. Hari explains his plans to Sayyid Ali, and Sayyid Ali grasps the lesson that Anita Desai's fable is designed to teach:

'Adapt – that is what you are going to do. Just as birds and animals must do if they are to survive.' It is a chastening lesson. He learns it, and at once topples backwards, and falls off the veranda into a hibiscus bush. He has tried to make Thul a wildlife sanctuary, a reserve for the baya birds and a reservation for the villagers. But Hari does not want his old life protected. He wants a new life, and a better life, and he will make it for himself. History, like Sayyid Ali's watch, is in his pocket. Sayyid Ali learns his lesson, and then goes back to bird-watching: 'with a cry of delight he was stumbling back to his marsh, having seen a little baya bird arrive with something in its beak for its young. He seemed to have forgotten Hari.'

He seems to have forgotten, but he has not. Anita Desai's novels have a single plot. The central characters build around themselves a quiet space, and into that quietness, just for a moment, the noisy life of India intrudes. Then it is quiet again, but the quality of the quietness has changed. Hari leaves his little fishing village for Bombay, where his ears are stunned by the noise of the traffic 'hooting and screeching and grinding and roaring past and around him'. Then he comes back to Thul, but he comes back a changed man. Hari is the central character in *The Village by the Sea*, but he is observed, seen from the outside. It is Sayyid Ali who is in close proximity to the novelist. His silent hours of bird-watching are interrupted by a short conversation with Hari. Then he goes back to his birds. But he too is changed. He has learned to recognise his own life as irrelevant to the larger life of India.

In *Fire on the Mountain* Nanda Kaul, widow of a vice-chancellor and a great-grandmother now, has retired from the plains to the quiet, unfashionable hill-station Kasauli. There, in the cool mountain air, she finds freedom at last from husband, children, servants and visitors. She devotes her old age to the perfection of an art that she has practised all her adult life. 'Each day, for an hour' she would retreat to her room, and lie with 'her eyes tightly clenched, her hands folded on her chest', and withdraw from the household noises – the giggles, the scrunch of bicycle tyres over gravel, the running taps, the hissed threats of an ayah – into her own stillness. In Kasauli she has found a place where she can surround herself with stillness all day long. She remembers just one moment in her adult life when she felt herself perfectly alone. It was night, the badminton was over, the guests had gone. She walked in the garden, and watched from the darkness as her husband returned after driving his mistress home. Then she walked again: 'That was one time she had been alone: a moment of private triumph, cold and proud.' In Kasauli she can stretch that moment into years.

But even there Nanda Kaul's isolation is imperfect. She is still at the mercy of letters and of the telephone. As the novel begins, the postman intrudes into 'the cool cave of her day'. He brings a letter telling her that her great-granddaughter Raka will be visiting her. After she has read it, the telephone rings. It is her childhood friend, Ila Das. First Raka and then Ila Das erupt into the cold, proud stillness in which Nanda Kaul had planned to live out her life.

She dreads Raka's visit – the demands it will make on her, the presence of a child who will 'shatter and rip her still house to pieces' – but the child, when she arrives, is as self-contained as Nanda Kaul herself. The old woman begins to feel a complicity with her: 'Raka, you really *are* a great-grandchild of mine, aren't you? You are more like me than *any* of my children or grand-children. You are *exactly* like me, Raka.' But, like Sayyid Ali's championship of the villagers, it is a false complicity. The self-centredness of the old, born of weariness, is quite unlike the self-centredness with which the young signal their amoral energy. Nanda Kaul recoils in her old age from a lifetime spent suffering other people's impingement on her. She believes that she is released from her debts to others because she has paid them in full. Raka, the child of one careless and one inadequate parent, has not yet learned that such debts exist.

Lila Das has spent her life clinging to that steep Indian slope that plunges from genteel poverty to indigence – slipping, clutching again, slipping, finding herself ever nearer the precipice over which India's unimaginably poor have fallen. She is in the same position as her rusty, broken-spoked umbrella, the last relic of her gentility, when it is snatched from her hand by laughing school-boys and kicked to the side of the road where it lodges precariously in the railings, saved – but only just – from a plunge of 2,000 feet. Lila Das has given piano lessons, been a domestic science tutor in the university that Nanda Kaul's husband governed, and now ekes out a meagre existence as a social worker in a village in the Himalayan foothills. When she visits Nanda Kaul, she brings with her a bitter knowledge; of babies dead of tetanus, children blind with conjunctivitis, and seven year old girls married to grey-haired landowners in exchange for a quarter of an acre and two goats.

Such knowledge is a jarring, discordant load to take up into the cool, pine-scented air of Kasauli – as jarring as Lila Das's voice. She is famous for her voice. When she lisped nursery rhymes, the noise 'curdled the blood of the adults who dandled her'. When she recited at school, 'teachers shivered, their teeth on edge, as if a child had squeaked a pencil on a slate or slid a nail down a glass pane'. As she sits in Nanda Kaul's garden taking tea, she bursts into a quavering song, and becomes for a moment a woman out of myth, an anti-type of Orpheus. At the sound of her voice pine trees let their needles fall, cicadas hide under stones and weep, pebbles roll downhill to escape the cacophony:

> Ye banks and braes o'bonny Doon,
> How can ye bloom sae fresh and fair.

The two old ladies take tea together, and Ila Das refreshes herself with a bath in the cool waters of memory; the vice-chancellor's house, well-groomed lawns, and badminton parties. Her memories are akin to those with which Nanda Kaul tries to win Raka's attention, but less crafted. When he set out to explore Tibet, Nanda Kaul's father took his family with him as far as the Zaji-la Pass:

> But one morning, when we had camped beside a river of green ice water in a meadow that seemed untouched by a single foot-print, and the sky seemed the purest, cleanest sky that's ever been, he got onto his horse, Suleiman, dressed in fur and leather, and rode away over the pass, leaving us alone.

Nanda Kaul makes her memories as hard and bright as dreams, but even so they distract the child only for a moment from the more pressing interest of things; a fat yellow snake, a broken tin can, a burnt-out bungalow. Lila Das is no more successful. Her memories stumble on something unmentionable. She remembers badminton, mixed doubles against the Vice-Chancellor and Miss David: 'Miss David was an *ace* player – ooh, she was good – and they beat us hollow . . . ' The forbidden name puts a stop to the conversation: 'and here were Ila Das and Nanda Kaul, both beaten, silent'.

Nanda Kaul does not invite Ila Das to live with her. When tea is over Ila Das walks back down the mountain to her shabby village home. But she never arrives. On the outskirts of the village she is raped and murdered by a villager who resents her interference in his marriage plans for his seven-year-old daughter. A policeman telephones Nanda Kaul with the news, and it has scarcely sunk in when Raka taps at the window: 'Look, Nani, I have set the forest on fire.' In the ravine below the house the brushwood is already aflame. Raka has always been fascinated by fire.

From her veranda Nanda Kaul can see the red-tiled roof of a school and the spire of a church. It is a more comfortable view than the one from the back windows, 'of the cliff plunging seven thousand feet down to the Punjab plains'. Raka delights in that gorge. The people of Kasauli use it as a midden. Rusted scrap-metal litters its slopes, snakes live there, and jackals – rabid jackals according to Nanda Kaul's servant, Ram Lal – and there too, according to him, are the *churails*, man-monsters, their feet turned back, who live on corpses. Jackals and *churails* haunt the gorge because in Kasauli is the Pasteur Institute where rabies serum is manufactured for the whole of India. The dead bodies of the animals on which the doctors have experimented are thrown into a chute from which they are debouched into the gorge.

The Institute is a factory in Shangri-la, a reminder that the stillness that Nanda Kaul finds in Kasauli, the stillness that she weaves around her, is not a natural but a manufactured product, an antidote to the madness of involvement refined as painstakingly as the doctors of the Institute refine their rabies serum. The memory of a childhood with a father who did not really ride into Tibet on his horse, Suleiman, and of a married life devoted to relieving her husband of domestic anxieties that might distract him from his lifelong affair with Miss David, are ejected into some mental gorge, put behind her while she broods contentedly on a red-tiled roof and a church spire. She nourishes this life of hers on carefully chosen reading: Waley's translations, a book on Indian birds, the *Travels of Marco Polo*, the *Pillow Book of Sei Shonagon*. It is a taste for the exotic, for detached elegance, the scent of pines rather than the fetid, pungent odours of the Indian plains. It is a refined and rather etiolated taste, and Anita Desai's prose is there to remind us that it is the taste of the author as much as of her heroine.

The story of the novel is the story of how Nanda Kaul's life of quiet self-containment is disrupted, by Raka and by Ila Das. Raka forces her to feel again a solicitude that she had given up as a bad habit. Raka loves exploring the gorge, and, as Nanda Kaul's eyes follow her, she is reminded of the clutter of tin cans, dead flesh, and primitive legend that she had rejected as incompatible with the elegant austerity of her chosen life. Then, with the murder of Ila Das, Nanda Kaul is forced to recognise the mindless brutality of a life that she had thought herself aloof from. Anita Desai's prose is a perfect match for Nanda Kaul in her aloofness. It is 'style' as a carefully refined antidote to the maddening welter of experience with which India, the India of the plains, assaults the mind and bewilders the senses. All impediments to its bright clarity have been excised, debouched into the waste-paper basket. When Nanda Kaul can no longer maintain her aloof detachment from life, Anita Desai is forced to relinquish her style. She looks for an alternative. Ila Das with her tattered gentility and awful voice infects the prose with a Dickensian extravagance, but this never reaches much higher than pastiche. The rape and murder are recounted with a blank factuality that derives from another school of writing – Muriel Spark at her nastiest. The novel gutters and dies in a medley of conflicting styles that can do no more than share in the central character's bewilderment. It is a less successful novel than the earlier *Clear Light of Day*.

Like *Midnight's Children*, *Clear Light of Day* is at once a family chronicle and a history of modern India. But there is a crucial difference. In *Clear Light of Day* history is glimpsed only out of the corner of the eye. In the partition riots Delhi is ablaze, but the fires are on the horizon. The novel takes place in Old Delhi's Civil Lines, 'where the gardens and bungalows are quiet and sheltered behind their hedges', and the residents only imagine that they 'hear the sound of shots and of cries and screams'. It is here that the family live, the four children – Raja, his two sisters, Bim and Tara, and Baba, the youngest son, the retarded baby of the family. Raja and Tara leave, Raja to marry the daughter of a rich Muslim businessman, and Tara to marry a diplomat and enter on the displaced life of the embassy, shifting from country to country, returning to India from time to time in a forlorn attempt to 'keep in touch'. Bim teaches history at the local college. Her life oscillates between history and memory, between the comfortably distant history of the Moghul empire that she teaches at college, and the memories that she broods over at home: sad memories for the most part, of her aunt's lapse into alcoholism, and of the rupture that took place between herself and her brother, embittering the love that she still feels for him.

It is a noisy house. Badshah, the dog on which Bim lavishes her affection, irritates the neighbours with his non-stop barking, and Baba plays over and over again at full volume his small collection of 1940s records. The noise grates on the nerves of visitors, sometimes on Bim's nerves too, but the noise works only to drown out the noises of the outside world. However paradoxically, it works to preserve a silence, the silence in which Bim has chosen to live out her days.

Time stopped for her in 1947. Then her sister married, and her beloved brother left home. She lives with her memories, two memories in particular – the one associated with her aunt, the other with her brother. The aunt – really a poor relation taken in by Bim's mother so that she need not be distracted by her children from her bridge – recommended buying a cow. The cow broke its tether, stumbled into the garden well, and was drowned. That image – the white cow, green slime and black water – haunted Bim's aunt as she lay dying. The white cow is balanced by a white horse. 'Can you remember', Bim asks Tara 'playing on the sand late in the evening and the white horse riding by, Hyder Ali Sahib up on it, high above us, and his peon running in front of him, shouting, and the dog behind him, barking.' It is the image that first inspired Raja with a vision of the grace of Islam, the glamour of India's Moghul past, and the beauty of Urdu. It gave him the ambition to become when he grew up a poet or a hero, a second Iqbal, or someone who might single-handed heal the wounds of his country's partition by the practice of a reckless magnanimity. Bim's emotional life is suspended between a white dream and a white nightmare, between love and bitterness.

Raja married Hyder Ali's daughter, became his heir, and wrote Bim a letter assuring her that he would not increase the rent she pays for the family house. Bim has never recovered from the shock of her brother, her hero, diminishing to a landlord. She keeps the letter by her, until, at the end of the novel, she destroys it, as a sign that she has recovered from her sterile obsession with the past. It is the progression figured in the novel's third white memory, a memory associated with Tara. Tara was running after her mother as her mother strolled through the rose garden. She spied something gleaming from under a heap of fallen rose petals, a pearl, or a silver ring. But what Tara finds when she bends to look is a 'small blanched snail'. 'Her face wrinkling with disgust her mother turned and paced on without a word, leaving Tara on her knees to contemplate the quality of disillusion'. The incident is recalled again later in the novel, but, as it is repeated, it is transformed. Tara stayed for a while on her knees 'crushed with disappointment, then lifted the snail onto a leaf and immediately delight gushed up as at a newly mined well at seeing the small creature unfold, tentatively protrude its antennae, and begin to slide forward on a stream of slime'. The loss of childish illusions need not after all be sad: it may mark the beginning of the adult's capacity to find joy in looking at the world undeceived. At the end of the novel Bim forgives her brother, forgives him for being not what she dreamed he might be, a pearl, a silver ring, a hero, but for being what he is.

In the novel's last scene Bim has left her house, left her garden She has not been released into a full possession of the great and wonderful land of India – Anita Desai's novels do not work like that – she has only gone next door, to listen to her neighbour singing. She still lives in her house as if in a shell, and she can only progress as snails do, slowly. But she is no longer self-enclosed her horns have emerged and are alert to the world around her After the neighbour, his teacher sings in his old man's voice: 'All the storms and rages and pains of his life were in that voice, impinging on every song he chose to sing, giving the verses of love and romance a harsh edge that was mocking and disturbing.' It is a voice that redeems by its beauty the ravages of time, the pain, and the disillusionment that it embodies: 'Vah! Vah! someone called out in rapture – it might have been the old man listening above on the veranda – and the singer lifted a shaking hand in acknowledgement.' So the novel ends, not with Baba playing over and over again his collection of 1940s records with their depressingly ironic titles – 'Don't fence me in' – but with an old man making beauty not by ignoring the passage of time, but by accepting it.

Bim's was a family overtaken by history, unprepared for life in an independent India. Her parents spent their lives playing bridge at the club, intently conning their hands, unaware of the movement of history that was bringing their way of life to an end. Their children were educated in English, in Christian schools, educated into a culture that in 1947 packed its bags and left, condemning them to live their lives as a futile exercise in nostalgia, dreaming like Bing Crosby on Baba's record of a white Christmas. Bim is offered no magic release. Even when she listens to the old man's song, what it brings to her mind is a line from Four Quartets. She and Raja will be friends again: the partition in the family will be healed. But the incident has no national implications, for *Clear Light of Day* determinedly refuses allegory. All that Bim is offered is a moment; a Hindu singing a song by Iqbal, Pakistan's national poet, and herself responding with a verse of T.S. Eliot's – a privileged moment in which her own, and India's, fragmented cultural heritage becomes one, and Bim feels at peace with herself and at peace with her land.

In Anita Desai's most recent novel, *In Custody*, Raja has slipped down the social scale, and reappears as Deven, struggling to support his wife and son on his meagre salary as a lecturer in Hindi at a college in Mirpore, an undistinguished small town outside Delhi. Like Raja, Deven has dreamed of devoting his life to Urdu poetry, and his dreams have collapsed around him, leaving not even wealth to reconcile him to his unglamorous existence. Deven is Anita Desai's version of a character common in modern Indian novels: the little man, often a teacher, trapped in a job that offers a precarious prestige, but not the salary to support it. One thinks of Narayan's *The English Teacher* and Ruth Jhabvala's *The Householder*. These are domestic novels. The householder, the poorly paid young teacher, learns to find in his wife and child the solace that supports him in the humdrum struggles of his life. They share with Victorian novels a sense of the redemptive virtue of domesticity, but whereas Dickens or George Eliot or Trollope find in domesticity the happiest expression of a national character, Narayan and Ruth Prawer Jhabvala celebrate domestic love as a private discovery, a wonderful surprise. Private love remains private: it is not pressed into service as the expression of a national value.

Deven has a sulky wife, Sarla, and a small son, Manu. His task, one supposes, is to transform his domestic relationships, to make his home a closed space where happiness can be kept intact, preserved from the meagreness and frustrations of his public life. After a dispiriting visit to Delhi, Deven returns home and takes his son for a walk. They go to the canal that 'separated the town proper from the chemically lush grounds of the Agricultural and Veterinary College', and look across the water at a flock of parrots exploding out of an acacia tree, 'acid green against the pale yellow of the sky'. Father and son are united in a moment of loving intimacy: 'It was as if the evening star shone through at that moment, casting a small pale illumination upon Deven's flattened grey world.' If Anita Desai is to be true to the pattern established

by her predecessors that moment will become the lodestar o
Deven's life. Instead, it remains a moment:'Of course it could no
be maintained, of course it had to diminish and decline.' Wher
Deven returns home, he finds a letter calling him back to Delhi
away from his family. It is as if Anita Desai has rejected domesti
happiness as an artificial solution, the creation of a closed space
lush but chemically lush, as dissociated from the urgent realities o
India as are the grounds of the agricultural college from the
stunted, barren, disorderly landscape of the town proper.

The letter is from the great Urdu poet, Nur, who invites Dever
to be his secretary. Deven conceives a project, to make a tape
recording of Nur. The novel charts the difficulties of the enterprise
Deven's technical innocence, an incompetent sound recordist
shortage of money, but most of all Nur himself – his insatiable
demands for biryani, rum and cash, the domestic chaos in which
he lives, his rambling conversation that flickers from poetry to
racing pigeons, wrestlers and brothels. For all that he writes in
Urdu, for Deven Nur embodies India. It is through Nur's poetry
that Deven understands his Indian experience, and is reconciled
with it. His project is akin to Anita Desai's, akin to that of all Indian
novelists: in recording Nur, he aspires to record India.

The result is a 'fiasco':

When the tapes could be induced to produce sound, there
seemed to be nothing to listen to – long intervals of crackling and
sputtering interspersed with a sudden blare of horns from the
street, the shrieking of nest-building birds, loud explosions o
laughter and incoherent joviality, drunken voices bawling
singing, stopping short. Where was Nur? Occasionally his voice
wandered in like some lost mendicant off a crowded street
offering a few lines of verse in a faint, foundering voice, ther
breaking off to say, much more firmly and positively, 'Fetch me
another glass of rum. What have you ordered for lunch today'
Has someone gone to collect it? I need more rum if I am to wai
for so long.' Or else wandering through some difficult and
involved tale of his vagabond days, stopping to groan and
complain of the agony piles were causing him, pleading for some
relief from discomfort, cursing his age, calling for palliatives in
the way of food and drink, then sinking into silence while some
admirer of his bawled out advice or encouragement with bawdy
undertones that made his audience yelp like a pack of jackals.

Deven's students, who understand electronics, help him to edit,
and the result is a single tape, 'a bizarre pastiche', made by
recording an excerpt from one tape and putting it together with an
incongruous bit from another, quite arbitrarily and fantastically'.
The final tape is 'completely useless from a scholarly point of
view', and yet not quite without value. It will be listened to by
devotees 'sufficiently interested to crawl by the amplifier with their
ears cocked'.

Deven loves Nur's verse for its 'perfect, unblemished shapes',
or how it places 'frightening and inexplicable experiences like time
and death at a point where they could be seen and studied, in
safety'. He had hoped that his tape recording might share the
formal beauty and the contemplative detachment of the verse. But
he finds that his project is not like a poet's, but like a novelist's,
and the novelist, the Indian novelist, must work with the immedi-
ate clutter of experience. What form results is at best a makeshift, a
bizarre expedient, desperate and more or less unsuccessful.

Deven's tape stands for the Indian novel, and yet it is not much
like the novel, *In Custody*, not much like any of Anita Desai's
novels. Hers is a fastidious talent. Had she lived in Britain, she
would have become, one guesses, a novelist something after the
manner of Barbara Pym. Living in India, writing about the country
where she lives, her subject becomes her own refinement, and the
barrier it creates between her and her material. She looks at India
like Nanda Kaul, from within the cool cave of her prose, or like
Bim, from behind an overgrown hedge, or like Deven, a pained
spectator of the messy chaos of Nur's life. She cannot escape
herself, and neither can she escape her subject. Her task as a
novelist becomes the forging of uneasy reconciliations between the
two. *The Village by the Sea* ends when Sayyid Ali recognises his own
irrelevance. In *Fire on the Mountain* all that Nanda Kaul can do is to
escape from the cold triumph of her detachment into pained
bewilderment and guilt. In *Clear Light of Day* and *In Custody* Anita
Desai is less self-deprecating. The culture that Bim and Anita Desai
share may function like a carapace, separating them from where
they live, and yet even without leaving its shell a snail can
tentatively protrude its horns. When Deven returns to Mirpore
and takes up his university duties again, he is still pursued by
Nur's demands for money. He had 'imagined he was taking Nur's
poetry into safe custody, and had not realized that if he was to be
the custodian of Nur's genius then Nur would become his

custodian too'. Their relationship, he realises, will never end. Even
when Nur dies 'the bills would come to him, he would have to pay
for the funeral, support the widows, raise his son . . . ' Deven, the
quiet man, will never be able to extricate himself from Nur and his
noisy household. It is a predicament that Anita Desai understands.
In seeking to be the custodian of India she has herself been taken
into custody, has placed her quiet, fastidious talent at the service of
a noisy, melodramatic land. It is a painful burden. So Deven feels,
and one senses that Anita Desai sometimes finds it so. But *In
Custody* ends not with a gesture of weariness, but with Deven
striding robustly forwards, confident that the burden he has
condemned himself to carry is also his highest honour.

5
The Politics of R.K. Narayan

know of only one substantial attack on R.K. Narayan's achievement. It might be of some interest simply as a novelty, but, coming as it does, from a man who has claims to be the best living writer in English, it deserves more serious attention than it has received. V.S. Naipaul admires Narayan, and his admiration survived, he tells us, the rainy season in India during which he slowly re-read *Mr Sampath, the Printer*.[1] It survived, but the account of the novel that follows leaves us in little doubt that it did not survive intact. Before the monsoon Naipaul had admired Narayan as a comic realist: after it he was left with an uneasy appreciation of Narayan's skill in disguising religiose fables to make them look like novels. *A Tiger for Malgudi* would not seem to him a retreat into quasi-philosophical whimsy forgivable in a writer near the end of a distinguished career, but the predictable outcome of tendencies present even in Narayan's strongest work.

Naipaul's problem has to do with the status of Malgudi. He knows that Narayan's fiction depends on the creation of Malgudi: his comedies were of the sort that requires a restrictive social setting with 'well defined rules', and he knows too that Malgudi is not Bangalore or any other real South Indian town: it is 'a creation of art'. But for Naipaul the value of fictional worlds depends on their maintaining a vital connection with the real world that they mirror. When he had read Narayan's novels in Trinidad and in London he had not doubted that connection: when he read *Mr Sampath* in Bombay, in Delhi, in Kutch, his sense of it snapped. He could not connect the India he read about with the India he saw around him. The cool sympathy with which Narayan views his characters and their doings, his 'ironic acceptance' of the oddity of men and women and the oddity of their ways, no longer seemed evidence of a Chekhovian sophistication, but the expression of a weary indifference to human pain, not the less offensive because it is presented to the reader as sanctioned by Narayan's religious sense of life, his Hinduism.

Towards the end of *Mr Sampath*, Srinivas, the central character, experiences a vision in which he sees the history of India pass before him, stretching back into the prehistoric past, forward into the unimaginable future. The vision leaves Srinivas in a state of elevated philosophical calm, a mood in which 'madness or sanity, suffering or happiness seemed all the same'. He then witnesses a primitive exorcism ritual in which a friend of his, a young artist called Ravi who has been driven mad by unrequited love, is beaten with a cane by an old priest. Srinivas has an impulse to protest against this cruelty, but finds himself 'incapable of any effort': 'The recent vision had given him a view in which it seemed to him as one whether they thwacked Ravi with a cane or whether they left him alone . . .' Ravi has, he now sees, all eternity to regain his sanity, 'though not in one birth, at least in a series of them'. All the same Srinivas is troubled by the noise of the thwacking: he goes outside.

Mr Sampath was written in 1949, and, as Naipaul notes, expresses a sense of India that had been fixed before Independence. Srinivas, dependent on his brother for money, on his wife for domestic comfort, is left free to cultivate his interest in the lofty spiritual doctrines of the *Upanishads*.[2] His spirituality is a flower of idleness. His character is less a product than a symbol of stultifying colonial dependence. When Narayan published *The Vendor of Sweets* India had been independent for 20 years, and the economic achievement of independent India could no longer be ignored. India had laid itself open to Western technology, and had become a major producer of industrial goods. Naipaul reads *The Vendor of Sweets* as Narayan's report on the new India. The Indian ability to absorb and to direct Western technology is coarsely parodied in the representation of Jagan's son and his fiction-writing machine: 'You see these four knobs? One is for characters, one for plot situations, one for climaxes.' Narayan evidently has no notion how such a machine might work. He ridicules machines from a position of invulnerable technological innocence. He is unable to see in the person of a young Indian educated in the West anything other than decadence – alcohol, girlfriends, unscrupulousness, a trivial aping of Western manners and dress, and a pathetic interest in machines that owe more to Heath Robinson than the microchip.

So ends Naipaul's critique, and for all his insistence that he remains an admirer, it is damning. His Narayan shelters from the fact of pain by cultivating a religiose indifference, and responds to hange only with uncomprehending mockery. At moments of risis he retreats, as Srinivas retreats from the noise of Ravi being hwacked, into a visionary India, a pastoral land, eternal, free from ‎ain – an India that can only be seen in a vision, for it is a country hat never existed. Such places of imaginative refuge are perhaps ‎ecessary for a colonial people, a people deprived of responsibility ‎r their own lives; but in modern India they are a harmful luxury, ‎r they get in the way of the duty to see the real world and to see it learly that the citizens of a self-regulating nation must accept if ver they are to make a better life.

India: A Wounded Civilization records two visits made by Naipaul ‎o India – the second, the visit with which the book is mainly oncerned, during the Emergency. Naipaul makes no mention of *‎he Painter of Signs*, and this is odd, because *The Painter of Signs* is ‎n Emergency novel.[3] In it, Narayan responds to the same crisis hat Naipaul records. Here, if anywhere, the truth of Naipaul's ritique may be tested.

The Painter of Signs is a re-writing of a novel that Narayan had ‎ublished 22 years earlier, *Waiting for the Mahatma*. The point is too ‎bvious to need detailed justification. Sriram and Bharati in the ‎arlier novel become Raman and Daisy in the later. Sriram and ‎aman are both of them impelled by love to become campaigners, ‎nd both are sign-writers. Sriram roams the countryside daubing ‎n every available wall Gandhi's ringing demand, 'Quit India'. ‎aman is a professional calligrapher, and the message has ‎hanged: 'We are two; let ours be two; limit your family'. The ‎elationship between the two novels signals Narayan's acceptance ‎f an argument that occupies Naipaul throughout his book. With he Emergency the pattern of India's development as an independ-‎nt nation decisively changed. Gandhianism had run its course, ‎nd the Emergency was the suitably dramatic signal that it had ‎een replaced by a new political philosophy, led and articulated, ronically enough, by someone also called Gandhi.[4]

Waiting for the Mahatma is the story of Sriram growing up. At the ‎eginning of the novel he is 'comfortably reclining on the cold ‎ement window-sill' of his grandmother's house. It is his favourite ‎osture: 'The window became such a habit with him that when he ‎rew up he sought no other diversion except to sit there, ‎ometimes with a book, and watch the street.' By the end of the ‎ovel he has broken his adolescent habit of disengagement from ife, and prepares to set up home with his bride, Bharati, and to

shoulder the responsibility of looking after 30 children, orphans o
the partition riots. But Sriram's growth into adulthood is entangle
with the development of India into nationhood. All through hi
adolescence Sriram is fascinated by a picture hanging in the swee
shop opposite his house, a 'portrait of a European queen witl
apple cheeks and wavy coiffure'. Before he can become a man h
must free himself from this vague Western ideal of womanhoo
and fall in love with Bharati, whose beauty is Indian, who is wha
her name means, the daughter of India. Bharati is a disciple o
Gandhi, and Gandhi, though only an occasional actor in the story
is the novel's dominant presence. Through Bharati he súper
intends Sriram's emergence into independent manhood just as h
presided over India's progress to independent statehood. Th
novel ends with the assassination of Gandhi and the marriage o
Sriram and Bharati. The coincidence is symbolic. Gandhi is not s
much murdered as translated: his work done, the children of th
new nation safely given into the hands of young India, Gandh
feels free to shrug off the burden of existence. It is not the death o
a man, but of a saint, foreseen by Gandhi and calmly accepted b
him. *Waiting for the Mahatma* is a weird hybrid, at once a comi
bildungsroman and a religious fable of national origin.

At times, the two work well enough together. A sharply
observed detail like the portrait of the apple-cheeked queen i
weighted by its significance within the fable. The portrait allow
Narayan to treat a potentially ponderous theme, the escape from
emotional and imaginative dependence on the colonial power
without disturbing the deft ease of his narrative. The fading of th
old imperial roll of honour and its replacement by a new nationalis
martyrology is caught in the contrast between Sriram's father
killed in Mesopotamia, whose memorial has shrunk to the meagr
proportions of the buff envelope that brings his monthly pension
and Bharati's father, killed in the Congress agitation of 1920
whose death is proudly remembered. Even the representation o
Gandhi is not monotonously fabular. It is enlivened occasionally
by the novelist's sharp perceptions. Narayan seems quietly
amused by Gandhi's penchant for delphic utterance – 'How do
you know he means that and not something else?' The spiritual
weight of Gandhi's presence, though awesome, can become
oppressive: 'The Mahatma's silence was heavy and pervasive, and
Sriram was afraid even to gulp or cough, although he very much
wanted to clear his throat, cough, sneeze, swing his arms about.'

ut more often than not the effect secured by the mingling of fable
nd novel is evasion. Narayan turns to the novel when he wants to
vade the consequences of his fable, and to the fable when the
ovel starts to drift into dangerous areas. *Waiting for the Mahatma*
s an evasive book, and what it is most anxious to evade is politics.

The most striking instance is Narayan's representation of
Gandhi. Few would deny that Gandhi's success had to do with his
mbiguous status as the leader of a movement that was at once a
eligious revival and a political campaign. When he returned to
ndia from South Africa he found a country with deep and
ontinuous religious traditions, but a country that was governed
y Britain, and was, in consequence, politically underdeveloped.
His achievement was to take those religious traditions and to make
hem serve in place of absent traditions of political association.
Narayan's effort is to undo Gandhi's project; to salute Gandhi as a
aint while leaving as vague as possible his other role, as a
tatesman. Narayan offers a Gandhianism with the politics left out.
The charka, for instance, functions in Narayan's fable as a religious
mplement, like a rosary.[5] In the novel it is a wickedly frustrating
ittle machine. Sriram's attempts to master it are rendered with all
Narayan's comic flair. What no one would guess is that hand
pinning had a crucial place in Gandhi's economic programme,
reeing India from dependence on the Lancashire cotton mills, and
ndicating that the best means for India's economic development
vas through village industries. Even giving oneself up to imprisonment scarcely seems a political act. Gandhi instructs Bharati
o surrender herself at the nearest police station. He does not tell
her why. She accepts his instruction as a religious command,
nscrutable, not to be questioned. She obeys not because she is
Gandhi's follower, but because she is his disciple. Obedience in
his religious view of things is not a means to the successful
putcome of a project, but an end in itself.

Sriram does not go with Bharati to prison. He decides, con-
veniently, that Gandhi has left his followers free, each to continue
he struggle as he thinks best. There follows the most enigmatic
section of the novel. Sriram falls in with Jagadish, a photographer
with ambitions to make movies – always a danger signal in
Narayan. Jagadish is a supporter of Chandra Bose and the INA,[6]
ess a Gandhian than a guerrilla, and, under his direction, Sriram
himself becomes a terrorist. There is a detailed account of him
aking some leaflets to distribute at a nearby military barracks, and

deciding, after he has scratched his arm on the barbed wir
perimeter, to make a dignified retreat. He tosses the leaflets int
the compound: 'The boys may pick up and read the messages a
their leisure tomorrow morning.' Sriram's subsequent career – h
becomes an arsonist, a bomber, he derails trains – is narrated in
single paragraph. The reason is clear. The first episode is availabl
for treatment in the dry, comic manner that Narayan favours, bu
the later incidents are not, and so they must be glossed ove
Sriram is a dreamy young man. Nothing much in the outside worl
except for Bharati impinges on his dreaminess. Narayan is we
practised in the depiction of such characters, and Sriram is utterl
convincing. But the chief function of the novelists's skill, here, is t
save the fabulist from the need to offer any serious account of th
political implications of Sriram's career. Narayan suggests clearl
enough that Sriram is wrong to be diverted from Gandhi's kind o
nationalism to Chandra Bose's, but since Sriram is scarcel
represented as a responsible moral agent, Narayan avoids th
obligation either to indicate why Sriram is wrong or to assess th
gravity of his error.

At the end of the novel Sriram asks Gandhi's permission t
marry Bharati. Gandhi asks Bharati if she finds the proposa
agreeable:

> Bharati bowed her head and fidgeted.
> 'Ah, that is a sign of the dutiful bride', said the Mahatma.

After her parent's death Bharati was 'practically adopted by th
local Sevak Sangh'. Her life has been devoted to the Independenc
struggle. She is strong-minded, fearless, and ignores most of th
traditional restrictions placed on the behaviour of Indian women
She walks alone through rough countryside to meet Sriram at th
ruined temple where he has his hide-out. She handles his inep
sexual advances quite unhysterically. She gives herself up t
imprisonment without fuss, and she risks death in the partitior
riots calmly. It is curious to see such a woman at the very end of th
novel revert to the stereotype of the coyly blushing Indian bride

This is just one example of what is surely the oddest fact abou
Waiting for the Mahatma. Narayan contrives to celebrate India'
independence, but only by representing it as having changed
almost nothing. When Sriram is released from prison, the waiter ir
a local restaurant and Jagadish both complain of the country'

isorganisation and the government's ineptitude: ' "We ought to ejoice that it is our own people that are blundering, isn't that so?" riram asked, some of his irresponsible spirit returning.' The tone f this whole passage is odd. There is the novelist's wry amusenent at the dashing of millenarian hopes, but there is also, one enses, a queer satisfaction, as though Narayan is reassured that vhat was a muddle when the British ruled will go on being a nuddle now that they have left. Walking down his own street riram sees life going on as it always had done. He thinks:

Why could he not have lived like these folk without worries of any kind or any extra adventures: there seemed to be a quiet charm in a life verging on stagnation, and no change of any kind.

This is a moment of lassitude, and yet one feels that Narayan's trange achievement is to invest what might seem the most lramatic moment in recent Indian history, India's independence, vith something of that quiet charm.

The surprising transformation of Bharati into a traditional Indian ride is one aspect of this: it is a somewhat desperate stratagem by vhich Narayan reassures himself and reassures the reader that the process by which India won its independence has not unloosed ny uncharming forces for social change. But crucial to the whole nterprise is the representation of Gandhi. It seems obvious that Gandhi, apparently despite his claim to be an orthodox Hindu, but n fact because of that, threatened a radical – for Narayan an larming – reorganisation of Indian society. Throughout the novel Narayan contrives at once to celebrate Gandhi and to defuse his hreat. One example must suffice. When he visits Malgudi Gandhi politely declines an invitation to stay at the municipal chairman's uxurious house, and chooses instead to stay in the outcaste colony, among the sweepers. It is a symbolic challenge to the caste system and Narayan unambiguously applauds it. But caste is the principle on which traditional Indian society, the society that Narayan sees as possessed of a quiet charm, relies for its stability. Narayan's response is to enclose Gandhi's symbolic challenge vithin the fabular life of a saint. Incidents in such a life are contemplated with religious awe, but they are invested with an autonomous rather than an exemplary value. Gandhi's action is proper, saintly: it is admired, but with an admiration that does not have uncomfortable social consequences. That is why Gandhi's response when Sriram confesses his terrorist activities is not at a surprising:

> 'We will hear if there has been anything so serious as to warran my going on a fast again. Do you know how well a fast ca purify?'

Narayan's Gandhi shows no concern to establish whether Sriran has killed or maimed, no concern for his victims. His worry is tha Sriram may have polluted himself: his concern is to fix on th appropriate purification ritual.[7] It is a response explicable only i terms of the caste feeling that, earlier in the novel, Gandhi has see it as his business calculatedly to outrage, and it is appropriate t the novel's benign conclusion, in which Narayan salutes the birt! of a new nation: the moment when everything has changed, and yet magically, charmingly, everything stays just the same.

In *The Painter of Signs* Bharati becomes Daisy, Sriram becomes hi near namesake Raman, and the place of Gandhi is taken by – n one. Narayan is not a rash man. Like Sriram Raman is an orphan He lives not with his grandmother but with an old aunt, and lik Sriram's grandmother the aunt leaves Malgudi to live out her las days in Benares.[8] Raman shares Sriram's detachment. In *Th Painter of Signs* it is signalled by Narayan's use of a narrativ technique in which Raman's actual words are supplemented b unspoken speeches in which he expresses those feelings that he i too polite, too timorous, or too canny to voice.[9] Like Sriram, too he is impelled by love to give up his familiar life for the uncomfort able lot of the political campaigner. He accompanies Daisy as sh tours the surrounding villages spreading the message of birt! control.

Bharati, whose name proclaims her Indianness, is replaced b Daisy – 'What a name for someone who looked so very Indian traditional and gentle!'[10] She has many of Bharati's best qualities She is careless of physical comfort, self-assured, independent, and utterly committed to her mission. But Bharati's struggle was t secure India's independence; Daisy's is to control the growth o India's population. Whereas the one project secures Narayan': hearty – if, as I have tried to show, oddly complex – approval, th other seems to him not so much mistaken as sacrilegious. Bharati i a disciple of the Mahatma, Daisy of some unnamed missionar, who has appointed her an officer in his campaign to sprea propaganda for birth control throughout India. But there is no need for me to imitate Narayan's reticence. Daisy is a Sanjayite. *Waiting for the Mahatma* is transformed into *The Painter of Signs* to mark the difference between the idea of nationhood inspired by Gandhi, and the idea that replaced it: the idea most strikingly embodied not in the person of Indira Gandhi, but in that of her son. Raman carries the tools of his trade in a shoulder-bag decorated with a 'bust of Gandhi printed in green dye'. It is a bag that the reader knows from another of Narayan's novels,[11] but it carries here an added significance. It signals that Gandhi has, as it were, been assimilated into the fabric of Indian life, that Gandhi's achievement was to enrich without damaging the complex web of social relationships in which Narayan finds his Indian identity incorporated. Narayan represents the new Gandhianism as an attempt to rend that fabric, to cut it with a surgeon's knife.

There is much that Narayan admires in Daisy, and, by implication, in the social campaign that she represents. He is aware, as Raman's survey of the venalities of Malgudi's public and business life makes clear, of the corruption that it opposes. He can admire, too, Daisy's steely idealism, her energy, her willingness selflessly to give herself up to a cause. She is, after all, a Sanjayite, and Sanjay Gandhi's achievement had this in common with the Mahatma's, that he activated the social consciences of a sizeable proportion of India's best young people. He took an idealism that a few years before might have dissipated itself in the futile and ugly violence of Naxalite revolution, and disciplined it, gave it an outlet in the service of the state rather than in its destruction. In his characterisation of Daisy Narayan accepts as much. To understand why Daisy, in some ways so admirable, is at last bitterly repudiated, we must understand Narayan's response to sex and to children.

In *Waiting for the Mahatma* nothing about Gandhi is stressed more than his love of children. He distributes the fruit and flowers he is given to the children that he meets. In Malgudi, at the municipal chairman's house, he shares his couch with a little sweeper boy and feeds him the chairman's oranges. The orphan children, victims of the partition riots, are his special care. Almost his last thought before he is killed is to ask after the health of one such child, a girl he has named Anar, pomegranate bud, and to give Bharati apples and oranges to take to the children. His love of children is not so much an aspect of his character as one of the proper badges of his saintliness. He is not like Marx, writing *Das Kapital* with children balanced on his knees. That image works to characterise Marx, to supplement his austere identity as a political philosopher with the human qualities of the family man. Gandhi's love of children is more like Christ's. He savours the frisky energy of young life with a holy relish, as a way of marking as movingly as possible his loving care of all humanity. Daisy is carefully estab-lished as his antitype: 'She never patted a child or tried any baby-talk. She looked at them as if to say, You had no business to arrive – you lengthen the queues, that's all.' At Malgudi station the stationmaster assembles his children before Gandhi 'as if on a drill parade'. 'Why don't you let them run about and play as they like?', asks Gandhi. When Daisy leaves a village the children are assembled to bid her goodbye:

> Daisy looked at them critically, 'Don't suck your thumb, take it out, otherwise you will stammer', she said to one. To another one she said, 'Stand erect, don't slouch.' She turned to their mother and added, 'Correct posture is important. Children must be taught all this early in life.' She was a born mentor, could not leave others alone, children had better not be born, but if born, must take their thumbs out of their mouths, and avoid slouching.

The contrast needs no underlining, nor, perhaps, does what it implies. Daisy's resistance to the growth of India's population is represented as a perverse refusal to accept and to rejoice in the processes of life. It is an attempt to substitute a stiff, sterile angularity for the prolific, leaping spontaneity that is found at once in the movements of playing children and in the patterns of Indian dance and architecture, and signifies in all three the divinely generous creativity that assures us of the presence of the gods within the world.

Narayan plays fair by Daisy. The spokesman for the religious point of view is a cantankerous, boastful, and thoroughly un-attractive old priest, keeper of an image of the Goddess of Plenty: 'Be careful, you evil woman, don't tamper with God's designs. He will strike you dead if you attempt that.' But Narayan's distance from the priest's style does not mark any serious disagreement with his point of view. Raman's aunt, as Narayan's old women often are, is the mouthpiece of the traditional wisdom: 'Isn't it by

God's will that children are born?' Raman responds with a joke: 'But our government does not agree with God.' It is a serious joke.

But what follows? Daisy visits a village where the population has increased by 20 per cent in a year. She responds vigorously:

'Has your food production increased twenty per cent?
Have your accommodations increased twenty per cent?
I know they haven't. Your production has increased
only three per cent in spite of various improved
methods of cultivation . . .'

Narayan pokes fun at this display of statistical earnestness, but to mock the style of Daisy's speech is not to challenge its substance, and what Daisy spells out in her gauche, bureaucratic manner is the fact of starvation. Narayan has nothing to say to this. He can offer in reply only Raman's bland assurance that though the children may be starving they appear perfectly healthy:

Malgudi swarmed with children of all sizes, from toddlers to four-footers, dust-covered, ragged – a visible development in five years. At this rate they would overrun the globe – no harm; though they looked famished, their brown or dark skins shone with health and their liquid eyes sparkled with life

One remembers Naipaul's weighty charge that in Narayan religion is an excuse for indifference to the sufferings of others, that his Hindu piety breeds, and is a disguise for, callousness.

To Narayan sexuality is first of all a threat, a dangerous impulse that must be struggled against. Sriram and Raman, pricked by sexual desire, both try to follow Gandhi's remedy for the control of lustful thoughts: 'Walk with your head down looking at the ground during the day, and with your eyes up looking at the stars at night.' But both fail. Raman tries to rape Daisy, and Sriram is only saved from raping Bharati by his sexual inexperience. When she visits him in his temple refuge, he notices 'her left breast moving under her white Khaddar sari', and makes a clumsy, frantic sexual assault on her. After it is over she rebukes him hesitantly, unhappily: 'He had never seen her so girlish and weak. He felt a momentary satisfaction that he had quashed her pride and quelled her turbulence.' Male sexuality is darkened, Narayan believes, by other desires – sadism, the urge to dominate. More than Bharati is threatened, for desire releases even in the mild and diffident Sriram impulses which, if unrestrained, would make impossible the continuation of any society that Narayan could recognise as civilised.

But Narayan is no ascetic. Sexuality threatens social stability, but it is also true that a test, possibly the crucial test, of a society's value is whether in restraining the sexual instinct it allows that instinct to be fulfilled. Lust must first of all become love. In *The Painter of Signs* the process is beautifully traced. 'Do you ever recollect the face of the woman whose thighs you so long meditated on at the river-steps?', Raman asks himself, and then he visits Daisy in her office:

> A side glance convinced him that the full sunlight on her face made no difference to her complexion, only he noticed a faint down on her upper lip and the vestige of a pimple on her right cheek.

When Raman notices that pimple it is the proof that his generalized capacity for lust has yielded a particular inclination to love. But love, even love genuine enough in its way, like Raju's for Rosie in *The Guide*, is still a dangerous and destructive emotion. It is redeemed only within marriage, when it is constrained within the larger social organisation.

Bharati agrees to marry Sriram only if Gandhi gives the couple his permission. Gandhi stands to her in place of father, and so Bharati does not more than show proper filial duty in requiring his consent. But for Narayan the convention embodies a deep truth: that love can be fulfilled only through an act of submission in which the lover submits his love to the higher duty of obedience. It follows that love is redeemed only within a society that exerts over its members a traditional authority. Daisy becomes Raman's mistress, and promises to be his wife. But the novel ends when she hears of a dramatic increase in the population of Nagari, packs her bags, and leaves Malgudi and Raman both. She could not behave otherwise. She is unable to make that obeisance to traditional authority without which, Narayan believes, love can never be other than a capricious and a destructive emotion, and she cannot do so because she has committed her life to a cause that requires her to view such authority as an obstructive and antiquated set of prejudices.

Like *Waiting for the Mahatma*, *The Painter of Signs* is both a novel

and a fable. It is a novel about a love affair that goes wrong, and a
fable about Sanjayism. At the end of *Waiting for the Mahatma* Sriram
and Bharati prepare to marry and accept responsibility for the
upbringing of 30 orphans. The life that they embark on so happily
is Gandhi's proper memorial, for his achievement was to instil in
his followers a sense of social responsibility, of the duty a man
owes his fellows, that, before Gandhi, had scarcely figured as a
part of the Hindu tradition. But Narayan could celebrate Gandhi's
success only because it had been accomplished without disrupting
that subtle interweaving of familial duty, proverbial wisdom,
custom and religious law that constitutes the authority which
guarantees the most precious of human freedoms, the freedom to
love. At the end of *The Painter of Signs* Raman, abandoned by his
aunt and abandoned by Daisy, cycles towards the Boardless Hotel,
'that solid, real world of sublime souls who minded their own
business'. That is, I think, the only bitter sentence in the whole of
Narayan's *oeuvre*. Daisy is left to devote her life to the expression of
a social concern unschooled by love, and such a concern inevitably
breeds hatred and violence. Raman is left with the shrunken view
that the sublimest state to which a human being can aspire is that
of minding his own business. It is a personal tragedy for Raman
and Daisy, but it represents a national tragedy for India.[12]
   Shiva Naipaul ends a vitriolic assessment of Sanjay Gandhi's
achievement by quoting these sad words spoken by a sociologist at
Delhi University:

> 'Sanjay did express a certain dark side of the Indian personality.
> I recognize that darkness in myself. Sometimes,' he said slowly,
> deliberately, 'when you look around you, when you see the
> decay and the pointlessness, when you see, year after year, this
> grotesque beggarly mass ceaselessly reproducing itself like some
> ... like some kind of vegetable gone out of control ... suddenly
> there comes an overwhelming hatred. Crush the brutes! Stamp
> them out! Its a racial self-disgust some of us develop towards
> ourselves ... that is the darkness I speak about...'[13]

Daisy is a zealot not a Kurtz, but for all that, there is much in the
anonymous sociologist's words to remind us of *The Painter of Signs*.
One thinks, for example, of Daisy's ill-concealed contempt for the
villagers whose lives she is trying to improve. That it is a racial
contempt is lightly indicated by her name, and by the impudent

transformation of her mentor into a Christian missionary. But
Narayan is less concerned to apportion blame than he is to lament
the outcome of a story in which Daisy and Raman are both of them
the losers.

It is odd that Naipaul, who, in recent years, has travelled the
world as a self-appointed missionary intent on the destruction of
all human illusions, and has found everywhere material to feed his
capacity for bleak and unforgiving disdain, should find in the
Emergency glimmers to inspire a wan hope,[14] whereas Narayan,
whose temperament seems of all major modern writers the
sunniest, should contemplate the same events and arrive, at last at
a mood very like despair. But the contrasting responses are the
product of profound differences between the two men. They are
differences of temperament and of religious belief, but they are
also political differences. 'Narayan,' William Walsh insists 'is not a
political novelist',[15] and there is obvious truth in his contention.
Raman speaks for Narayan in finding Daisy's lack of humour
wearing – 'Why shouldn't we also laugh a little while preventing
births?' – and a lively sense of humour does not fit easily with
disciplined political commitment. Political writing characteristically
flattens language in an effort to render it a medium fit to
communicate unambiguous meaning. Narayan loves language for
its playfulness, its mischievous tendency to subvert the flat,
univocal intentions of its user. 'Quit India', writes Sriram on every
available wall. What message could be plainer – until a passing
Indian asks why he is being asked to leave his own country, and
another, troubled by the uproar that Sriram's arrival has caused,
suggests that he add an 'e' to his message, and appeal instead for a
little quiet. Raman is an artist in his way. Calligraphy is a joy to him: he
delights in 'letters, their shape, and stance, and shade'. Narayan
shares with his hero the belief that art has an intrinsic value as
unrelated to any extrinsic purpose the artist might serve as Raman's
pleasure in his craft is to the motives of the businessmen who
commission his signs. When Raman abandons all his other trade and
binds himself to the endless reproduction of Daisy's single message,
he is, among other things, a type of the artist who puts his talent at the
service of a political campaign, and Narayan feels any such decision
as constricting. But George Orwell reminds us that for a writer to
choose to be non-political is itself a political act, and it seems clear that
in Narayan's case the rejection of politics is the expression of a deep-
rooted conservatism, a comprehensive hostility to radical change.

Narayan's novels begin when Malgudi is threatened by some newcomer, which may be the Mahatma or the movies, a taxidermist or a dancing girl. Narayan flirts with the danger, but the novel ends only when the threat has been removed, when it has been blunted by the repressive tolerance of traditional India, or when it has been exposed as a rakshasha, an evil demon that, because it is evil, necessarily destroys itself. The admiration that Naipaul felt for such a writer was never likely to be other than fragile, puzzled, for Naipaul's achievement is as clearly built upon his sense of himself as deracinated, his painful and proud insistence on living in a free state, as Narayan's is founded on his participation in the values, the prejudices, the culture of the society that he depicts. The vision of two writers so essentially opposed could never tally.[16] We can ask of each only that he submit his vision honestly to the test of an undoctored reality. In *Waiting for the Mahatma* Narayan studiously, and with considerable flair, avoids so difficult and dangerous a procedure. In *The Painter of Signs* he does not. There is reckless honesty in his refusal to counter Daisy's statistics with anything more substantial than Raman's dogged insistence that starvation is perfectly compatible with glowing good health. And there is honesty, too, in the flimsiness of the consolation he offers – to himself, to his readers, and to those suffering from the ministrations of Daisy and her less scrupulous real-life colleagues. It is written on a ribbon-wide slip of paper, and offered for sale at a price of five paisa by a 'professor' who sits each day by the fountain outside the Malgudi town hall. It consists of just three words, 'This will pass'.

Bharati and Sriram marry, Daisy and Raman separate. Union and disunion are both of them symbolic. When Sriram marries Bharati, when he makes the daughter of India his wife, he weds his own life with the life of his nation. When Daisy leaves Malgudi, Raman retreats into a life of embittered privacy. Narayan is a major novelist, his achievement is much greater than Kipling's, or Rushdie's, or Ruth Jhabvala's, or Anita Desai's, and it is appropriate that in his novels the movement and counter-movement, the pattern of expansion and contraction, that characterise the Indian novel should achieve their most complete expression. But it is a dilemma that I have so far represented as either aesthetic or as temperamental, as having to do with the problem of writing a novel about India, or as deriving from the personality of the novelist. Both these explanations seem to me true, but both seem in themselves inadequate. I do not want to argue only that these patterns are characteristic of Indian novels and Indian novelists, but that they are characteristic of India.

In the following two chapters novels, individual fictions, will become only fragments of the 'collective fiction', to use Rushdie's expression, that is India. The enterprise is difficult, and it is also dangerous. To try, however tentatively, to explore the imaginative life of a nation is inevitably to run the risk of re-discovering a racial stereotype, but this is a risk that I have to accept. The alternative is to remain trapped within an experience of literature that never overflows into an experience of life.

Nations live imaginatively when daily activities are invested with symbolic value. I will take just two such activities, two kinds of travelling. One traveller journeys to see his country, another journeys to find himself. In India, the first kind of traveller goes by train, the second on foot. When Kim and the Lama travel to Benares they take the train, but whenever the Lama finds the mechanical clatter of its motion irksome, the two descend and travel for a while on foot. It is that rhythm that makes their journey so comprehensively Indian.

6

Indian Trains

There is a scene in a film by Satyajit Ray. Children are running through long grass, going further from their village than they have ever been before. They come to the edge of the grass, hear a noise, and crouch down as the train roars past. Then they walk silently home, wide-eyed, sharing a secret too big to talk about. When they left home that morning their world was their village. They come home heavy with the knowledge that the village is a small place in a huge land. Their world is now less secure, but it is also bigger, more exciting. It has trains in it.

The beginnings were small enough. On 18 November 1850, the first train in India ran from Bombay to a small town a few miles distant. The next year Lord Dalhousie, the Governor-General, issued a minute calling for a system of railways throughout the country. The response was sceptical The tracks would be washed away in the monsoon floods, or, if they survived, the sleepers would be eaten by white ants. And, in any case, it was unlikely that so conservative a people as the Indians could easily be accustomed to the idea of rail travel. But Dalhousie pressed on, and by 1868 a rail network linked the great cities of India. This was only the first stage of the plan. In the following decades branch lines were built that spread throughout the country, 18 000 miles of track by 1893, 35 000 by 1914. The boast was, then, that there was no village in India more than 50 miles from a railway.

Fears of conservative resistance to travel by railway were quickly shown to be unfounded. As early as 1855 an editorial in the *Indian News* was commenting snootily on the new fad: 'The fondness for travelling by rail has become almost a national passion among the inferior orders.' In 1867 there were nearly 14 million passengers, by 1932 over 600 million. India had become a nation of travellers, and Indians travelled by rail.

Dalhousie's aims were practical. The railways made it possible to garrison India more efficiently: troops could be moved quickly from one province to another. Trains opened up India's arable hinterland, freeing Britain from dependence on American cotton.

They made the whole of India a market for British industrial goods. They also made it possible to transport food from one province to another, and so helped to control the local famines that from time to time devastated whole areas of the country. Thanks to Dalhousie the administration and the economy of India became dependent on the railways. The railway unions are the most powerful in India, but their power is paradoxical. It is so great – the nation is so dependent on its rail service – that no government can allow it to be used. In 1974, confronted by a nationwide rail strike, Indira Gandhi responded by arresting and imprisoning all the union officials, a number variously estimated somewhere between 20 000 and 50 000.

The railways have a huge economic importance, but that was not what impressed the children in Satyajit Ray's film. Trains were not for them a means of distribution, they were a new idea.

Life in a village is circular, bound in time by the cycle of the seasons, and in space by the fields grouped around the village at their centre. The life of the village is a self-contained, inward-looking life, and it offers those who live it a place within a social fabric rich enough to make nostalgia for the village the commonest, and not an entirely factitious, emotion even in the prosperous city-dwellers of modern India. But such a life is not, and never has been, enough. This explains, I think, one of the most charming aspects of Hinduism, the reverence for rivers – not just the great rivers of the Indian plains, the Ganges which sprang from Siva's hair, the Indus and the Jamuna, but also for the local river, the river alongside which the small town or village grew up. The river, its waters rising in the hills and flowing to the sea, interrupts the circular life of the village. It has a place in the village's religious festivals, but it has a place, too, in the life of every day. The villagers who bathe there in the morning, the children who play there, the people who take their walk there in the evening, or sit gossiping on the sands, are connected by the flowing water with the large spaces of India. Through rivers, one might say, Indian villages become provincial. But when Ray's children found the railway track, and saw the train scream by, they stumbled on one part of a great network that spread throughout a subcontinent. They came home excited by the idea of a life beyond, they felt the first stirrings in them of the idea that they belonged to a nation.

Dalhousie planned the railways to tighten British rule of India, to make it more efficient. But the trains had one effect that Dalhousie surely did not foresee. They made possible the birth of the idea that was finally to put an end to the Raj, the idea that India was a nation. Trains connect the inward-looking life of the village with the life of the whole country. The roar of the train jerks Ray's children out of the dreamworld of childhood, and makes them attend to what is outside their experience. To see a train is to be forced to recognise an outside world. The Indian imagination is, I suspect, as dependent on trains as is its economy.

In his autobiography, *My Days*, R.K. Narayan records how he came to write his first novel, *Swami and Friends*:

> On a certain day in September, selected by my grandmother for its auspiciousness, I bought an exercise book and wrote the first line of a novel: as I sat in my room nibbling my pen and wondering what to write, Malgudi with its little railway station swam into view, already made, with a character called Swaminathan running down the platform peering into the faces of passengers, and grimacing at a bearded face . . .

All Narayan's novels are set in and around Malgudi, but the economy of his fiction depends on the fact that Malgudi has a 'little railway station'. Trains stop at Malgudi, newcomers arrive and disrupt the dreamy contentment of Narayan's heroes. Without their intrusion the novels would have no plot, and, more than that, they would have no point.

The hero of *The Guide* is called Raju. He was born near the station, and his earliest memories are of trains:

> The railway got into my blood very early in life. Engines, with their tremendous clanging and smoke, ensnared my senses. I felt at home on the railway platform, and considered the station-master and porter the best company for man, and their railway talk the most enlightened. I grew up in their midst.

When he has grown up, he runs the station shop, and adds to his income by acting as a guide to tourists who come to Malgudi. He is known as 'Railway Raju'. He stands for all Narayan's central characters. They are all, willingly or unwillingly, placed like Raju, in Malgudi but vulnerable to the world outside. It is in this way that Narayan can be at once a defiantly provincial novelist, and yet retain his national and his international appeal. It is because the central characters are like Raju that it is appropriate that novels so steeped in Tamil culture as Narayan's should all the same be written in English. And it is also because of the railway that Malgudi never quite becomes a fictional place sealed against contamination by the real India. Malgudi is linked to the real India by a railway track – a train runs from Malgudi to Madras.

Narayan transferred the scene at the station in *Swami and Friends* from the beginning of the novel to the end. Swami runs along the platform as the train chugs out of Malgudi with his friend, Ramu, aboard. Swami is a boy; his has been the seamless experience of childhood, and, as the train pulls out, he feels for the first time that the continuity of his life is broken. The child's cyclical sense of time, in which change is the condition of permanence, is brought up sharp against the adult sense that time is linear, and that change means loss. All children, Indian or otherwise, learn that, but Narayan seems to me characteristically Indian in associating this new sense with a railway track.

Ved Mehta was not yet five when his father sent him to the school for the blind in Bombay. The Frontier Mail stood at Lahore station, the train whistled, and his father handed him, crying, through the window of his compartment: 'The last words Daddyji said to Ved (and the first words I remember hearing) were, "You're a man now." ' Little Ved becomes a man because he is removed from his family circle, breaks out of it, as most young Indians break out, in a train.

Because Ved is blind through meningitis, he learns the lonely adult sense of himself as 'I' too early. His father had been a college student when he made the same discovery. He witnessed a painful quarrel between his parents, and suddenly decided that he could never again live under his father's roof. He had a vague plan of working his passage to America as a deck-hand, and so he bought a third-class ticket on the Frontier Mail to Bombay. He arrived in Bombay with six rupees, and lived for a few days on a starvation diet, until a kindly British magistrate forced him to confess his story and packed him off home. It was just a childish escapade, and, back in Lahore, Daddyji resumed his studies. But it was also something more important. When Daddyji returned home his relationship with his father had decisively changed. 'Please do not worry about me', he said.

To board a train alone is to make a journey through the shadow line separating youth from manhood. It is an initiation rite, sometimes literally so. After the marriage of Ved Mehta's sister, Pom, her family go with her to the station to see her safely installed in the coupé, the two-berth compartment in which she and her new husband will travel to their new home. As the train pulls out, Ved heard his father's voice 'through the clatter and thunder, the sounds of finality itself'. Daddyji was speaking to the groom, 'Kakaji, take the journey gently . . . She's very innocent.'

The screech of the train signals the death of Pom's old life, as a daughter, within her family. It is just one of a series of such scenes that impressed themselves on Ved Mehta's mind until he remembers himself thinking, 'whenever I took the train something died in me'. The train tears the continuous web of his life, and the train journeys he remembers, he remembers as so many little deaths.

The platforms of Indian stations are crowded. It is as if everyone boarding the train has a family and friends to shout to through the window, to wave to as the train pulls away. Travelling on a train is a serious matter. It needs the presence of family and friends to solemnise it. On the platform, smiling at well-wishers, trying to look serious as he is offered advice, his arms filling up with little packages of food to sustain him on the journey, the traveller is a son, or a daughter, a neighbour or a friend, tightly caught in the subtle tissue of family and social relationships in which every Indian is swaddled at birth. As the train pulls away, and he settles back in his seat and looks around him at his travelling companions, he must find a new identity.

It is on this fact that devotees of progress pinned their hopes of the Indian railway. Marx looked to trains, and the modern industry that would result from them, to 'dissolve the hereditary divisions of labour upon which rest the Indian castes, those decisive impediments to Indian progress and Indian power'.[1] The liberal historians who compiled the great *Cambridge History of India* pointed to the railways as 'the most powerful educative force in India'. Trains 'necessarily tended to break down the barriers of ages, to stimulate movement, and exchange of thought'. In railway carriages 'Brahmans and Sudras, Muslims and Sikhs, peasants and townsmen sat side by side.'[2] The traveller in the compartment of a train loses the reality of his family or caste identity. He has to re-define himself, find a place within the larger life of the nation.

It is not, of course, a place within a homogeneous, egalitarian society. In a train the Muslim may sit next to the Sikh, but both will be distinguished from other passengers within the most complex hierarchy of ticket classes that any nation has seen fit to devise. There are the first, the second, and the third classes, but these are only the principal notes, and around them, as in a raga, are woven intricate variations. It is possible for the traveller to signal in the ticket he buys not only the extent of his wealth but its kind; first-class coupé for the old-fashioned rich man who owes it to himself to travel in the slippered ease of a private compartment, air-conditioned chair car for the young executive whose prestige is better supported by purchasing in a train the odourless discomfort of air travel.

Boarding a train can be for an Indian a fraught experience: the compartment he enters signals his place within a national hierarchy. When the young Gandhi defiantly insisted on travelling in a third-class compartment, Gokhale, Gandhi's patron, and then one of the two most famous political leaders in India, insisted on seeing him off at the station. Gandhi asked him not to trouble himself, 'I should not have come if you had gone first class, but now I had to', Gokhale replied. It is a sensitiveness that the Indian traveller takes with him when he goes abroad. Ved Mehta's Daddyji stood paralysed on the platform of Union Station in Washington. The train was divided into cars marked 'Whites only' and cars marked 'Blacks only'. He asked the conductor which he should take, and the conductor said 'Hindu? You're white'.

It is tempting to think that if the South African conductor who examined Gandhi's first-class ticket as his train stood at the station in Maritzburg one evening in 1893 had made the same decision, India might never have been born. Instead, the conductor insisted that Gandhi leave the compartment and travel in the guard's van. Gandhi refused, was ejected from the train by a policeman, and spent the night shivering in the station waiting-room. The next morning he caught the first train to Charlestown. From there, Gandhi had to take a stage-coach to Johannesburg. He agreed to take his seat on the outside of the coach, though his ticket entitled him to travel inside, with the whites. Then, in the afternoon, the conductor decided that he would like to sit in Gandhi's place. He spread some dirty sacking on the footboard, and told Gandhi to sit there. Gandhi refused, and the conductor beat him up. Gandhi had only just arrived in South Africa. That journey from Durban to Johannesburg changed his life.

Gandhi arrived in South Africa a failure. He had insisted, with the single-mindedness that characterised him throughout his life, that his family – provincial Gujerati notables and none too well off – send him to London to read for the bar. He returned to India a qualified barrister only to find that he was too painfully self-conscious to address a court. His shyness was not a sign of diffidence, but of utter self-absorption. He had developed already the narrow, intense range of interests that stayed with him throughout his life – dietetics, alternative medicine, and sex, the typical preoccupations of the self-obsessed. He had, it is true, great gifts. He was very intelligent, had enormous energy, and a terrifying obstinacy. But he was also – thanks to the peculiar English notion that barristers needed social rather than intellectual qualifications – eccentrically self-educated. His encounters with English intellectual life had been pretty much confined to vegetarians and theosophists. He seemed set fair to develop into one of those cranks who seem harmless, even charming, until they corner you in a bar and reveal themselves as intolerable monomaniacs.

What happened to him on that first South African journey was horrible. But it needed to be. Gandhi was a proud man, but even so I doubt whether any insults less gross than those casually delivered by the average Boer in his everyday dealings with his non-white neighbours could ever have breached Gandhi's armour of complete self-absorption. Shivering in the station waiting-room at Maritzburg, clinging to his seat on the stage-coach while the white man punched his head, something happened to Gandhi. He became an Indian. When he stepped down from the coach in Johannesburg he was already a nationalist leader. I find it a proper coincidence that this, the crucial event of Gandhi's life, should have begun on a train.

It was Gandhi who created India. Nehru's title for him, 'Father of the Nation', was the right one. It is a title that the British have claimed for themselves. Colonel Robert J. Blackham, an old India hand, speaks for all the other old India hands when he ends his rather plummy account of the subcontinent with the words, 'I must insist that India was only a geographical expression until she was welded into the beginning of a nation by the genius of British administrators . . .'[3] What the colonel means is that Britain gave India a more or less unified legal and administrative system, and such a system, it is true, is a necessary condition for the existence of a nation. But it is not a sufficient condition. India could never have become a nation until India existed not just as an administrative unit but as an idea present in the minds of people who lived in thousands of scattered villages, and it was no part of British policy to assist in the spreading of such an idea. That was Gandhi's work.

It was work he accomplished without ever losing his cranky obsession with what went into his body and what came out of it. He kept that to the end of his life – bitterly regretting his inability to give up goat's milk, insisting that his young female disciples sleep naked with him to test his vow of chastity, recording in a long newspaper article his shock and puzzlement when, in his late sixties, he experienced a nocturnal emission. He always believed what he wrote at the beginning of his autobiography, that 'all his ventures in the political field' were incidental to one, private, apparently quite unpolitical end, the desire for 'self-realization, to see God face to face, to attain Moksha'. Moksha, release from the cycle of birth and death, can be achieved only by the man who has total control over his own mind and body. What happened to Gandhi as he travelled from Durban to Johannesburg was that this ambition merged with the demand that his countrymen win control over their own country: self-realisation became dependent on swaraj.

What Gandhi did when he returned to India was to transform the nature of the Congress party. He found it a party, led by Gokhale and men like him, that represented the urban middle classes of India, and was inspired by a Western ideal of parliamentary democracy. He made it into a party of the masses, and he did so by establishing himself as, in the strong sense of the term, a charismatic leader, which is to say that he came to represent in his own person the national identity of his people.

He prepared himself for his role. In 1901 he took what seemed to his patron, Gokhale, a quixotic decision. He toured India travelling in third-class railway carriages, all his luggage stored in a 'canvas bag worth twelve annas'. It was the first of many such tours, though, after 1918, Gandhi travelled second class, no longer thinking himself fit enough to withstand the rigours of third-class travel. Gandhi criss-crossed India on trains. Where the train did not go, he walked. He is the only Indian politician who has ever been able to say without gross exaggeration that he knew India, and it was through Gandhi's knowledge of India that India came to know itself.

Charismatic leadership can only express itself symbolically, and Gandhi was a subtle and inventive symbolist. As he bent over his charka, his spinning wheel, he extruded a thread that he would wind around each one of his countrymen, binding them to him. The khadi movement was not just an economic programme, it was a vision of every Indian recognising his own responsibility to spin and weave the social fabric of the nation. The typical Gandhian action is at once severely practical and symbolically resonant. He undertook his first tour of India as a way of 'acquainting himself with the hardships of third class passengers'. The only remedy for the 'awful state of things' in third-class carriages is that 'educated men should make a point of travelling third class'. They will dissuade by their example the other passengers from spitting, smoking, and otherwise behaving badly, and they will be able to insist that the railway authorities offer a reasonable standard of comfort. That is the practical programme, but Gandhi also travels in trains as a way of linking himself with the lives of all those who share his carriage, as a way of asserting his identity with them and theirs with him.

The carriages of a train are separated yet linked, the passengers are grouped but divided, the engine, the power that keeps them together, is visible to the passengers only at rare moments, when the train takes a bend. India is so diverse that it is hard to see how any structure simpler than a train could appropriately figure its unity. In Ruth Prawer Jhabvala's *A Backward Place*, Sudhir, an idealistic young Bengali, throws up his job in Delhi to work in a Literacy Institute in a backward province. As his train cuts through India, his fellow passengers, who had first struck him as irritating and banal, come to seem

> a manifestation of all the variety and unexpectedness of the fertile lives that sprang out of this soil, which was in itself so various and unexpected, and was now desert and now flourishing fields and now the flattest plains and now the highest and most holy of mountains.

He has a vision of the diversity of India, and it is through this vision that Sudhir recognises himself as an Indian. He sees the variety of the people he travels with and the land he travels through, and it is through that variety that he feels himself at one with them. He has learned to read the significance that Gandhi attached to trains.

India was Gandhi's idea, and some would say that it died before he did. He refused to celebrate India's Independence day. He

observed the occasion sadly, in fasting and prayer. The India tha
was coming into existence was not the India that he had though
of. In the last months of his life the partition riots brought hin
closer than he had ever been to despair. We will never know how
many died. They died in the streets of Lahore, in mud huts ir
villages, and in tenements in Calcutta. The dead clogged the river:
that formed the boundaries between India and Pakistan. Other:
died on trains. The trains carrying Muslim refugees to Pakistan an
Hindu refugees to India were some of them ambushed, and their
passengers murdered.

It is the deaths on trains that are remembered. The partition o
India and the killings that accompanied it have impressed themselves on the imagination in a single image, as an attack on a train
Khushwant Singh's documentary novel, *Last Train to Pakistan* i:
perhaps the classic account. But the scene has become a cliché. Ir
the *Raj Quartet* it is enlivened by some theatrical heroics. The trair
is stopped, and a mob bangs on the compartment door screaming
for Muslims. Kasim, the son of a staunch Muslim Congressman, i:
anxious to spare his European travelling companions the incon-
venience of seeing him hacked to death. 'It seems to be me the
want', he says, and steps out of the compartment. The image has
become so dominant that when Ved Mehta recalls the nights in the
early months of 1947 that he spent in a room in Lahore, huddled
together with the women and children of the Hindu families of the
neighbourhood, listening to the noise of the Muslim mob approach
and recede, he remembers himself feeling as if he were in the
compartment of a train.

Narayan's handling of the scene is typically reticent. In *Waiting
for the Mahatma* Sriram travels from Malgudi to Delhi on the Grand
Trunk express. It is a bad journey:

> His greatest trial had been when two men appeared suddenly
> from somewhere when the train was in motion, and scrutinized
> all the people in the compartment: when they came to him, they
> stopped in front of him and asked him a question. He could
> catch only the words 'Mister' and 'Hindu' with a lot of other
> things thrown in. They were rowdy-looking men. He said
> something in his broken Hindi, and Tamil and English, which
> seemed to make no impression on them. They came menacingly
> close to him, peering at his face; Sriram was getting ready to
> fight in self-defence. He sprang up and demanded in the

language that came uppermost, 'What do you mean, all of you staring at me like this?'. As he rose, one of the two pulled his ear-lobe for a close scrutiny, saw the puncture in it made in childhood, and let go, muttering, 'Hindu'. They lost interest and moved off. After they were gone, a great tension relaxed in the compartment. Someone started explaining, and after a good deal of effort in a variety of languages, Sriram understood that the intruders were men looking for Muslims in the compartment: if Muslims were found they would be thrown out of the moving train: an echo of the fighting going on in other parts of the country. Sriram lapsed into silence for the rest of the journey.

Narayan's prose is so limpid, so easy, that one has to keep reminding oneself how active it is. He focuses here on India's linguistic diversity. When the 'rowdy-looking men' leave, and the tension relaxes, the different languages become just a badge of human variousness. They cause difficulties, but with 'a good deal of effort' these can be overcome, and they do not prevent the people from recognising their shared experience as travellers. But when the two rowdies confront Sriram, he is saved not by his broken Hindi, nor by his fluent Tamil and English, but by a puncture in his ear-lobe, by a sign that when he was an infant, at some time before his memory begins, he underwent a ceremony that stamped him as a Hindu.

Sriram is saved by a pierced ear. The incident marks Narayan's sense that the partition riots were a regression from citizenship to tribalism. The train figures India's admission to what Forster calls 'the drab nineteenth century sisterhood' of nations, but it seems drab only to those like Forster, so sophisticated that they have grown weary of the exercise of a political responsibility that most of the world has never known. On the train Indians who belong to different cultures, and speak different languages can still forge a sense of common identity. But that sense is fragile, vulnerable. It takes only two rowdy-looking men for the passengers to find themselves unable to look to each other for support. Instead, each turns inwards, and finds in his primitive, tribal identity the only safe refuge in an insecure world. Then the eyes of those children that Satyajat Ray filmed begin to shine not with wonder but with hatred. The train becomes a threat to the tribal group, not a promise of a bigger world. The lines are torn up, the train is stopped, and the tribe enacts its ancient ritual of murder.

After 1947 the train represented a smaller idea of India. Trains no longer ran between Bombay and Lahore, between Calcutta and Dacca. Nehru rode the trauma of partition much more robustly than Gandhi. He was younger, of course, and had never been committed to non-violence as a sacred principle. But it was also, think, because the riots laid bare paradoxes at the heart of Gandhi's character. He had been for many years what Mulk Raj Anand calls him, 'the greatest liberating force of the age', but he had also been a reactionary with the extravagant ambition of dragging India back to the twelfth century. It was as if, in the partition riots, in the attacks on trains, the two aspects of his personality declared war on each other. It left him wanting to die. That prayer at least was granted.

Gandhi was afraid of flying. Even when he was urgently needed in some distant part of the country, he would travel only by train. Nehru, on the other hand, was fascinated by aeroplanes. Unlike Gandhi, he was committed to machines. His ideal was economic prosperity in an industrial society, and he was right. India has been able to maintain the appallingly low living standards that it offers hundreds of millions of its people only because Nehru inaugurated a programme of massive industrial expansion. Without that, millions of Indians would not be poor, they would be dead. But Nehru's achievement had a cost. Nirad Chaudhuri spells it out in the waspish attacks on Nehru that punctuate his *The Continent of Circe*. Nehru industrialised India by allowing one tiny segment of its population, the educated, anglicised Hindus, to dominate the whole country. If Chaudhuri is unfair – and I think he is – it is because Nehru did not act to serve the interests of his own caste, he allowed the anglicised Hindus to monopolise power because he could see no other way of doing what he knew had to be done.

Nehru's autobiography was provoked – Nehru says as much – by his need to break free of Gandhi's hold on him. Its saddest moment is the moment that marks Nehru's success. Throughout the book Gandhi has been 'Gandhiji', until, in the final pages, he is suddenly referred to with cool formality as 'Mr Gandhi'. It is not that Nehru has stopped loving him, but that he has accepted that in crucial matters he and Gandhi are political opponents. Nehru is utterly out of sympathy with Gandhi's reactionary and religious romanticism, and he can no longer find it in himself to subscribe to a paradox as though it were a policy.

Nehru wins a bitter victory, and it is the more bitter because he realises that in winning free from Gandhi he is winning free from the Indian people. Gandhi, he recognises, is 'the quintessence of the conscious and subconscious will of the peasant masses of India', and he achieved that position not in spite of, but because of the fact that he was a compendium of startling paradoxes. 'Almost he was India', writes Nehru, and in his wonderment, just for a moment, he slips into the syntax of an Indian rather than a Cambridge man. But it is only for a moment. Significantly, even though Gandhi has more than a decade to live, Nehru uses the past tense.

Gandhi's leadership was charismatic: it was secured by his inability to distinguish himself from the people of India, and their inability to distinguish themselves from him. Nehru's leadership was glamorous. He wonders wryly how much of his popularity he owes to the rumour that he and his father send their laundry to Paris every week. Glamour, unlike charisma, is rooted in difference.

The class that gained power under Nehru still rules India. One meets them on Marine Drive in Bombay, in Delhi's Connaught Place, and in the novels of Ruth Prawer Jhabvala and Anita Desai. They are foreigners in their own country, whose only contact with the India that Gandhi knew is the peasant craftwork that he encouraged, and that they have transformed into interior decoration. It is as if India has suffered a second partition. Before it, Indians travelled in different compartments, but in the same train. There was the maharajah's state carriage, for the zamindars there was a first-class compartment with its surplus of uniformed waiters, and there was a third-class unreserved where four people couched on a single luggage rack and the normal mode of entry and exit was through a window. But all the carriages were pulled by the same engine. Now the new rulers of India do not often travel by train. They have found alternative means of transport.

Paul Scott's *Staying On* is set in the hill station, Pankot, where Tusker and Lucy Smalley live in retirement in a bungalow in the grounds of Smith's Hotel. India is much changed since the time when Tusker Smalley was quartermaster to the Pankot Rifles. The train from Ranpur still arrives in Pankot at 8 a.m., but few passengers take a taxi from the station to the Shiraz, the new luxury hotel: 'Most of the Shiraz's guests arrived late in the day by private car or by the Indian Airways bus that picked them up in mid-afternoon at the airfield down in Nansera.'

The train unites India: the plane fragments it. That is too simple
of course, but it will serve to indicate the ambivalence of Western
technology in its impact on India. Western technology enable
nations to come into being: it establishes the conditions withou
which it is hard to think how a sense of nationhood could come t
exist. But at the same time it threatens to divide a nation into tw
distant groups; those who have appropriated the articles c
Western manufacture, and those to whom they remain foreign
mysterious, and unattainable. It was, I think, his understanding c
this danger that prompted Gandhi's quixotic and futile hostility t
machines. Trains have become Indian: the railway remains th
most impressive single expression of India's national identity. A
India remains a foreign acquisition; its mascot for many years
cheery, chubby maharajah, a significantly Western token for Indi
its food a bland westernised substitute for Indian cuisine, it
hostesses chosen exclusively from among the daughters of India'
middle class with an eye, if I am not mistaken, for a Europea
complexion.

But there is another way, too, in which the West threaten
India's sense of itself. For many Westerners India is less a countr
than a state of mind. It is significant that novelists as diverse a
L.H. Myers and Hermann Hesse have written novels of spiritu
quest set in India. India was chosen because it already had
tendency to exist less on the map than in the mind, because
threatened less forcefully than other countries their autonomou
imaginative visions. India has always been a favourite goal fc
those who travel not to experience another country, but in fligh
from the constrictions of living within a real world. But why do s
many such people pick on India? Is their choice arbitrary, or
there something about India that beckons them?

7

Indian Fugues

At the beginning of Ruth Jhabvala's *Heat and Dust* a missionary is talking to a young English girl just arrived in India, talking with the urgency of night-time conversation between those who cannot sleep:

> One day I saw a terrible sight. He can't have been more than thirty, perhaps a German or Scandinavian – he was very fair and tall. His clothes were in tatters and you could see his white skin through them. He had long hair, all tangled and matted, there was a monkey sitting by him, and the monkey was delousing him. Yes the monkey was taking the lice out of the man's hair. I looked in that man's face – in his eyes – and I tell you I saw a soul in hell.

I once saw such a man. There was no suffering in his face, nor any sense of his own degradation. Neither pain nor humiliation is remarkable to someone who is living in India. What I saw was emptiness, the vacancy of a man who had let go, relinquished, in the hope that in abandoning the sense of self that the West had given him he might be flooded with some spiritual light. But what his eyes revealed was that he had been rewarded neither with divine illumination nor human knowledge. He had found himself empty, with nothing to say, with only an awareness of himself as meaningless in a meaningless world.

Ruth Jhabvala's missionary came to India out of love for Jesus, so that she might show her love by serving the poor, and share her love with those who knew nothing of it. She still clings to Jesus. But he is no longer what opens her heart to India, he is what protects her against it: 'And through it all I've learned this one thing: you can't live in India without Christ Jesus... Because you see, dear, nothing human means anything here. Not a thing.' Jesus has become the only defence she has to offer against the threat of what she sees in that young man's eyes.

Later in the novel, the young English girl meets Chidananda,

Chid for short, who wears the saffron robes of the holy mendican
the saddhu, but who speaks in a 'flat Midlands accent'. He ha
come to India to pursue his interest in the Hindu scriptures, foun
a guru to 'strip him of all personal characteristics' and re-name hir
Chidananda, and has now set out on a pilgrimage to the holy cav
of Amarnath. In Satipur he stays with the English girl for a while
irritating her with his demands for food and sex, and boring he
with his religious ramblings. Then he sets off again on hi
pilgrimage. Months later he returns. He is sick, but not just in hi
body. India, the food, the climate, and the people, all of it, nov
fills him with disgust. He lies in a hospital bed, his eyes tightl
shut, and waits to be well enough to fly home.

Chid and the blond young man are representatives of a new kin
of traveller who came to India in the 1960s and 1970s. They cam
not to find but to lose, not to enrich themselves but to abolis
themselves. For them travel was flight, a species of fugue. Th
victim of fugue forgets who he is, or assumes a false name, becaus
what he is fleeing from is himself. He travels because he is in th
grip of fear, and the natural impulse of the afraid is to run, but h
must also travel to maintain his necessary fiction, that he is no
himself but someone else. He travels to avoid friends, family
anyone who would remind him of his name, his wife, his socia
obligations. Fugue is a temporary state, a mood rather than
condition. It may last only minutes, or it may last months. It
victim flees from himself in panic, and when he comes to, when h
finds himself in a strange place, not understanding how he cam
to be there, he is disturbed, frightened. A fugue begins and end
in fear. It begins in the fear that our life, with all its difficultie:
its frustrations, its sufferings, is fixed, unchangeable, and ha
shackled us to an identity that we feel inadequate to maintain.
ends in the fear that the firm sense of ourselves to which we clin
as the mark of our sanity is just a sham, an illusion that might a
any moment be shattered. When the victim of fugue remember
who he is, his problems may only have begun.

Ruth Jhabvala abandons the blond European in Bombay, leave
him staring out of his vacant eyes forever as a monkey picks lic
from his hair. But the man that I saw probably left India, wrote t
his parents, like Chid, for a plane ticket to take him home. On
does not see so many white boys with saffron robes in Indi
nowadays, nor so many derelicts, the flimsy uniforms with whic
they once signalled their contempt for a life of conventional routin

now tattered, who came overland to India for the hashish, and stayed for the heroin. Those who remain seem no older than those I saw in 1970, which suggests that they are the successors, not the survivors of the first and stronger wave of those who were attracted to India not by a country but by the negation of a country, by their need for a place that offered release from consciousness, a place where one might live 'stripped of all personal characteristics'.

They were people in flight – in flight from materialism they might have said, not realising that the materialism of the hungry has a sharper edge than anything the West has to offer. But in truth they were in flight from thought not things, from the burden of individual consciousness that no Westerner can evade, and that seemed to them too heavy a load to carry. Chidananda, in Birmingham, Wolverhampton, or some other dreary Midlands town, was attracted by the Hindu scriptures, and came to India at their call. In India he meets two other English people, who have come to India after hearing a swami lecture on universal love, which he compared to 'an ocean of sweetness that lapped around all humanity and enfolded them in tides of honey'. They came to India as to a spiritual treacle well in which they might drown themselves. They came looking for embrocation to ease their modern aches, and they found dysentery, ringworm, and pick-pockets. Their careers are a brutal comedy of disillusion. But if all they wanted was the calm of feeling their minds dissolve into a fine mist of meaningless abstractions, there were purveyors of spirituality nearer home who could have served their purpose. Why did they ignore the possibilities of mental befuddlement offered by any one of a legion of bizarre versions of Christianity, and choose rather to go half way across the world, and look for the peace that obviates understanding in some bizarre version of Hinduism? Fashion, of course, counts for much, but there may have been more to it than that. It is possible that they were attracted by a dim recognition that their own experience had something in common with the experience of many Indians.

The novel of R.K. Narayan that I always press on those I am recommending him to is *The Bachelor of Arts*. This is his second novel, not his best, but it has always seemed to me his most beguiling. It tells the story of Chandran, and it is in two parts. The first takes Chandran through his final year at college. In the second he makes the more difficult passage to maturity. After graduating, Chandran has no notion what to do, except for a vague plan of going to England to pursue his studies. His days pass dreamily, lazily, pleasantly, until one evening, as he takes his walk along the sands of the River Sarayu, Chandran falls in love. He falls in love without ever having spoken to the girl, without knowing her name, before even he has seen her face clearly. He finds out that her name is Malathi, and, with some difficulty, he persuades his parents to arrange a marriage between them. Everything seems to be going well. The girl's parents are pleased by the proposal. But then Chandran's dream is shattered, wrecked by a discrepancy between the Drig and the Vakya almanacs. Both point to, the baneful influence of Mars in Chandran's horoscope, which will prove fatal to his bride. But according to the Vakya system the malign influence will persist until it is neutralised by the ascendancy of the sun when Chandran is 25. According to the Drig Mars lost its potency when Chandran was 20. Malathi's father is an advocate of the Vakya almanac, and feels it impossible to entrust his daughter's life to a rival system in which he has no confidence. Malathi is soon betrothed to someone else.

Chandran is inconsolable. He goes to Madras, where he meets Kailas, who has money that he made in Malaya, keeps two wives in his village, and visits Madras every few months to drink whisky and visit brothels. But Chandran has promised his mother that he will never drink alcohol, and at the door of a brothel he gives Kailas the slip and runs away. He takes a bus to Mylapore, pays a barber to shave his head and provide him with two pieces of cloth dyed in ochre, and becomes a sanyasi. For some months he wanders the countryside begging food from the villagers. Then, as he sits under a banyan tree, he is enlightened. He realises that the food he has taken from the villagers has been obtained on false pretences, that his renunciation was not spiritual, but only a childish 'revenge on society'. He goes home, gives up his plan of studying in England, and throws himself into a new career as an agent collecting subscriptions for a newspaper. Then his mother takes him to see a girl called Susila. Chandran falls in love again and is soon married.

Chandran's schooldays are happy. Like all young men he feels a tension between his own need for self-assertion and the demand of his parents and teachers that he conform, but it is a function of love to ease such strains, and Chandran's is a loving family. Only when he falls in love with Malathi is the harmony of his life threatened. He does not know what caste she belongs to, at first, but, wonderfully, he finds that her caste is his. His parents had hoped

for a more splendid match for him, and it is
the boy to make the first move in such
proves equal to the emergency, and all th
are made, only for Chandran's happir
discrepancy between the Drig and
time in his life Chandran bumps
festly indifferent to his wishes.
less painful for being suffered
Chandran's response is dis.
fugue. He takes flight from the.
desires and the pattern of the stars
after dressing in the appropriate clo
now disguised as a religious quest.

Chandran recovers the balance of his b.
takes a train with his mother to see Susila, a
smiles his acceptance of the bride his parents have . . . .t.
Malgudi, Narayan's town, offers happiness to the quirky entric
people who live there. The town imposes the compromise between
assertion and acceptance on which, Narayan believes, happiness is
founded. But the compromise is delicate, easily disturbed, as the
story of Chandran makes clear, and the characters in Narayan's
more recent darker novels, unlike Chandran, are not allowed a
second chance.

In 1967, 30 years after *The Bachelor of Arts*, Narayan published *The
Vendor of Sweets*. It is still a comic novel, but the comedy has turned
sour. It traces the crisis that prompts Jagan, the sweet-vendor of
the novel's title, to abandon his business and his family, and set
out on a fugue from which there will be no return. As a young man
Jagan was a disciple of Gandhi – he even followed Gandhi to jail.
But now, as he approaches 60, his Gandhianism has become a
comfortable habit, and coexists easily enough with his life as a
prosperous merchant. Jagan is a bundle of paradoxes – a
sweet-seller who imposes on himself a diet of unusual austerity, a
religious man who studies the *Gita* as he sits in his shop, distracted
from his reading only by the chink of a coin or the glimpse of a
customer not being attended to – but the paradoxes have been so
often repeated that they have lost their edge. Suspended between
the *Gita* and the chink of coins, between spiritual wisdom and
business sense, his life has achieved an unruffled stability, disturbed only by his love for Mali, his son.

As a child Mali is spoiled, idle and stupid. When he returns from

America, where he has insisted on going to take a course in creative writing, he is a good deal worse. Narayan seems not to have been outraged by the Raj. Its representatives, the principal of Chandran's college, a planter in *Waiting for the Mahatma*, are not dangerous, only comical in their irrelevance to the real centres of Indian life. But all Narayan's contempt for the West since 1947 is pressed into his characterisation of Mali. It is a blanket contempt for Western technology – Mali brings back to India an absurd project to manufacture on franchise a fiction-writing computer; for Western habits – Mali has taken to drink, and as the novel ends he is in jail for drunken driving; and for Western morality – Mali brings back with him a Korean girl, he introduces her as his wife, but they are not married. It is this last that snaps Jagan's love for his son:

> Mali had proved that there was no need for ceremonials, not even the business of knotting the thali around the bride's neck. Nothing, no bonds or links or responsibility. Come together, live together, and kick away each other when it suited them. Whoever kicked harder got away first.

America has infected Mali with a hard Western individuality. He dispenses with ceremony, and with it all the bonds, the links, the obligations that bind people together. Watching his son Jagan sees a vision of life become chaos, an anarchy of conflicting egos each clattering against the other. 'Reading a sense into Mali's actions was fatiguing, like the attempt to spell out a message in a half-familiar script', and Jagan is too old, too tired, to make the effort. He takes a bus to Mempi where he plans to begin a new life of holy poverty, assisting a stonemason carve the statue of a goddess. Narayan judges Chandran's fugue severely. His was not a spiritual renunciation, but a 'revenge on society'. It seems a harsh description of a boy's bewilderment, more appropriate to Jagan's state of mind. But in the later novel Narayan shares his hero's disgust, and smiles kindly on his flight.

Chandran flees because his love is frustrated by the stars, Jagan because his son has been corrupted by the West. But the two fugues have more in common than this suggests. It has been impossible for more than 200 years to imagine an intelligent Westerner for whom an interest in astrology is anything more than a whimsical affectation. In India it is common, even among the sophisticated. 'So sorry to keep you waiting, I had to see my astrologer', an urbane Indian businessman once said to me, amused not at all by his confession, but by my embarrassment. I blushed to meet so unexpectedly with a sign that he and I, who had seemed to get on together so easily, could be so unlike each other. I had stumbled over a radical difference between the Western and the Indian perceptions of human identity. Western identity is secured by difference, by a sense of the self as unique, the model of its association with others a contract, an agreement to cooperate to secure some end. But Indians know of another kind of identity, not grasped in an act of introspection by which the self becomes aware of its difference from all others, but acted out in all those customs and ceremonies in which the individual is assured of his place within the group. The Western sense of identity is guaranteed by the individual's freedom, the Indian by the system of constraints within which the individualist is bound. A belief in astrology is as impossible for the one way of thinking as it is natural to the other. If the individual finds himself in accepting his social function, then this act of acceptance is at once authorised and made majestic when the social pattern and the constraints it imposes are mirrored in the pattern of the eternal stars.

But I have been speaking loosely. Chandran and Jagan were both educated in English. For them, as for all Indians like them, an 'Indian' sense of identity can only coexist with a sense of themselves indistinguishable from that of Westerners. As Chandran walks by the River Sarayu, he falls in love with a girl in a green sari, careless of her caste, knowing nothing of her social place. His love is an assertion of his right to feel not as the son of a district judge, nor as a man with the surname Iyer, but as an individual. What threatens is a crisis that will tear apart his two identities, his two ways of understanding himself. For a while the crisis is averted. The girl turns out to be of the proper caste, both families agree to the marriage, but then the horoscopes are exchanged and Chandran falls apart. To live the life of Kailas, drinking whisky, and using prostitutes, would be to annihilate himself. But so too would his sense of himself be lost if he accepted the decision of the astrologers, for then he would have given up his right to feel, to love, as an individual. Suspended between two identities, unable to choose either, he jettisons both, puts on saffron robes, and finds in them the release he needs from the impossible problem of who to be. When he recovers and returns to Malgudi, his life resumes its proper balance. To sell his newspapers he devises a sales campaign of American panache, and he marries the bride his mother has found for him.

Jagan's crisis is delayed. As a young man he defied his family, and went to prison. But he acted then as a follower of Gandhi, and Gandhi, the England-returned lawyer and the devout Hindu, resolved in his own person Jagan's problem. Jagan could go to prison as an assertion of his right to citizenship, and also as an act of obedience to a mahatma. Gandhi offered millions of Indians what he offered Jagan: a way in which their discordant senses of themselves might be reconciled. But his achievement did not survive him. Since his death Jagan's two selves have been held together in comfortably loose solution, until he is confronted in his son with a nightmare version of an aspect of himself. He cannot cope. All he can do is to take flight in what for him can only be a parody of the disengagement from the world traditionally recommended to the Hindu in the last stage of his life. As he retreats into mendicancy he takes with him that most characteristic possession of Western, individualised man, his cheque book. For him there can be no escape from the world, only flight: no reversion to a simple, traditional identity, only fugue.

It is not a big step from Chandran and Jagan to Ruth Jhabvala's characters, Chidananda and the blond European. The spiritually sick only pretend to go in search of a cure, what they are really looking for is a sanction for their disease. Young Westerners came to India in flight from the burden of individuality, of self-consciousness, that the West imposes on its citizens as the condition of the industrial society that secures their prosperity. They came out of nostalgia for a life 'without personal characteristics', but they did not come to a country where such a life existed. They did not travel to some primitive tribal society, but to India, to a country that is the eighth largest producer of manufactured goods in the world. If that European had lifted his eyes from the Bombay pavement he would have seen skyscrapers. On his pilgrimage to Amarnath, Chidananda could have stopped off to inspect a nuclear power station. Their mistake was too absurd not to be deliberate. They were not looking for a country where their dream might be realised, but for a land where it was shared.

In India a very rapid industrial expansion had been imposed on a society elaborately organised to one end, the preservation of itself unchanged. The first impulse came, no doubt, from the need of the first Indo-European settlers to preserve their way of life from contamination by the aboriginal inhabitants of India, but it has been sharpened over the centuries by the need to defend the identity of the race against successive waves of conquerors, first Muslim and then European. What developed was a complexly and rigidly stratified society, in which each member's sense of himself was secured by the certainty of his place within the whole, and that society persisted, persists, within an India that now makes quite different, even contradictory, demands of its citizens. Citizenship assumes a Western notion of individuality: caste denies it. The result is a radical instability, a flickering between rival identities. Jagan's and Chandran's fugues are representative, and they are what attracted Chidananda from the Midlands and the blank-eyed European, for in such Indians they recognised their compatriots.

In *India: A Wounded Civilization* V.S. Naipaul records his conversations with Sudhir Kakar, a psychologist at Jawarharlal Nehru University.[1] According to Kakar the Indian ego is 'underdeveloped': 'The mother functions as the external ego of the child for a much longer period than is customary in the West, and many of the ego functions concerned with reality are later transferred from the mother to the family and other social institutions.' This is as revealing as it is perceptive. Kakar persists in using a Freudian terminology, in defining the seat of self-awareness as the 'ego', but Freud's scheme, as Freud's later writings seem to acknowledge, describes a psychology generated by a particular set of social circumstances. Freud's 'ego' is the sense of himself possessed by the citizen of an industrial state. It is a misleading term to apply to a sense of identity generated not by a sense of oneself as unique, separate, but by a knowledge of oneself secured by the performance of the duties prescribed by the community. But it would be just as misleading if Kakar were to avoid the term, for Indians are citizens of an industrial state, and simultaneously they inhabit a quite different country.

And so, of course, do we all. Western countries were industrialised much more gradually than was India, and the feudal societies that industrialism disrupted were much less rigid. But still, in every Westerner, there lurks a nostalgia for another world. The English do not take astrology seriously, but every popular English newspaper offers its readers daily horoscopes. They are read smilingly, but they are read, as, for a minute or two, we dally with a dream, a release from individual responsibility to a life where what will be is written in the stars. Horoscopes press on what Major Minnies would call 'the weak spot'.

Major Minnies is the political agent to the Nawab in the 1920s plot of *Heat and Dust*. After his retirement to Ooty, he publishes what amounts to a gentlemanly, English version of Kurtz's last monograph. India should be loved and admired, but only with a 'virile, measured, *European* feeling'. To go further is to run the risk of being 'dragged over to the other side'. India, despite his love for it, 'remained for him an opponent, even sometimes an enemy, to be guarded and if necessary fought against from without, and, especially, from within: from within one's own being'. Many Europeans, even the finest, have 'a weak spot': it is there that India seeks them out and pulls them over into 'the other dimension'. The Major thinks it virtuous to resist, Chidananda thinks it spiritual to succumb, but they share a sense that India, if only the European will let it, has the power to demolish the foundations on which the Western sense of identity is built. India offers Chid a ceremony in which he is stripped of 'all personal characteristics', which is what he wants, for a while. It condemns Major Minnies to a lifetime's struggle to preserve his Englishness, to regulate his feelings. Chidananda in India is in fugue, in flight from himself. Major Minnies seems his opposite, and yet in India his need to preserve his habits of 'virile, measured, *European* feeling' becomes fugue-like, a flight from the discovery of some 'other dimension', which is there in India, and which threatens him, because it is present too within his 'own being'.

E.M. Forster, Ruth Jhabvala, Paul Scott, and V.S. Naipaul have all noted how in India the Englishness of the English became insecure. The pipe, the whisky soda, windsor soup became props needed for the acting-out of a notion of Englishness that had become illusive, theatrical. Naipaul notes a peculiarity in India's imperial architecture; the Victoria Memorial in Calcutta, the Gateway of India in Bombay, even Lutyens's sublime New Delhi. These are monumental buildings, massively wrought out of stone, and yet they also have the peculiar quality of stage sets. For all the solidity of their building materials they seem somehow fragile. Naipaul is especially sensitive to this, for he finds nothing equivalent to it in the English dealings with his native Trinidad.[2] In Trinidad England's legacy is a language, institutions, a legal system. In India it is an idea of Englishness, an idea so potent that it survived the Raj, and could be expertly acted out as recently as

1971 in those urbane exchanges between the Indian and Pakistani commanders-in-chief – 'I hope you are as handy with your sten as you are with your pen' – that brought the war in Bangladesh to an end. So it was that a modern war – sordid, vicious, a war in which the ceremony of innocence was not drowned, but raped, bayoneted, and had its throat cut with a rusty blade – ended theatrically, archaically, with a snatch of dialogue that might have been, perhaps one ought to say was, invented by Kipling. In India, being English stopped being a description of national origin, and became an ideal of behaviour, a style, a role.

When Chidananda comes back to Satipur, he has abandoned his saffron robes for 'a pair of khaki shorts and a shirt and a pair of shoes'. He is 'a Christian boy' again, with parents who can be written to and asked to send a ticket home. He has come to, recovered himself, but from now on he will be eerily conscious of the self he has recovered as a disguise, a costume proclaiming him a Christian as theatrically as his saffron robes once proclaimed him a Hindu. What happened to prompt his transformation he cannot say, he only repeats that he 'can't stand the smell'. He lies in a hospital bed with his eyes tightly shut, and waits to be well enough to fly home. But for him Birmingham will no longer be home, only a refuge from some intolerable experience. The English girl's friend, Maji, laughs when she hears he has gone: ' "Poor boy", she said. "He had to run away." Her broad shoulders shook with laughter.' He comes to India, running away from Birmingham. He goes home, running away from India. One fugue has ended, but only for another to begin.

Chidananda is a pitiable eccentric, but the structure of his experience is typical. In her essay 'Myself in India' Ruth Jhabvala describes her own experience of India as a crazy shuttling between one flight and another. In India she sits in a room with the blinds drawn, reading Tolstoy, Stendhal, Joyce, intent on preserving her European self in an alien landscape. From time to time she flies back to Europe, but only to find that Europe no longer seems real to her. She comes back to India in flight from the flimsy unreality of the West, and draws the blinds and opens her Flaubert. At the end of *An Area of Darkness* V.S. Naipaul records how he fled from India in panic, and as the plane rose India dropped away from him like a bad dream in the morning. But in Rome airport he watched a stewardess, smart, self-confident, and had a moment of sick vertigo:

How could I explain, how could I admit as reasonable, even to myself, my distaste, my sense of the insubstantiality and wrongness of the new world to which I had been so swiftly transported? This life confirmed that other death; yet that death rendered this fraudulent.

There had been something in his bad dream of India that undermined his confidence in the solid Western world.

We might be passed in the street by a man walking along the road, and never know that that man was in fugue. 'In long fugues,' the psychiatric handbook notes 'the patient travels far, appears self-possessed, and lives in every way like a normal person, except that he is not where he should be.' He is in New York when his home is in Kansas, or in Paris while his wife and children wait for him in a semi-detached in Basingstoke. When he comes to, he will panic, finding himself in surroundings that he does not recognise. But he can be reassured, go home, and resume a normal life. There is no such simple cure for the victim of the kind of fugue that I have tried to describe, what seems to me a distinctive Indian fugue. Where should Chidananda be – in Satipur or in Birmingham? Is Jagan's proper place in his shop, or with the stonecarver in the wilderness? Naipaul lived in London and visited India, but when he returned he did not come home. His visit had worked to confirm him in his own 'homelessness', in the knowledge that he belonged nowhere. He is the descendant of all those Englishmen who served their 40 years in the Indian Civil Service dreaming of retirement to Eastbourne, only to find that when they came home and bought their bungalow their nights were full of dreams of Ooty, Simla, Darjeeling. But he is related to Indians, too. My businessman friend consults his astrologer, and then, perhaps half an hour later, he is on the phone to New York. He cannot choose to be of the East or West, he must be both, and the two identities fall apart from each other, each exposing the other as fraudulent.

Contradictory selves cannot be reconciled, but they may both be accommodated. Chandran in *The Bachelor of Arts* and the young English girl, the narrator in *Heat and Dust*, both succeed in this, and for both their success is an achievement of style. The English girl will bear and raise her child by Inder Lal, the government clerk. She has come to India and loved an Indian without restricting herself to a 'virile, measured, *European* feeling', and she has done so without being dragged over into any other dimension. She

emains what she always was, a decent, good-natured English girl.
What saves her from Chidananda's fate is her ordinariness. She
accepts Hindu mysticism: 'Maji was in a state of samadhi. To be in
that state means to have reached a higher level of consciousness
and to be submerged in bliss.' But she keeps her English decencies.
When she visits Chid in hospital, she notices that the man lying
next to him is in distress, he has been left for hours lying on a
bedpan:

> I removed it from under him and went to empty it in a bathroom.
> The state of those latrines has to be seen to be believed, and
> when I came out I did feel a bit sick. I tried to hide this so as not
> to hurt anyone's feelings, but it seems I had already done
> enough. Everyone looked at me as if I had committed some
> terrible act of pollution . . .

She is the novel's heroine, but what secures her heroism is that
insipid prose, which is scarcely prose at all for it is spoken on to
paper rather than written, a prose so incapable of inflection that it
can hold together any inconsistency within its tumbling monotone.
Chandran's achievement, too, is an achievement of style,
Narayan's style. Narayan writes a prose commonly described as
'gently ironic'. The adverb marks the reader's sense that it is an
irony without hostility. Narayan has to write ironically, because
only an ironic prose can play between contradictory sets of values
without repudiating either. His irony acts as a suture, not a scalpel,
and in *The Bachelor of Arts* it stitches together Chandran's discordant identities so neatly that the scar is scarcely visible.

But Narayan's achievement is unique, and Ruth Jhabvala signals
in the gauche, sub-literary prose that she devises for her narrator
that the ease with which the English girl accommodates East and
West is unavailable to her creator. There is, I suspect, a crucial
difference between the impact of the West on India, and its impact
on other countries colonised in the nineteenth century by the
European imperial powers, or yielding in the twentieth to the
economic might of the United States. Elsewhere, when Western
modes of thought came into conflict with incompatible ways of
thinking, the Western mind proved dominant. But in Hinduism it
met a tradition too strong to be driven underground, too vital to
die. In India rival realities persist together, and each renders the
other absurd. Narayan's Jagan finds in the end that it is an

absurdity that he can no longer maintain. He retreats into the wilderness, and into a pure Hinduism uncontaminated by the West. But the West has not just got a hold of his son, it has a hold in him. He can no more dispense with it than he can bring himself to throw away his cheque book. Naipaul retreats from India, and flies back to a Europe that is inhabited by 'whole men'. But when he arrives, he finds that there is a piece of him missing, that India, Hinduism, had offered him 'something true which I could never adequately express and never seize again'. Jagan takes a bus in one direction, Naipaul takes a plane in the other, but it is the distinctive quality of the Indian fugue that it leaves one unsure which of the two men is its victim.

8

An Area of Darkness

It was not until 1972 that V.S. Naipaul's mother told him how his father had gone mad: 'He looked in the mirror one day, and couldn't see himself. And he began to scream.'[1] Naipaul's father had made himself into a writer, a journalist. It had been an extraordinary achievement. He transmitted his vocation to his son, and with it, as a 'subsidiary gift', his hysteria, his 'fear of extinction'. Hysteria is what Naipaul takes with him when he travels abroad. He looks at alien cultures as into a mirror, tense with the fear that he will not find there any comforting reflection of his own humanity, that the mirror will be empty, and he will start to scream.

Travel books are now of two kinds. They record adventures – voyages in bizarely constructed boats, treks through perilous terrain, or amongst the more savage of primitive tribes – or they are reflective. But there is something ersatz about prearranged adventures, carefully planned and usually sponsored by a major industrial company. And there is something callous in the reflections of travellers from the prosperous nations of Europe and America who find in the wretchedness, the cruelty, and the meagreness of more fragile countries the drug they need to enliven the comfortably upholstered tedium of their lives. Naipaul is the only great travel writer of this century, and it is his hysteria that makes him so. He travels at risk, but the risks are not frivolous or wilful. They are a necessary by-product of what he calls 'exposing himself to new people and new relationships'. *An Area of Darkness* remains his best travel book, not because it is the best written – there are passages in a style riper than anything Naipaul would now allow himself – nor because it is his most intelligent commentary on an alien culture, but because Naipaul has never since placed himself at such risk. His later travel books record the experience of a man who is playing safer, whose hysteria is kept more firmly in check, who is trying to expose a country to his reader without exposing quite so much of himself.

In the first chapter of *An Area of Darkness*, Naipaul tells the story of Ramon. Ramon was a classmate of Naipaul's in Trinidad 'Proper Brahmin', Ramon had murmured admiringly wher Naipaul had refused to use a pipette that was being passed arounc the class from mouth to mouth. Naipaul was not a propei Brahmin, religion bored him. Caste-consciousness lingered only as a vague feeling of superiority, and an exaggerated fastidiousness about personal hygiene. But Ramon had recognised, wher Naipaul quietly passed the pipette straight on to the next boy, tha Naipaul, however loosely, still belonged to something. Ramon dic not. He had no caste, no family attachments. He had only one thing, a love of cars. He drove them without a licence, he pilfered bits and pieces to repair them, and he was always caught. When i was no longer possible to be with cars in Trinidad, he came tc London, leaving his parents, his wife and children, and his pregnant girlfriend with scarcely a regret. It was in London tha Naipaul met him again. He had a room in a Chelsea boarding house, he was unshaven, he was 'of a piece with the setting, the green grown dingy of the walls, the linoleum, the circles of dir around door handles, the faded upholstery of cheap chairs, the stained wallpaper'. But he was not unhappy. He had come tc London for the cars, and in London he was able to be with cars. He was soon in trouble with the police again, and drifted in and out of prison, and then he died in a car crash.

Naipaul has a clear sense of the difference between travel writing and writing novels, but in *An Area of Darkness* the distinction is blurred. One result of this is the book's obliqueness. Naipaul does not explain why he finds place in a book about India for the story of Ramon, but the story provides the only explanation he offers of the motives that drew him to India. When Ramon dies, Naipaul felt a need to see to it that his body was handled 'with reverence', 'according to the old rites'. He was not at the funeral, but he imagined the scene: 'a man in a white dhoti speaking gibberish over the corpse of Ramon, making up rites among the tombstones and crosses of a more recent religion, the mean buildings of a London suburb low in the distance, against an industrial sky'. The pathos of Ramon's death, the spurt of pity it inspired, opened up to Naipaul the pathos of his own life in London. Trinidad had only ever been for him a place to escape from, in Trinidad he had growr up with the belief that life was what went on elsewhere. To escape to London was to arrive at the centre of the world, and Naipaul had arrived:

And I was lost. London was not the centre of my world. I had been misled; but there was nowhere else to go. It was a good place for getting lost in . . .

In London, in the 'neutral heart' of the city, Naipaul found himself 'confined to a smaller world than I had ever known': 'I became my flat, my desk, my name.' He felt an exile, but an exile for whom nowhere was home. It is unsurprising that, feeling this, he should have turned to the land that his grandfather left 60 years before, the mythical place, the 'area of darkness', that had fed his imagination as a boy. He went to India in terror of the meaningless, private extinction that had overtaken Ramon. He went looking for a home, for a country and a people that he could belong to.

His ship docked at Bombay, and he found himself one of the crowd hurrying into Churchgate Station, for the first time in his life indistinguishable from the mass of people around him.

It was like being denied part of my reality. Again and again I was caught. I was faceless. I might sink without a trace into that Indian crowd. I had been made by Trinidad and England; recognition of my difference was necessary to me. I felt the need to impose myself, and didn't know how.

He bought some extremely expensive sunglasses, and they broke. Denied a part of his reality in London, where he was only a flat, a desk, a name, Naipaul went to India, where his face became suddenly not distinctive, and for that reason not his own. He was caught between two different kinds of extinction, two mirrors in neither of which he could see himself. The predicament generated a hysteria that rarely left him throughout his stay.

So many Indian novels are built out of the opposition between the plains and the mountains – *Kim, Heat and Dust, A Fire on the Mountain* – and in this, too, *An Area of Darkness* works like a novel. The first part is set in the heat of Bombay and Delhi. Naipaul spends his time scuttling away from the sun into small pockets of coolness, shuttered rooms or air-conditioned offices. Out in the sun every impression is like a hallucination. His conventional inhibitions are burnt out of him: 'I was shouting now almost as soon as I entered government offices.' He sees middle-class schoolchildren at the Gandhi Memorial shamelessly begging from kindly Americans: 'I advanced towards the schoolboys, simple murder in my heart.' His violence feels like an 'exultation', but he knows that his mood is phoney, a product of the temperature From Delhi he takes a train to Kashmir, to Srinagar, and a hotel or the Dal Lake, in search of a coolness that will allow him the detachment he needs to record his experiences. The second part of the book deals with his stay in Kashmir. In the third he comes down to the plains again, to the heat, and even before he catches his bus in Srinagar his hysteria returns. He quarrels with the tonga driver over the fare, and 'I found, to my surprise – it must have been the earliness of the hour – that I had seized him by the throat.'

In Kashmir, Naipaul finds coolness, and also an India reduced to dimensions that his imagination can cope with. He brought with him to India an imagination nurtured on a small island, a dot on the map of the world. He sensed in Indians 'an easy, unromantic comprehension of size' that he could not share. He felt an 'islander', in need of the 'small and manageable', and he found what he needed in Mr Butt's hotel on the Dal Lake. The hotel is a 'doll's house': it is not only the temperature but the diminutiveness of Kashmir that is healing. It is in the weeks that he spends there that Naipaul's experience of India is at its most benign. His hysteria still sometimes bursts out as anger; when he is presented with an exorbitant bill, when a holy man's followers destroy the hotel lawn, when a young man from Bombay insists on listening to the film songs on Radio Ceylon. But, for the most part, he keeps his hysteria in check. Here, where India is reduced to Mr Butt, Aziz the head servant, the cook, and the odd-job boy, Naipaul can be gracious; typing testimonials, talking pleasantly to prospective guests, and badgering the tourist office to grant the hotel official recognition. Aziz, in particular, he courts. He tries to make Aziz his friend, and when Aziz invites him to his family home and gravely entertains him, he thinks that perhaps he has succeeded.

The sheer scale of India has always been an incitement and a threat to those from small countries, whether Trinidad or Great Britain. Almost every islander who visits India has sat on a train steaming over the great plain, and watched a landscape that curves away only with the curve of the earth, a space so impossibly extended that it mocks the belief that landscape is given order by the people who live in it, and threatens more insidiously the notion that the fate of an individual human being, within a terrain so vast ιat it reduces human proportions to those of an ant, could ever be matter of very much significance. The huge extent of India can be terror to eyes bred on small fields and near horizons, but it is not ιst a matter of space. It is a country that stretches through too ιany climates, from the silent ice of the Himalayas to the dry heat ∢f Delhi, and the even less tolerable wet heat of Bombay and ∶alcutta. There are too many physical types. To travel from Delhi, city dominated by massive turbaned Sikhs, to a city of the South ke Madras is to make a voyage from Brobdignag to Lilliput. You ιep down from the train in the morning and find that you have hanged size overnight. What is beautiful is too beautiful, and √hat is ugly is too appalling. The wealth is more flagrant and the ∘overty more degrading than one had believed possible. Naipaul's ιland imagination is under terrible strain in India, and it is to rest ιs imagination as much as his body that he goes to Kashmir. But, s I have tried to show, this terror of a country too big to be nagined is not confined to visitors from Trinidad and Great ∙ritain. It is a part of the Indian experience, too. Naipaul exposes imself to all of India, retreats to the doll's house in Kashmir, and hen exposes himself to India again. Such alternating reflexes can e traced in almost all Indian novels.

During his stay in Kashmir, Naipaul joined a pilgrimage to the ιoly cave of Amarnath 13 000 feet up in the Himalayas, sacred to hiva because of the stalagmite that forms there each summer in he shape of a lingam. He was one of 20 000 pilgrims slowly √inding their way upwards, settling at night into huge, chaotic amps. His attention keeps shifting from the mountains to the ∘ilgrims; from streams and valleys and snow to 'pilgrims defecat- ιg behind every bush': 'The woods were already littered with ιncovered excrement: hanks and twists of excrement crowned very accessible boulder.' The mountains are a part of his dream of ndia: he remembers his grandmother's religious pictures and their ∶ones of white against simple, cold blue'. The mountains are ndia, but behind every bush there is a squatting pilgrim, and that ∶ India too. Just once, as he nears the cave, the two Indias are econciled:

At the end of the valley, where the ice, less protected, was partly broken, one remembered picture came to life: a sadhu, wearing only a leopard skin, walking barefooted on Himalayan snow, almost in sight of the god he sought. He held his trident like a

spear, and from the trident a gauze-like pennant fluttered. H
walked apart, like one to whom the journey was familiar. H
was a young man of complete, disquieting beauty. His skin ha
been burned black and was smeared with white ash; his hair wa
reddish-blond; but this only made more unnatural the perfectio
of his features, the tilt of head, the fineness of his limbs, the ligl
assurance of his walk, the delicate play of muscles down his bac
and abdomen.'

But it is an isolated moment.

When Naipaul reaches the cave, its entrance is blocked by
seething mass of worshippers. The holy cave of Amarnath i
transformed for the day into Churchgate Station, and Naipaul wi
not risk extinguishing himself in such a throng: 'No sight of th
God, then, for me: I would sit it out.' Aziz reported that there wa
no lingam in the cave – either it had not formed that year, or th
press of worshippers had melted it – but the pilgrims are nc
disappointed. For them, the empty cave is a perfectly adequat
symbol of the absent symbol of the absent God, a 'spiralling
deliquescing logic' that Naipaul cannot begin to share. Th
downward journey was quick. The next day Naipaul was back i
Mr Butt's hotel. The pattern of the pilgrimage – slow, painfu
approach, swift flight, and in between a moment that reveals t
Naipaul only his own difference – that is the pattern of the whol
book.

In the mountains the pattern is traced wryly, tolerantly. On th
plains it becomes violent. On a train going south Naipaul meets
Sikh, who reminisces of evenings he has spent in the Bambi Coffe
House in the Finchley Road. 'You know my trouble?', says th
Sikh, gazing around at the small dark-skinned South Indians o
the train, 'I'm colour-prejudiced.' 'But how awkward for you'
Naipaul replies. The Sikh's remark seems sophisticated, bantering
it opens the way to intimacy. When Naipaul leaves the train, h
and the Sikh exchange addresses and agree to meet again. Whe
they do, Naipaul realises that he had got it all wrong. What he ha
taken for self-mocking irony was rage and contempt – 'niggers'
'blackies', 'Let a couple of those Dravidians loose and they spo
the race for you.' The Sikh's colour prejudice may be absurd, but
is real and alarmingly intense. He is eaten up with a contempt fc
others that can only have its origin in a radical contempt of himsel
and, in the Sikh's company, Naipaul, monstrously, begins to b

infected by the Sikh's contempt: even as it happens he knows that he will 'carry the taint of that moment'. In a restaurant the Sikh imagines that some 'bloody Dravidians' are staring at him. He knocks one man to the ground. Naipaul walks out, and then returns to find the Sikh gone. He goes back to his hotel. There is a telephone call. The Sikh threatens to come over and beat Naipaul up. He comes, they talk, and then they break with each other. Here is the pattern again; the slow approach to intimacy, and then the flight, and in between a sudden realisation of difference, a realisation that the quality of Naipaul's disillusion with India is quite different from the Sikh's crazy rage.

As in a dream, everyone Naipaul meets becomes a parody of himself. A parody is both alike and different, so that to deny the likeness or to accept it is to be equally untrue. The pilgrims to the cave of Amarnath parody Naipaul's quest for a homeland that never existed except in his childhood imaginings, and yet they, unlike him, are satisfied with the emptiness that they find. The Sikh travelling south to vent his contempt of his non-Aryan compatriots caricatures Naipaul's voyage to India to vent his spleen against his forefathers. Then there is Laraine, an American girl who has drifted to India from out of the pages of a Scott Fitzgerald story. She is alone, in trouble, and Rafiq comes to her rescue. He is a young sitar player. One minute after their meeting they are in love, but it is a hysterical love punctuated by violent, frenzied quarrels. They marry and spend their wedding night at Mr Butt's hotel, but when Naipaul next sees Laraine she is alone again, on her way to join an ashram. Soon afterwards she returns to America. At first she replies to Rafiq's letters, and then they are returned unopened: 'Still he wrote: and months later he was still grieving.' Laraine is the child of a broken family, rootless and empty. She came to India looking for spirituality, something to fill her inner space. But she is a careless traveller: she leaves casualties, like Rafiq, in her path. Laraine's relationship with Rafiq, in which love cannot disentangle itself from violence, is a commentary on Naipaul's relationship with India. When she flees back to America, and retreats into the vast carelessness of the richest nation on earth, she makes a bleak comment on Naipaul's eventual flight from India, from the streets of Delhi to the spacious elegance of Madrid.

The history of India becomes itself a parody of Naipaul's Indian year. The Raj was a theatre, a stage on which the British played at

being British, carefully ignoring the Indians on the other side of th
footlights. When they packed their bags and left, they wei
abandoning a country that they had never bothered to get to kno
or become a part of. It had been more important to them i
preserve their difference, their theatrical Britishness. It is not s
very different from Naipaul at Churchgate Station, denied th
sense of his own difference, and responding by hurrying off to bu
a pair of Crookes sunglasses. The British are gone, and all that
left of them is a habit of mimicry, army officers called Bunty feelin
bushed. But writers, too, have imperial power, and one wondei
how many travellers remain trapped within Naipaul's vision, s
that wherever they go in India they see only Indians mimickin
Naipaul's perception of them. The bottle of Metaxas and the bottl
of Scotch that Naipaul carried with him when he disembarked i
Bombay were impounded by the Customs. The story of Naipaul
attempt to recover them is *Bleak House* in miniature. At last h
penetrates to the office where a permit he needs is issued. Paper
everywhere:

> on shelves rising to the grey ceiling, on desks, on chairs, in th
> hands of clerks, in the hands of khaki-clad messengers. Foldei
> had grown dog-eared, their colour faded, their spines abraded t
> transparency, their edges limp with reverential handling; and t
> many were attached pink slips, equally faded, equally limp
> marked URGENT, VERY URGENT, or IMMEDIATE.

To imagine with such Dickensian vigour is to imagine once and fc
all. There for all time is Indian bureaucracy, and every governmer
office in India becomes a pale imitation of the office Naipaul visite
during his first week in Bombay.

To be in India, for Naipaul, is to suffer 'the delirium of seein
certain aspects of myself magnified out of recognition'. Th
pilgrims, the Sikh, Laraine with her skirt of Indian cotton and he
conversation sprinkled with fragments of mispronounced Hind
the monuments of the Raj – everybody and everything that Naipat
sees in India is a caricature of himself, a mirror that reflects back t
him his own likeness gone wrong. He begins to lose the stabl
sense of himself that he needs if his responses are to be consisten

Driving in the south with the Sikh, Naipaul became aware tha
the Sikh's anger and contempt was 'feeding on everything he saw
He tried to 'transmit compensating love to every starved man an

.oman [he] saw on the road'. But his love is more fragile than the
.kh's hatred, and before the drive had ended he had yielded to
.e rage of the man beside him, and was in the grip of 'a self-
.cerating hysteria in which [he] was longing for greater and
.eater decay, more rags and filth, more bones, men more starved
.d grotesque, more spectacularly deformed'. India is a country of
.azy mirrors, moral mirrors that plunge him into moral giddiness,
.sick spinning between hysterical violence and equally hysterical
.ntimentality.

In Madras, Naipaul read the newspaper headlines: 'CHINESE
.AUNCH MASSIVE SIMULTANEOUS ATTACKS IN NEFA AND
.EDAKH'. 'Newspaper headlines can appear to exult', he com-
.ents, and he sees himself in that mirror too: 'The famous Fourth
.ivision was cut to pieces; the humiliation of the Indian Army,
.dia's especial pride, was complete.' His sentences can seem to
.ult. Against Chinese discipline and Chinese guns India offers
.mbols of defiance, and there is a part of Naipaul that takes a
.align glee in the spectacle of Indian symbolism brutally shattered
./ Chinese fact. And again the only retreat from brutality is into
.e sentimental. India:

> permitted a unique human development to so many. Nowhere
> were people so heightened, rounded, and individualistic;
> nowhere did they offer themselves so fully and with such
> assurance. To know India was to take a delight in people as
> people; every encounter was an adventure.

.t the end of his stay, Naipaul visited the village that his
.randfather had left for Trinidad more than 60 years before. It was
.ot the climax of his tour, but a 'duty' that he was not looking
.rward to. After a year in India Naipaul was emotionally ex-
.austed; his violence withered into peevishness, his sentimentality
.to a weak nostalgia as he heard someone singing a Hindi love
.ong he remembered from his childhood. He met Ramachandra,
.e village headman, who fulsomely acknowledged his obligations
. the grandson of the man who had used his Trinidadian wealth
. build three shrines in the village and to buy land there, and then
.amachandra suggested that he was in need of some money to
.ursue a law suit. Naipaul felt only boredom, irritation, and
.nbarrassment: 'I don't think I can keep this up much longer.' As
.e was about to leave in his government jeep, a young boy

appeared, freshly washed and in his best clothes, and stoc
around waiting to be offered a lift into town. 'Shall we take him
asked the civil servant who was acting as Naipaul's guide. 'No. L
the idler walk.': 'So it ended, in futility and impatience,
gratuitous act of cruelty, self-reproach and flight.'

Eight years later, in 1972, Naipaul pieced together the story
his father's madness. His father had written articles in his pape
the *Trinidad Guardian*, revealing that Indian farmers were in th
habit of protecting themselves against outbreaks of cattle diseas
by making sacrifices to Kali rather than obeying the governmer
regulations and having their cattle vaccinated. He received
threatening letter promising that unless he himself made a sacrifi
to Kali he would die within a week:

> In the week that followed my father existed on three planes. H
> was the reporter who had become his own very big front-pag
> story: 'Next Sunday I am doomed to die.' He was the reform
> who wasn't going to yield to 'ju-jus': 'I won't sacrifice a goat.' /
> the same time, as a man of feud-ridden Chaguanas, he wa
> terrified of what he saw as a murder threat, and he was prepare
> to submit. Each role made nonsense of the other. And my fath
> must have known it.[2]

He could not hold together his different identities. As he stoo
sullenly by while the goat had its throat cut, he lost sight of who F
was. He became depressed, and then one day he looked in th
mirror, couldn't see himself, and began to scream.

Naipaul's grandfather had gone to Trinidad from a village i
Uttar Pradesh, but he had never, Naipaul believes, seen Trinida
at all. His only concern had been to create in the new place the li
of his Indian village. It was not like this for Naipaul's father. H
could not ignore Trinidad, and in the end he was broken by hi
inabililty to hold together his Trinidadian and his Indian identitie
'I had learned my separateness from India, and was content to be
colonial', Naipaul writes of his last weeks in India. But this is to pu
the matter too calmly. He comes to insist on his separateness fror
India as the only refuge from his hysteria, the only guarante
against the predicament that made his father mad. India, he write
'brought out concealed elements of the personality', and made hir
ask, 'Was this me?' He felt himself invaded by Indian habits c
mind, even though it was not until he was safe back in Europe tha

realised 'how close I had been in the past year to the total Indian
negation, how much it had become the basis of thought and
feeling.' He chose, in the end, to reject the part of himself that
recognised India, and, though the rejection entailed loss, it was a
loss that he could survive. But what of those Indians whose minds
have been invaded by the West? They cannot take flight from the
West as Naipaul fled from India, nor can they reject their Western
habits of thinking and feeling, and they cannot do so, because
India, their country, is itself the product of both East and West; of
Hinduism and parliamentary democracy, of mantras and transistor
radios, of bullock carts and nuclear power. Unlike Naipaul, they
must find some way of holding together their dual personalities,
and the story of how they have tried to do so is best told in their
autobiographies.[3]

9

Indian Autobiography

I

Makunda Lal Ghosh was born on 5 January 1893, in Gorakhpu
He is better known as Yogananda, 'bliss through divine union', th
name with which he was invested by his guru. Swami Yogananda
later Paramahansa or 'master of spiritual discrimination' Yoganand
was the first Indian guru to establish himself in America. Throug
his yoga classes and his autobiography he did more than anyone t
establish the fashion for Eastern mysticism in the West. Even no
it is common enough to find young Westerners travelling in Indi
with a copy of *Autobiography of a Yogi* tucked into their rucksacks.
is a pleasant enough book. Yogananda emerges as an amiable mar
high-spirited, pleased with himself and well-enough pleased wit
the rest of us. His plump, smiling, somewhat epicene face beam
from the book's photographs with a complacent innocence tha
ought, one would have thought, to disarm criticism. But I was no
much surprised by the snort of angry derision that was an India
friend's only comment when he saw what I was reading. For all h
affability, Yogananda strikes one as a rather vulgar, feeble-minde
man, and my friend was as outraged by the notion that such a ma
might be thought to typify the religious life of India as I would b
were I to find someone educating himself in the religious life c
England by studying the works of Doris Stokes. All the same, it i
an interesting book.

The materials of Ghosh's life are fascinating. His mother die
when he was eleven. Thereafter, he made a series of attempts t
run away from his family home. He used to set out for th
Himalayas, where he hoped to be initiated into the yogic arts
When he finished school, his father agreed to his joining
monastery in Benares, but he could not get on with his fello
monks. Just when he was finding his situation intolerable, he me
the man who was to become his guru, Sri Yukteswar. Yukteswa
encouraged him to continue his education, and he went on t
graduate from Serampore College, but all his spare hours wer

pent with his guru. After some years of discipleship he experienced *samadhi*, the divine experience of cosmic consciousness, and was initiated by Sri Yukteswar into the swami order. Ghosh set up a school in which the children were educated according to yogic ideals. Then he travelled to America, ran yoga classes there, and established his successful Self-Realization Fellowship.

It is a life that prompts questions. How did Ghosh so early come by his single-minded ambition to be an adept in yoga? Why, when he speaks of himself as a loving son and brother, was he so given to running away from home? How did the ambition to convert America to yoga occur to him, and how did he, arriving in America unknown and without much money, achieve what he did there? How did he adjust so quickly to America, and America to him? Ghosh's life may prompt such questions, but his autobiography answers none of them, or, rather, the answers amount only to an insistence that the questions are irrelevant. He became a yogi because it was prophesied by the 'omniscient guru' Lahiri Mahasaya when Yogananda was still a baby. He went to America in obedience to a vision, and his mission was successful because its success had been prophesied by Babaji, inventor of *kriya yoga* the 'scientific technique of God-realization' in which Yogananda specialised.

Autobiography is, one might suppose, essentially exploratory. It addresses itself to the puzzle of how it was that the writer came to be who he is. But for Swami Yogananda there are no puzzles, there are only miracles. All that can be done with miracles is to record them, and that is what Yogananda does – miracles that he has performed, miracles that he has witnessed, and miracles that he has only heard about. A policeman impetuously chops off the arm of a sadhu he has mistaken for a murderer. 'Son, that was just an understandable mistake on your part', says the sadhu with a surprising lack of rancour: 'He pushed his dangling arm into its stump, and lo! it adhered.' There are saints who never eat, and saints who never sleep, levitating saints, and saints who appear in several places at the same time. There are stories of the well-known saint Sadasiva, who was once carried away by a flood: 'Weeks later he was found buried deep beneath a mound of earth near Kodumindi in Coimbatore District. As the villagers' shovels struck his body, the saint rose, and walked briskly away.' There is even a roguish saint who has the facility to dematerialise any object he touches and make it reappear in his pocket. It is a gift that he uses to travel free on trains. Yogananda's father, who was an official on the Bengal–Nagpur railway, remembers that his own company had been 'one of the firms victimised' by the saintly trickster. The miracles Yogananda performs are less striking. He makes a boil appear on his arm, he miraculously passes exams without doing any work, and he several times arranges for people to offer him feasts when he is feeling peckish. But all such events for Yogananda are 'strange and beautiful manifestations of the Intervening Hand'. Some manifestations seem pointless even to him. There is, for example, the famous Trailunga Swami, who lives in Benares, is more than 300 years old, and will sit for days either on the surface of the River Ganges or beneath it. But what impresses Yogananda is that he can maintain a massive body weight – it 'exceeded three hundred pounds' – although he eats very seldom. 'A master,' Yogananda comments 'easily ignores all usual rules of health when he desires to do so for some special reason, often a subtle one known only to himself.'

The miracles are various, but all the stories are the same. Some sceptic appears, often a scientific man, who smilingly or contempt-uously doubts the powers of the yogi. A miracle shocks him out of his materialism and leaves him begging to be initiated into the secrets of *kriya yoga*. Not to do so is dangerous. A vet was miraculously saved by Sri Yukteswar after his doctor had given him up for dead. Yogananda was a friend of the vet's son, and had put in a special word for him. Even the doctor is amazed: 'Never before have I seen a dying man make such a comeback. Your guru must indeed be a healing prophet.' But after his recovery the vet continues to eat meat, rejecting as 'unscientific' Sri Yukteswar's advice to the contrary. Six months later he drops dead. The term of his life had been extended simply because of Yogananda's 'earnest supplication', and Yogananda records the event as an instance of his guru's 'boundless kindness'.

It would be reasonable to suppose from all this that Yogananda sets great store by miracles. But apparently not so. He is not impressed, for example, by the 'perfume saint', a yogi whose speciality is to 'make a person's skin exude delightful fragrance'. The yogi excuses this apparently childish activity by arguing that his purpose is 'to demonstrate the power of God', but Yogananda will have none of this: 'Sir, is it necessary to prove God? Isn't he performing miracles in everything, everywhere?' Yogananda is severe with the saint – 'you have been wasting a dozen years for fragrances which you can obtain for a few rupees from the florist's hop' – and, even though the perfume saint includes amongst his followers 'many members of the Calcutta intelligentsia', Yogananda remains indifferent to him. Such miracles as he performs are spectacular but spiritually useless. Having little purpose beyond entertainment, they are digressions from a serious search for God'.

Yogananda's book is a catalogue of miracles, but he is careful to intersperse here and there a sentence disclaiming their importance. There is no connection between the two positions. Yogananda alternates between them just as the mood takes him, and this is entirely typical of him. Religion is very often used to expose the pretensions of the scientist. Yukteswar mocks an agnostic chemist: 'So you have inexplicably failed to isolate the Supreme Power in your test tube!' But just as often science is called in to authenticate the claims of religion, as in this bizarre use of Einstein to explain the miraculous powers of yogis:

Light velocity is a mathematical standard or constant not because there is an absolute value in 186,300 miles a second, but because no material body, whose mass increases with its velocity, can ever attain the velocity of light. This conception brings us to the law of miracles. Masters who are able to materialize and dematerialize their bodies and other objects, and to move with the velocity of light, and to utilize the creative light rays in bringing into instant visibility any physical manifestation, have fulfilled the lawful condition: their mass is infinite.

Miracles are awe-inspiring or trivial. The role of the scientist is to be put out of countenance by the yogic master, or to give scientific respectability to religious experience. There seems no logic here, but there is: it is the logic of public relations. Occasionally this becomes grotesquely obvious, as when an astral palace constructed by Babaji, the supreme yogi, is described as 'this shimmering palace, superbly embellished with jewels', and the estate agent's rhythm shoulders its way through the exotic vocabulary. When Babaji prophesies Yogananda's success in America another kind of prose takes over, a style peculiar to the salesmen of newfangled religions: 'Kriya Yoga, the scientific technique of God-realization', he finally said with solemnity, 'will ultimately spread in all lands, and aid in harmonizing the nations through man's personal, transcendental perception of the Infinite Father.'

Yogananda may be a naive theologian and an incompetent

philosopher, but he always has a shrewd eye for the market. When
he meets Ananda Mayi Ma, the 'joy-permeated mother' of Bengal
he is quick to see an opportunity, and invites her to America: 'An
Indian woman saint would be sincerely appreciated there by
spiritual seekers.' America is Yogananda's market, and he know
it. He correctly senses in the West a weak-minded reverence for
science and an equally weak-minded suspicion of it, and he
devises a religion that appeals to both impulses, a 'scientific
technique for God-realization' and at the same time a refuge for the
Westerner anxious that his way of life has somehow lost contact
with the things of the spirit. In New York there are skyscrapers: in
India there are saints, or, as Yogananda calls them, 'spiritual
skyscrapers'. In America there are radio and television, but in
India yogis have perfected the art of 'astral radio and television'
Yogananda is never happier than when he can slip between East
and West via metaphors, because metaphors are slippery enough
to accommodate both his requirements. The 'spiritual skyscrapers'
of India can confirm his American follower in his suspicion that
American technology is not everything, and at the same time
reassure him that, after all, skyscrapers are the proper measure
of all human achievement. Swami Yogananda invented the metaphysical pop that Gita Mehta has christened *Karma Cola*. He melts
East and West into a solution that manages to vulgarise both
traditions. It is an achievement of sorts.

II

Yogananda called in on Gandhi when he made a tour of India in
his reliable Ford car with an American follower. He felt it fitting, I
suppose, that he and Gandhi should be acquainted, as one
spiritual skyscraper with another. Unfortunately, it was Gandhi's
day of silence – he passed Yogananda polite notes. Nothing of
interest happened, but, anxious to impress his Western readers
with Gandhi's spiritual achievements, Yogananda records two
anecdotes. When operated on for appendicitis, Gandhi, it seems,
refused anaesthetics and 'chatted cheerfully with his devotees
throughout the operation'. Much earlier in his life, he had chosen a
life of simplicity, and given up 'an extensive legal practice which
had been yielding him an annual income of more than $20,000'.
What is telling here is not that both stories are untrue, but that,

even had they been true, they would still have been trivial. In such gossip Yogananda betrays an essential vulgarity, a vulgarity that Gandhi himself was incapable of. It is necessary to say this at the outset, because I want to go on to claim that the two men have something in common.

For Gandhi as for Yogananda religious experience was of primary importance, but the religion of both men was remarkably unsophisticated. In an acerbic aside in his *Hinduism* Nirad Chaudhuri remarks that if Gandhi's religious thought were subjected to the same procedures that archaeologists use to date pots, he would be confidently ascribed to the fourteenth century. To suggest that he might post-date Vivekananda would be to invite scholarly mockery. Understatement is not one of Chaudhuri's vices, but it is certainly true that Gandhi shows no awareness of the reform movements that transformed Hindu religious thought in the nineteenth century. The same is true of Yogananda, though for a Bengali who lived for many years in or near Calcutta to remain as primitive a theologian as Yogananda suggests a more culpable intellectual laziness.

It is again Chaudhuri who points out that what distinguishes Hinduism in its popular form from other religions is its intense worldliness. The goal of the believer is happiness and prosperity in this world, whether it be in this or some future life. The only alternative ambition is that at some point the precariousness of worldly happiness may be exchanged for the security of personal extinction. The spiritual adept is distinguished by his power. That is why miracles are so important to Yogananda. Through miracles the yogi reveals his power over this world. Yogananda made the discovery that there was a market in America for a religion that offered happiness in this world rather than in some future existence difficult to imagine: a religion that at its best abutted on the province of the psychotherapist and at its worst invaded the sales pitch of those who promise wealth, self-confidence, and sexual success to anyone willing to attend half a dozen moderately priced lectures. Yogananda was able to discover this not in spite but because of the primitiveness of his religious thought. A more sophisticated variety of Hinduism would not have served his purpose.

Gandhi's achievement was, of course, his potent fusion of political and religious leadership, and this too might not have come so easily to him, and perhaps not come at all, had his religious thought been more advanced. Vivekananda, who is much the most powerful Hindu thinker of the last hundred years, is the proper measure here. He visited America before Yogananda, and made a considerable impression, but without attracting to himself the band of devotees who followed Yogananda. Vivekananda also addressed himself to political issues. He was a nationalist impressive for the clarity and common sense of his views, but he never achieved anything like the political authority that millions accepted in Gandhi.

The fast was the most potent of all the means by which Gandhi directed religious activity to political ends. But the very first fast that he undertook was not political at all. It took place at Gandhi's South African ashram, the Phoenix Settlement. There Gandhi fasted first for 7 and then for 14 days. In his autobiography he records his reason vaguely: he had heard of the 'moral fall' of two of the ashram's children. Gandhi does not say so, but what had happened was that they had been caught engaging in some kind of homosexual activity.[1] Gandhi decided to fast because the teacher is 'responsible, to some extent at least, for the lapse of his ward or pupil', and because in this way 'the parties would be made to realize my distress and the depth of their fall'. But the decision seems so odd that one suspects a more mysterious motive. He fasted, I suspect, in obedience to a popular Hindu tradition according to which self-inflicted austerities are a means of acquiring power. Fasting was his way of re-asserting and reinforcing his spiritual power over the group. But his mystical motive went together with a sharp sense of the efficacy of fasting as a technique of moral blackmail. That strange combination of simple mysticism and practical shrewdness is entirely characteristic of Gandhi. He found the second fast hard, he says, because he 'had not then completely understood the wonderful efficacy of *Ramanama*', the name for God that Gandhi thought the most potent of mantras, and because he did not then know 'the necessity of drinking plenty of water' during a fast. It is grotesque, of course, to compare this with the combination of naive credulousness and sharp business sense in Yogananda – it has a quite different moral character – and yet it is not entirely unlike.

Yogananda's and Gandhi's autobiographies are both books that contain only one character, the author. Hundreds of other people are mentioned, but none of them ever comes alive. A vivid sense of other people has its origins, I suppose, in the child's slow recog-

ition that his parents have a separate life, a life not wholly
ubsumed in their relationship to the child. That must be why so
nany novelists offer in their first novels characters modelled on
heir parents. It is a rite of passage that must be performed before
he novelist can enter his artistic maturity. Neither Yogananda's
nor Gandhi's parents become people. Mother and father are
emembered as circumambient presences, and the affection that
he children express for them is pious. Chaudhuri argues that the
ousiness of describing one's father, that is, of seeing him as an
ndependent person is even harder in India than it is in the West.
Almost the first Sanskrit tag a boy used to learn, he recalls, declares
Father is Heaven, Father is Morality, Father besides is the Highest
Prayer'. He adds that it is common to find even in doctoral theses a
ledication in Sanskrit, 'To my Father the God'. But if one cannot
ee one's father is it possible ever to see anyone else? And without
eeing other people is it possible even to see oneself?

Gandhi includes in his account of his childhood failings a
onfession of theft. He used to steal coppers from the servants to
ouy cigarettes. Later he was guilty of a 'much more serious
offence'. The story, as Gandhi tells it, is worryingly vague. His
meat-eating brother' had run up a debt of 25 rupees. Had he
oorrowed the money to buy meat? The brother wore a gold armlet;
It was not difficult to clip a bit out of it.' Was this done with the
orother's agreement, or when he was asleep? 'Well, it was done,'
vrites Gandhi, 'and the debt cleared.' But he was overcome by
guilt, and wrote to his father confessing what he had done, and
asking for 'adequate punishment' and 'forgiveness'. His father
ead the note and cried 'pearl-drops of love'. It was, Gandhi now
ecognises, an example of 'pure Ahimsa' (non-violence). It is an
opaque story. Why is it much more serious to use his brother's
gold to pay his brother's debt than to steal money from servants? Is
t just that the gold was more valuable? But more puzzling is the
onfession. It is hard to see how Gandhi could have confessed
vhat he had done without explaining why he had done it, and any
explanation would have revealed that he had acted out of love for
nis brother, or at least out of concern for his brother's reputation.
There might be several reasons why Gandhi's father read that
etter and cried. All that Gandhi tells us is that the confession
made my father feel absolutely safe about me, and increased his
affection for me beyond measure'. The omissions and vagueness in
he story do not seem at all disingenuous, but they do suggest an

odd lack of self-awareness, as if Gandhi's ability to understand his own actions is somehow crucially limited. One remembers Yogananda's failure to offer any but a supernatural explanation for his habit of running away from home.

There are odd occasions in his autobiography when Gandhi contrives to sound very like Yogananda. To speak of the 'science of *satyagraha*' (literally 'firmness for truth', but the term Gandhi gives to his own technique of passive resistance) is not much different from Yogananda's 'science of kriya yoga'. Both seem attempts to filch the prestige of science without submitting to its discipline. Gandhi's title, 'The Story of My Experiments with Truth', if familiarity had not blunted the impression, would surely strike us as verging on the high-soundingly meaningless. What can it mean to experiment 'with' truth? Truth is, of course, the key idea for Gandhi, but he defines it so variously that it all but loses content. Truth is inconsistent with marital infidelity, the enjoyment of food, breaking oaths, copying in class, luxurious living, a refusal to compromise, and improperly kept accounts. It is identical with God, and with non-violence, it is properly expressed by suffering, and it was the ground of Gandhi's youthful loyalty to the Empire just as surely as it was the ground of his later opposition. It would seem as pointless to try to make consistent sense of such a sequence of remarks as to try to clarify Yogananda's theology. And yet it is impossible to read Gandhi's autobiography without recognising that one is in the presence of a formidable intelligence.

When Gandhi returned to South Africa after a visit to India, he was met at the quayside by a white lynch mob. He was advised to leave the ship secretly, but he refused. As soon as he disembarked he was set upon, and was only saved by the brave intervention of the wife of the superintendent of police. A posse of policemen escorted him to a friend's house, but the mob surrounded the building. The superintendent suggested that Gandhi slip away from the house in disguise, and while the superintendent diverted the mob by leading them in a rendition of their song, 'Hang Old Gandhi on the Sour Apple Tree', he made his escape. Gandhi tells the story, and then pauses to examine his own inconsistency. When the danger to his own life had been only potential, he had insisted on confronting the mob openly. When it had become actual, he had agreed to make his escape in disguise:

Who can say that I did so because I saw that my life was in

jeopardy, or because I did not want to put my friend's life and property or the lives of my wife and children in danger? Who can say for certain that I was right both when I faced the crowd in the first instance bravely, as it was said, and when I escaped from it in disguise?

It is idle to adjudicate upon the right and wrong of incidents that have already happened. It is useful to understand them, and if possible to learn a lesson from them for the future. It is difficult to say for certain how a particular man would act in a particular set of circumstances. We can also see that judging a man from his outward act is no more than a doubtful inference, inasmuch as it is based on insufficient data.

This passage, and it could be matched by dozens of others in the autobiography, is as good an illustration as any of what I mean by Gandhi's intelligence. Intellectual power is a part of it, but only a part. It needs also a rare honesty, moral seriousness, and a refusal of all easy postures. Gandhi investigates himself and his own motivations with an attentive scepticism, but he has a firm sense, too, that there is a point beyond which such investigations should not go, or they become exercises in perverse self-fondling. For him the point is reached when his enquiry has confirmed him in a cautious and limited tolerance, of his own behaviour and that of everyone else. It is, of course, a passage quite beyond the range of Yogananda, and it fits very oddly with my previous contention that there is a sense in which Gandhi never knew himself. But Gandhi was what Nehru called him, 'a mass of contradictions'. The only way to think about him is to decide which contradiction is central.

When they were boys, Gandhi and a friend took up secret smoking. They collected dog-ends, bought cigarettes with pilfered coins, and found a plant with a porous stalk that could be smoked:

But we were far from satisfied with such things as these. Our want of independence began to smart. It was unbearable that we should be unable to do anything without the elders' permission. At last, in sheer disgust, we decided to commit suicide!

The exclamation mark makes light of the incident, categorises it as a childish prank, and the story of the suicide attempt confirms this. The boys gather some seeds that they believe to be poisonous, but

they dare swallow only two or three. At that point they decide to
give up both smoking and thoughts of suicide. Gandhi was 'twelve
or thirteen' then. He can remember what happened, but seems to
have lost all sense of the powerful emotions that must have been
gripping him. As a boy his imagination fed on a picture of
Shravana carrying his blind parents in a sling attached to his
shoulders, and he dreamed of proving his love for his parents in
some similar act of service. But at the same time he could find the
obligation to obey 'unbearable'. It is a conflict that Indian children,
who are bonded to their families so much more closely than
children in the West, are almost bound to feel. But in Gandhi it was
strong enough to drive him to an attempt at suicide, however
feeble, and it marked him permanently. All his life he felt
simultaneously, and with great intensity, two impulses; the one to
give himself up in the performance of some self-denying act of
service, the other to impose his own will on the world. He needed
both to serve and to dominate.

The Gandhi who, in his father's last illness, delighted in
massaging his father's legs is continuous with the Gandhi who
attended the 1901 Congress in Calcutta. Despite the prestige that
his South African activities had earned him, he served happily as a
humble clerical assistant to the Congress secretaries. One of them
allowed Gandhi to button his shirt, and perform other little acts of
personal service. 'The benefit I received from this service', he
writes 'is incalculable.' Gandhi was rarely happier than when he
was nursing the sick, be they plague victims, Zulu insurgents,
members of his family, or chance acquaintances.

But the other side of Gandhi's personality was also evident
throughout his life, the side that, according to Nehru, reduced
those who disagreed with him to a 'psychic pulp'. Two anecdotes
are revealing. On a voyage from South Africa to England, Gandhi
noticed that his South African friend, Kallenbach, was unduly
attached to a pair of binoculars:

> 'Rather than allow these things to be a bone of contention
> between us, why not throw them into the sea and be done with
> them?', said I.
> 'Certainly, throw the wretched things away', said Mr Kallen-
> bach.
> 'I meant it,' said I.
> 'So do I', came the quick reply.

And forthwith I flung them into the sea. They were worth some £7, but their value lay less in their price than in Mr Kallenbach's infatuation for them.

Gandhi must have been very charming to get away with such behaviour. The second incident took place in Champaran, at the start of Gandhi's first political campaign in India. A number of lawyers offered their services to Gandhi and moved in to his campaign headquarters, but the 'irregularity' of their habits worried him – they brought their servants with them, and dined luxuriously, often 'as late as midnight'.

Ultimately it was agreed that the servants should be dispensed with, that all the kitchens should be amalgamated, and that regular hours should be observed. As all were not vegetarians, and as two kitchens would have been expensive, a common vegetarian kitchen was decided upon. It was also felt necessary to insist on simple meals.

Gandhi's choice of those impersonal, passive tenses – 'it was felt necessary' – is so outrageous that it is disarming.

All through his life Gandhi was heroically self-denying and heroically self-assertive. What concerns him is not to reconcile these two impulses, but to make sure that they leave him free to act. His decision to give up sex, first entertained as early as 1900, and sealed in 1906, when Gandhi took the vow of brahmacharya, has always intrigued Western observers. They tend to trace the decision to a knock on Gandhi's bedroom door. Gandhi was 15 and making love to his pregnant wife (he was married when he was 13). His uncle was knocking to tell him that his father had died. Gandhi bitterly confesses 'the shame of my carnal desire even at the critical hour of my father's death', and adds that the child his wife was carrying lived only a few days – 'Nothing else could be expected.' But I doubt whether this incident did any more than exacerbate feelings that would have developed in him anyway. He consistently speaks of sexual desire as something that invades him, an urge to which he succumbs. Just as consistently he speaks of the sexual act as imposed by an aggressive male on a passively enduring woman. It is as if, in his sexuality, Gandhi's impulse to surrender himself and his impulse to impose himself merge. This was exciting Gandhi remained unusually preoccupied throughout his life

by the nature of his own sexuality – but it was also, he found
inhibiting. Gandhi makes it clear that for him a vow of chastity wa
necessary before he could dedicate his whole life to public action

Gandhi left India before he was 20 and did not finally retur
home until he was a middle-aged man. In those intervening year
he lived, except for brief Indian interludes, in the West, in Englan
and then South Africa. Those years left their mark. There was
part of Gandhi that would always see India as a Westerner sees i
V.S. Naipaul, who makes this point, knows too that nothin
separates East and West more forcibly than their different attitude
towards human waste. In India a pronounced ritual horror i
commonly associated with an easy personal indifference. In th
West these proportions are, in most of us, reversed. The secre
truth that Naipaul lets out is that for Western travellers memorie
of India will always be accompanied by the sweet and sickly stenc
of human excrement.[2] Gandhi responded like a Westerner. H
campaigned as long and as hard to reform Indian sanitary arrange
ments as he did to remove the British government, and, thoug
there may have been much that was cranky in Gandhi, there wa
nothing at all cranky about this.

Gandhi knew about cholera, and he knew how necessary it wa
for Indian agriculture that use should be made of the one freel
available fertiliser. He was nothing if not a practical man, and hi
tough-minded, blunt practicality bursts through in the mos
unlikely places. A passage in which he speaks of his reverence fo
cows and his interest in cow-preservation ends only when h
points out that in him this creates a concern to introduce scientifi
breeding techniques to improve the stock. Even the strange stor
of his boyhood suicide attempt comes to a typically tough con
clusion: 'I realized that it is not so easy to commit suicide as t
contemplate it. And since then, whenever I have heard of someon
threatening to commit suicide, it has little or no effect on me.' It i
this side of Gandhi that won the grudging respect even of har
Boer politicians and stolid British administrators. But Gandhi was
moralist before he was a practical man, and his interest in sewag
was, first of all, a moral interest. He recognised untouchability a
the great moral evil of India, and he knew that it could be don
away with only by breaking through the elaborate system of taboo
that governed the handling of human waste. He performe
himself the duties of what, in India, is called the scavenger, and h
demanded that his wife, his children, and all his followers do th

ame. He led by personal example, but even Gandhi's personal
xample would never have been enough to threaten traditions
housands of years old. What he did no one else would have
hought of. He made scavenging into an act invested with religious
ignificance, he made a ritual out of the breaking of rituals.

Nothing is more characteristic of Gandhi, nothing marks him
nore clearly as a man both of India and of the West. In him the two
dentities remained unreconciled, even incongruous, but the pur-
uit of a harmoniously integrated self would have seemed to
Jandhi too merely aesthetic an activity. If he was content with
vinning through to only a limited self-awareness, that was
because self-awareness for him was never more than a means to an
nd, and his end was action in the public world. Truth was not
omething to be grasped in an act of introspection, it was
omething to be accomplished. He defines best what he means by
ruth when he tells how in London he made a decision to live as
imply as possible, on bread, cocoa and porridge. Such a diet he
ound 'more truthful', because it 'harmonized my inward and
outer life'. Truth was always for him something to be found in
iction. He must attend to his 'inward life', but only up to a point,
ip to the point at which he is able to decide how to act. Truth may
begin in a moment of self-awareness, but it ends properly only in a
campaign to change the world.

III

n comparison with Gandhi's, Nehru's is a conventional political
autobiography. It differs from others of its kind only by being so
hugely superior. This is partly a matter of chance. Nehru wrote his
autobiography in the eight months from June 1934 to February the
following year. He was 45, at the height of his powers, and his years
as India's first prime minister were still ahead of him. Autobiography is not for him an opportunity for settling old scores and
manufacturing disguises for political blunders and moral lapses in
the hope that, got up like this, they will impress future historians
as exemplary instances of high statesmanship and unshakable
probity. Nehru's autobiography benefits too from the odd habit of
the British in the last years of the Empire of preparing nationalist
leaders for office by sentencing them to spend long years of their
early manhood in prison. In some, no doubt, this training bred a

hardness that revealed itself unfortunately when they came int
political power, but in others – and Nehru was one of them – th
years in prison fostered habits of reflection that preserved then
from the curious human flimsiness that one senses in the commo
run of politicians.

Gandhi and Nehru are by far the greatest men of modern India
and, for most of us, to look at India is inevitably to choose to loo
with one of their two pairs of eyes. For me there is no choice. Thi
is partly a matter of temperament – Nehru's incomprehensio
verging on impatience in the face of most kinds of religiou
sentiment is a cast of mind I feel immediately comfortable with
but it may also be a matter of race. Nehru knew that he wa
consistently treated better by the authorities than other Congres
prisoners, and he understood why. Officials could not rid them
selves of the feeling that a man educated at Harrow and Cambridg
must be, despite everything, one of them. Perhaps that feelin
lingers in me.

But motives are, in any case, less important than reasons, and
single incident is enough to show the reasons for my admiration o
Nehru. In 1928 he led a Congress demonstration in Lucknow
against the visit of the Simon Commission.[3] The day before th
Commission was due to arrive Nehru was walking to a meetin
with a group of supporters when they were attacked by mounte
policemen. Nehru's first instinct was to run, but 'some othe
instinct' held him to his place. There was a mêlée, and Nehru
found himself isolated in the middle of the road: 'Automatically
began moving slowly to the side of the road to be less conspicuous
but again I stopped and had a little argument with myself, anc
decided that it would be unbecoming for me to move away.' It wa
his pride that stopped him, he supposes: 'Yet the line betweer
cowardice and courage was a thin one, and I might well have beer
on the other side.' Just then a policeman trotted up. Nehru turned
his head away – 'an instinctive effort to save the head and face' –
and received 'two resounding blows on the back'. It was his firs
experience of the *lathi*, the steel-tipped stave with which policemer
control crowds in India, and the experience left him feeling
exhilarated. He had stood up to it, and, even more important tc
him, his mind had remained throughout, 'quite clear'. That nigh
he telephoned his father to reassure him that he had not been hurt,
but his father could not sleep for worry, and drove through the
night from Allahabad to Lucknow, arriving early in the morning,

ust as Nehru was setting out to join the massive demonstration
hat would greet the members of the Commission when they
rrived at Lucknow station. The demonstrators assembled on the
maidan in front of the station, and were charged by three lines of
avalry. They held firm, and then the beating started. Nehru felt
ometimes 'a dull anger' and sometimes 'a desire to hit out', but he
vas restrained by 'long training and discipline' and by the
nowledge that any resistance would encourage the police to open
ire. While all this was going on the train arrived, and the
Commission members 'secretly crept away'. Nehru was left
ruised, and very tired, but not badly hurt. He came away with 'a
omewhat greater conceit' of his capacity to withstand punishment, and a memory of the hate-filled faces of the policemen:

> And yet, we had no grievance against each other, no ill-will. We
> happened to represent, for the time being, strange and powerful
> forces which held us in thrall and cast us hither and thither, and,
> subtly gripping our minds and hearts, raised our desires and
> passions and made us their blind tools. Blindly we struggled, not
> knowing what we struggled for and whither we went. The
> excitement of action held us; but, as it passed, immediately the
> question arose: To what end was all this? To what end?

t is not a great piece of writing, but it is good enough. It brings
Nehru before us, and what impresses, as throughout the autobi-
graphy, is the fullness of his presence. There is the courage, of
ourse, so admirable because so finely understood, and worn with
o winning a touch of self-deprecation. But there is much more
han that. There is, for one thing, the depth of family attachment,
ignalled in the telephone call to his father, and wonderfully
reciprocated by Motilal Nehru, as the old man travels through the
night, not at all intent on dissuading his son from doing what both
now must be done in the morning, but just to be there near him.
More than anything, there is Nehru's alertness, both to what is
going on inside himself and to what is happening around him.
And perhaps most striking of all there is his ability to recognise
hat on this day he and all those with him were heroes, and then to
pass on from that. He ends with questions: 'To what end was all
his? To what end?' It sounds like a rhetorical flourish, but that is a
imitation of the prose only. Nehru means these questions. His
whole book is an attempt to find answers to them, to give content

and direction, as he puts it, to the nationalist sentiment that had sprung up so vigorously in his countrymen.

Nehru's autobiography, unlike Gandhi's and Yogananda's, has characters in it, two of them. One is Nehru's father, Motilal, and the other is Gandhi himself. It is a political autobiography, and so it is inevitable that Gandhi should be its central character, for Gandhi was Nehru's political father. But it is with Motilal that it is best to begin.

From 1919 until his death in 1931 Motilal Nehru was one of the three or four most powerful figures in the Congress party. Before then he had been a wealthy lawyer, proud of his success; an admirer of Western ways; moderately nationalist in his politics but admired alike by Indians and Englishmen. Then came the Amritsar massacre, martial law in the Punjab, and a meeting with Gandhi and, in his late fifties, Motilal Nehru threw himself into Congress politics. He abandoned Western dress, gave up whisky, simplified his life, and, when the time came, joined his son in prison. He became a radical in late middle age. Even so, his politics remained at variance with his son's. It was inevitable that a man who had devoted his life to the law should be by instinct a constitutionalist whereas Jawaharlal was convinced early on that the British Empire would never offer its colonies a constitution within which it was possible to work for the Empire's dissolution. Father and son often disagreed politically, and sometimes found themselves on opposing sides in Congress, but neither allowed this to obscure the love and respect they felt for each other. The story of Nehru's autobiography is the story of his failure to achieve the same relationship with Gandhi that he had with his father.

Everything that Nehru writes about Motilal is shot through with pride that he should have had such a man for his father. In his account of a time when he had sided with Gandhi on an issue on which his father was Gandhi's chief opponent, what he best remembers is showing Gandhi a photograph taken after his father had shaved his moustache. Gandhi had commented that seeing the firmness of that mouth and chin had made him realise for the first time what manner of man they were up against. Motilal was a hero to Nehru until the day he died, when he insisted on sitting up in a chair to say his farewell to all the old comrades who had come to take their leave of him: 'There he sat like an old lion mortally wounded and with his physical strength almost gone, but still very leonine and kingly.' But there is nothing blind in this hero-worship. Motilal is brought vividly to life, with his huge laugh and frightening temper, managing a length of the swimming pool he had installed in the family house 'with set teeth and violent and exhausting effort', or, many years later, serenely informing the prison governor at Yeravda that he would take only 'very simple and light food', and going on to list requirements that would have seemed simple, no doubt, 'at the Ritz or the Savoy' but would certainly stretch a prison's catering resources.

In comparison, Gandhi's and Yogananda's expressions of filial devotion seem no more than ritual piety. Nehru's is an adult love, founded on a recognition of his father as separate from himself. And this is a sign – I would rather say a cause – of Nehru's ability to take an adult's objective interest in the world around him. When he travelled on the same train as General Dyer, the perpetrator of the Amritsar massacre, he saw Dyer leave the train in Delhi wearing 'pyjamas with bright pink stripes, and a dressing gown'. Gandhi would not, I think, have noticed that. Neither would he in his prison cell have looked closely at lizards catching wasps: 'Twice I saw them stalk them with enormous care and seize them from the front. I do not know if this avoidance of the sting was intentional or accidental.'

Nehru wrote his autobiography, he tells us, 'under peculiarly distressing circumstances, when I was suffering from depression and emotional strain'. He was in prison, his wife was ill, he had lots to be depressed about. But what provoked him to tell the story of his life was a crisis in his relationship with Gandhi.

Nehru had returned to India after more than seven years in England. He was at Harrow for two years, took a degree at Cambridge, and then spent a couple of years in London studying for the bar and running into debt. His father thought that he was 'rapidly going to the devil': 'But as a matter of fact I was not doing anything so notable.' He was busy turning himself into a fashionable young man about town. He returned to India a rather conceited young man, something of a dandy, and 'a bit of a prig' – and he was soon bored. The social life of Allahabad must have seemed to him very narrow, and Indian politics at the time were 'dull'.

Then, in 1919, came Gandhi. Nehru had met him three years before, but had thought him 'distant' and 'unpolitical'. In 1919 with the Amritsar massacre and the passing of the Rowlatt Act, a misguided attempt to rule India by suppression, Gandhi assumed the political leadership of all India. 'Go to the villages', he told young men like Nehru, and Nehru went. It was his first direct contact with the Indian peasantry, and it changed his life: 'somehow I had not fully realized what they were and what they meant to India. Like most of us, I took them for granted.' From that moment, he writes, 'my mental picture of India always contains this naked, hungry mass'. Nehru had found his country, or rather, he had been given it by Gandhi.

India came to exist for Nehru through Gandhi, and for 15 years he was unable to distinguish the country from the man. India, Nehru had recognised, was its peasantry, and Gandhi was 'the great peasant', the 'complete peasant' but at the same time he was 'utterly unlike a peasant'. Gandhi was India made accessible, as if by magic, in the person of an intelligent and articulate man, someone Nehru could argue with, be comforted by, love. It was not only Nehru who felt this: it was a feeling common to the educated, politically aware class that Nehru belonged to. Nothing else explains the extraordinary position that Gandhi occupied in Congress politics throughout these 15 years. It was Gandhi's habit in these years to refuse office, and sometimes he did not even attend the annual sessions of Congress. Yet nothing could be done without him. 'No struggle could be effective without Gandhi's lead' writes Nehru, and the sentiment becomes a refrain. Gandhi is a 'magician', a 'wizard': the words are clichés, but, used by so confirmed a sceptic as Nehru, they are revealing. They expose Nehru's scarcely conscious belief that Gandhi's leadership was secured by something more mysterious than his political effectiveness: 'Always we had the feeling that while we might be more logical, Gandhiji knew India far better than we did. If we could convince him, we felt that we could also convert the masses.' This is a rational-enough feeling, but Nehru insists so forcibly that Gandhi was the 'ideal embodiment' of the masses, the 'personification of their conscious and unconscious will', that one suspects that he scarcely distinguishes between persuading Gandhi and persuading the millions. To consult Gandhi's wishes was to practise a primitive, magical democracy.

Sometimes Gandhi did not know what his wishes were. Nehru once taxed him with his habit of 'springing surprises' on his colleagues. 'There was something unknown about him', Nehru said, and it frightened him. Gandhi's response – it would be amazing in any other politician, but it is entirely characteristic of Gandhi – was to accept the charge: 'He admitted the presence of this unknown element in him, and said that he himself could not answer for it or foretell what it might lead to.' Gandhi just waited for what he called his 'inner voice' and then obeyed, and Nehru, although he had no time for inner voices and heartily disliked the phrase, waited too, because for him that voice had become identical with the voice of India.

In 1919 Nehru had been a convinced Gandhian. Learning that some peasants had looted a landowner's house in the name of the Mahatma, he summoned a meeting and called upon the guilty parties to raise their hands: 'and, strange to say, there, in the presence of numerous police officers, about two dozen hands went up'. Gandhi would have been gratified: Nehru was left feeling vaguely guilty at 'having exposed those foolish and simple folk to long terms of imprisonment'. Even then he could not say with Gandhi, 'Truth is God': he did not believe in God. As the years passed he became ever more aware of his differences from Gandhi. He was unhappy at Gandhi's habit of blending political argument with the heady language of religious prophecy. He was at odds with Gandhi's vision of an ideal India, free from machines, where all lived a simple village life – such a life, he notes, would for him be worse than a prison – and he was outraged by Gandhi's insistence on the holiness of poverty.

In the end, two small incidents were decisive. On 15 January 1934, the town of Muzzafurpur was destroyed by an earthquake. Nehru was staying not far away, and was quickly on the spot. He was awed by the devastation. Then he read a statement by Gandhi to the effect that 'the earthquake had been punishment for the sin of untouchability'. In April, in prison again, Nehru read Gandhi's statement withdrawing civil disobedience. Nehru accepted the decision – the current agitation had run out of steam – but he was outraged by the reason Gandhi gave for his decision. It had been 'due to a revealing information I got in the course of a conversation about a valued companion of long standing who was found reluctant to perform the full prison task allotted to him, preferring his private studies to the allotted task'. Nehru did not believe that reluctance to go to prison was a sin – 'I have been guilty of it and I am wholly unrepentant' – but, in any case, it seemed to him 'monstrous' and 'immoral' to decide the course of a national

movement on the basis of the conduct of a single individual: 'With
a stab of pain I felt that the chords of allegiance that had bound me
to him for many years had snapped':

> And now? Suddenly I felt very lonely in that cell of Alipur Gaol.
> Life seemed to be a dreary affair, a very wilderness of desolation.
> Of the many hard lessons that I had learnt, the hardest and the
> most painful now faced me: that it is not possible in any vital
> matter to rely on anyone. One must journey through life alone:
> to rely on others is to invite heartbreak.

These are childish sentences, in a way: they have a child's intensity
of pain, and something of the child's capacity for bitterness. But
they are the last childish sentences that Nehru can properly write,
for with the snapping of the 'chords' of allegiance – how odd that
spelling is, as if 'cord' were too patently umbilical a word – Nehru
is released into political adulthood. It is a lonely feeling. Under
Gandhi's leadership he had come to feel for the people of India as
for his family. To cut loose from Gandhi was to lose the sense, that
had become precious to him, of all Indians as members of his own
family: 'I felt lonely and homeless, and India, to whom I had given
my love and for whom I had laboured, seemed a strange and
bewildering land to me.'

It is only in the final pages of the autobiography that Nehru
recovers his staunchness. He recognises now that he can never be,
like Gandhi, wedded to the people of India. He will always be an
outsider, always therefore lonely. But now he is prepared to accept
that loneliness is only another word for the independence proper
to a grown-up man. His critics complain, he writes, that he does
not represent 'mass-feeling':

> Indeed, I often wonder if I represent anyone at all, and I am
> inclined to think that I do not, though many have kindly and
> friendly feelings towards me. I have become a queer mixture of
> the East and West, out of place everywhere, at home nowhere.
> Perhaps my thoughts and approach to life are more akin to what
> is called Western than Eastern, but India clings to me, as she
> does to all her children, in innumerable ways; and behind me lie,
> somewhere in the subconscious, racial memories of a hundred,
> or whatever the number may be, generations of Brahmans. I
> cannot get rid of either that past inheritance or my recent

acquisitions. They are both part of me, and though they help me in both the East and the West, they also create in me a feeling of spiritual loneliness not only in public activities but in life itself. I am a stranger and alien in the West. But in my own country also, sometimes, I have an exile's feeling.

Nehru has been thus far India's greatest prime minister. Reading his paragraph it becomes impossible to doubt that. But it also becomes appropriate that Nehru was the first prime minister of independent India, because he reveals himself here as the 'ideal embodiment' of the new India, the India that he was to do so much to bring into being.

IV

'An insufferable man, conceited and silly', said an intelligent, kindly professor, when I mentioned to him my admiration for Nirad Chaudhuri. Perhaps the two had met, and the meeting had not gone well. I did not ask. What I remembered were the first two months I spent in Bombay, when I lived as if unaccountably hemmed around by some cliché-ridden documentary film. I date my discovery of India, its transformation into a country that could be thought about and explored, from the day when I picked up from a Bombay pavement bookstall a grubby, Jaico paperback of Nirad Chaudhuri's *Autobiography of an Unknown Indian*. Reading it again, I am more conscious of what it is in the book that provokes responses like my professor's. Chaudhuri's self-assertiveness is abrasive, sometimes brutal, and, just occasionally, a little vulgar, as if he feels it necessary to bolster his sense of his own dignity by demeaning his country, his countrymen, and their leaders. But Chaudhuri's autobiography remains for me an extraordinary achievement, one of the handful of great books that have come out of modern India.

Chaudhuri did not begin writing it until he was past 50. He had been a student of brilliant promise, but from the time that he failed his MA degree his life had been one of failure and poverty. For most of that time he eked out a meagre living with jobs on short-lived magazines. He took little part in the great national events through which he lived. He once saw Gandhi pass by in a car, and once had a short, formal conversation with Nehru, but he lived a

private life, dominated by the demeaning struggle to find th
wherewithal to feed and clothe his wife and children. He was a
unknown Indian, but he does not present his autobiography as th
diary of a nobody: it is, he claims, 'more of a national than persona
history'. It ends with 'An Essay on the Course of Indian History
from the time of the Aryan immigration to 1947. The autobi
ography rests on a premise next to which the fiction of *Midnight*
Children seems modest: that Chaudhuri's life contains the histor
of a civilisation 3 000 years old.

Of course, no book could satisfy such claims, but the originalit
and the liveliness of Chaudhuri's autobiography depend on th
daring with which he makes connections between the story of hi
own life and the history of India. Chaudhuri understands how i
was that he came to fail his MA. He suffered from the 'insan
ambition' to be both India's Gibbon and India's Mommsen, t
produce a historical work that would be at once a miracle o
painstaking analysis and a 'stupendous synthesis' – 'No wonder
crashed.' But the ambition never left him, and in his autobiograph
it finds its only possible expression, in a book that is at once th
detailed history of an individual life and a complete history of
civilisation. The charm of Chaudhuri's autobiography lies in it
particularity, in a memory of how he and his brothers chased afte
the family cow to the river: 'We took up the water in our folde
hands, and, sniffing it, found it charged with the acrid smell o
cattle.' But its energy comes from Chaudhuri's determination t
understand the place of his own experience within the broades
movements of history. When he was eleven, Chaudhuri rea
about the battle of Trafalgar, and Nelson's signal so rang in hi
head that as he walked home from the river he kept shouting
'England expects every man to do his duty.' An elderly man on a
elephant stopped, and asked Chaudhuri what he knew abou
these words, and young Chaudhuri was able to answer him. As
memory this has a splendid vividness – the small town in Eas
Bengal, the elephant, and Nelson's signal – but it is out of this, an
material like it, that Chaudhuri constructs his understanding of th
place of England in the Indian imagination.

In his account of his ancestral village, Banagram, Chaudhur
describes how Durga Puja, the chief festival of Bengal, wa
celebrated there. It was quite unlike the genteel urban celebration
of the festival that I have witnessed, and I doubt whether th
festival is still celebrated anywhere in the form that Chaudhur

emembers it. But I know of no other piece of writing that so precisely conveys the power of Hindu ritual.

The festival involved animal sacrifice. A number of goats, and, inally, a buffalo were decapitated and their blood offered to the goddess. A priest remarkable for his powerful physique was specially imported to deal with the buffalo, for if the head was not severed in one blow, it was a sign that the goddess was displeased and had refused the offering. The sacrifice of the buffalo was the climax of the bloody portion of the ritual, and it was followed by an orgy of blood. The worshippers fell on the carcass, 'smeared hemselves and each other with its blood, kneaded the dust of the yard into a dough with blood, and pelted one another with the mixture'. Then they began to sing, 'song after song, songs of nortals to the Immortal, of the helpless and the weak to the Strong, of the weary and heavy-laden to the Comforter'. And they sang songs, too, that were ascribed to the demons vanquished by Durga, in which the demons sadly contemplated the inhuman violence of the goddess, and in doing so voiced the bewilderment of the worshippers themselves 'after that bloody sacrifice'.

But Durga Puja was a festival of light as well as a festival of blood. There were 'crystal-glass chandeliers, branched wall brackets, glass balls of different colours – clear, red, green, amber, some of which had lamps burning and others candles', and also here were 'Japanese and Chinese lanterns of coloured paper', and t was amidst all these lights that the ritual of the waving of light ook place, when a priest swung five brass lamps in the face of the gods and goddesses.

The festival also had its distinctively male and female aspects. It ncluded a war ceremony in which the family's ancestral weapons were blessed, and a priest touched the forehead of each male with a scimitar. For the women the festival marked the three days that Durga spent with her mother, Menaka. The final day of the ceremony when the gods and goddesses were immersed in the tank marked the day on which Durga left her mother's house to eturn to her husband. It was a poignant moment for the women who shared the bitter knowledge that, after marriage, their visits to heir own home would be brief and rare, and that in marrying they had exchanged the steadfast love of a mother for the more doubtful affections of a mother-in-law. As the images sank, the worshippers greeted each other, touched the feet of the elders, and embraced: This was the evening on which we were expected to forgive every

injury, bear no malice, and have love in our hearts for all man-
kind.' But it was also an evening of sadness. They joined in a procession that visited each of the family's ancestral shrines, and then,
after dark, they returned home. They passed the worship-hall, all
its lights now extinguished except for a 'little earthen lamp', and
they could not bear to look at it. They hurried into the inner house
where the older women were waiting with 'handfuls of grass and
grain to bless us': 'To be near them was some comfort.'

It is not necessary to be religious to recognise how intense and
complete an experience such a ritual offers those who perform it. A
more interesting question is why Chaudhuri, despite his complete
lack of religious faith, is able so powerfully to convey this, whereas
no other writer that I have read achieves anything like it. The
answer lies, I think, in Chaudhuri's sense of history. He is alert to
the abrupt changes of mood within the festival because he is aware
of the complete ritual as the result of a long process of accretion, so
that the ceremony lasts five days, and, looked at another way,
extends through all of 3000 years, containing within itself a
complete history of the evolution of Hinduism.

Chaudhuri's family were in the habit of visiting Banagram only
once a year at the time of the Durga Puja. All the rest of the year
they lived in the small town of Kishorganj, some six miles away.
Yet, if asked where they lived, they would reply by giving the
name of their ancestral village. They thought of Kishorganj only as
a place of temporary encampment:

> It was a remarkable tribute to the power of the old tradition that
> through it even the children's feeling for the place where they
> were born, in which they were steeped, and which seemed all in
> all to them, was swamped at times, and accompanied always, by
> the loyalty to the absent village.

All the power of this 'old tradition' is compacted into Chaudhuri's
account of the Durga Puja. Immediately afterwards he writes: 'my
father never seemed to feel quite at home in his ancestral village'.
In fact he disliked it, and so did Chaudhuri's mother. To think
about that dislike, and of how it coexisted with an unbreakable
loyalty is to move towards the centre of Chaudhuri's book.

When Chaudhuri's father left Banagram to set up house in
Kishorganj, he exchanged a life in which he was supported by the
rent from the family estates and the services of feudal retainers for

a life in which he earned his living as a lawyer. He exchanged an extended family in which the emphasis is on the duty owed towards the elders for a nuclear family, in which the primary obligation is that of the parents towards their children. He also abandoned a religion founded on the correct performance of the prescribed rituals in favour of a religion defined by its theology. He and his wife were adherents of Brahmoism, the reform movement that shook Hinduism in nineteenth-century Bengal. They were monotheists, and so hostile to superstition that they refused to allow horoscopes to be cast for any of their children. Their Brahmoism was allied to an earnest, puritanical, personal morality, a disinterested belief in the value of education, and a love of literature, both Bengali and English. The quality of Chaudhuri's admiration for his parents, its clear-eyed unsentimentality, is again a product of his historical understanding. He recognises his parents' virtues as the products of what he thinks of as the bravest experiment in the recent history of India, the Bengali renaissance: the attempt, originating in nineteenth century Bengal, to effect a radical reform of the religious, moral, and cultural life of India.

Chaudhuri's parents are the unknown heroes of his book. Its public heroes are the architects of the Bengali renaissance; Rammohun Roy, Michael Madhusudan Dutt, Bankim Chandra Chatterji, Vivekananda and the Tagore family. What these men tried to do, Chaudhuri argues, was to reform Indian life by assimilating European, and specifically English, traditions. Brahmoism is Hinduism subjected to the critique of Protestant Christianity, and the 'new Hinduism' of a man like Vivekananda is only a less radical, or more subtle, product of a similar experiment. The cultural achievement was made possible by the importation of English literary forms. The new emphasis on a strict personal morality had its roots in the Victorian values of nineteenth-century England. Chaudhuri insists on this so emphatically that it is hardly surprising to find his whole project construed as a calculated affront to nationalist sentiment. It would be rash to argue that such a motive was wholly foreign to Chaudhuri's nature, but there is something more serious at issue than any simple wish to tease. Chaudhuri is anxious not only to celebrate the Bengali renaissance, but to explain its failure.

Its ambition was to create a synthesis of East and West. That ambition, Chaudhuri argues, was impossible, and for this reason, that the ancient traditions of India that were to be synthesised with

Western habits of thought were themselves the products of Western scholarship. The traditions of India were made available to Indians by Westerners, and thus already 'subtly transformed by being passed through the filter of European thought and scholarship'. It was Orientalism rather than the Orient that was compounded with the West, and the result was predictable. It was a movement that might re-make some individuals, but it could never have re-made India because there was nothing Indian about it. There was bound to remain a gap between the achievement of those brave reformers and life as it was lived by the many, and for Chaudhuri the emblem of that gap is the six miles that separates Kishorganj from Banagram. Kishorganj, with its civic pride, its neighbourliness, its amateur productions of *Julius Ceasar*, and the austerely rationalist religion that Chaudhuri's parents practised there, remained a place where the Chaudhuri family 'lodged'. Their sense of it always coexisted with, and was sometimes swamped by, their sense of Banagram, the ancestral village, and its different obligations, different social ties, and different religion. There was no reconciling one place with another – they remained six long miles apart.

Chaudhuri is his parent's son, the offspring of that nineteenth-century movement of which he is the elegist. The failure of his adult life, its poverty and meagreness, is the most poignant proof he offers of the failure of the whole movement. In modern India there is no place for him, he is as obsolete as the historical forces that produced him. And yet, when Chaudhuri records in his preface his friends' opinion that he is a failure, he adds: 'I do not concede the point', and his book ends, surprisingly, in a burst of joy. For most of his life, he writes, his one bitter satisfaction has been a sense of his own defiant separateness from the India around him. But in the past five or six years he has come to a quite different conclusion: 'I am only a particle of the universe, and remain so in every particle of my existence':

> Thus on the one hand I have been disenthralled by knowledge. On the other I have believed in order to understand, and have been rewarded with joy.

The knowledge that has disenthralled Chaudhuri is historical. He has come to understand the forces that shaped him, and that shaped India, and in understanding he has won freedom.

Surveying his newly independent countrymen, he makes a lofty boast: 'They are freed men, I am a free man.' But he has been able to understand his country's history only because he has found that history written in himself. The discovery that frees him from his country restores him to it. Chaudhuri's knowledge of history and its methods comes to him from the West; as a historian he is the product of a Western tradition of scholarship. But he is the historian of himself. He has found the one scholarly field available that does not come to him 'subtly transformed by being passed through the filter of European thought and scholarship'. Chaudhuri's account of Durga Puja could not have been written, I think, by anyone who was not a trained historian, but neither could it have been written by anyone who was not an Indian. Who else would know that when the festival had ended, and the procession had visited the ancestral shrines, the boys would hurry indoors to the women to receive their blessing, and feel that 'to be near them was some comfort'? Chaudhuri may mock at the possibility of any synthesis of East and West, but in such passages he seems to me to do just that, and it may be that the 'great flood of faith, hope, and joy' that bears him up as he finishes his book signals his sudden recognition of his achievement.

V

In November 1937, when Ved Mehta was three and a half, he contracted meningitis. He recovered from the illness, but he was left blind. Just before he was five, he was sent on a journey of 1500 miles, from Lahore, where his parents lived, to Bombay, to Dadar School for the Blind. In 1943 he came back to live in Lahore, until, at the partition, his whole family fled to India as refugees. In 1949 he left India for America, to attend the Arkansas School for the Blind in Little Rock. Since then, except for three years at Oxford, Ved Mehta has lived in America.

When he was 22 Ved Mehta published his autobiography, *Face to Face*, and must have realised quickly that in this, his first book, he had used up his best material. He has written much else since, but his major project has been the re-writing of that early autobiography. Five volumes have appeared so far, and Ved Mehta has got as far as the end of his schooldays in Arkansas.[4] He is already at work on the next volume.

The bare facts of Ved Mehta's life indicate why it is that he should have spent so many of his adult years constructing his autobiography. His early life was a long sequence of cruel jerks – from normal vision to blindness; from the Punjab to a school 1500 miles away where the boys spoke to each other in Marathi, a language that Ved did not understand; from the affluence of the Mehta household in Lahore to India, where the family had to start all over again as refugees; and then, when he was 15, he travelled alone from Delhi to a school in, of all places, Little Rock, not an easy place to be in 1949 for a boy who was neither black nor white. Given such a life, it is not surprising that for Ved Mehta the crucial need is to assert the continuity of his own experience, and it is not very surprising either that the single volume of autobiography published when he was 22 left that need unsatisfied. It is a life so strange that for Ved Mehta, one suspects, it can be grasped only in the act of being written down. Its continuity can be felt only in the process by which each disruption is accommodated within the smooth, effortless simplicity of Ved Mehta's prose.

The critical moments in the sequence occur when different parts of his life collide against one another. Once, in America, Ved Mehta was taken with the crazy notion that he could see. He persuaded a girlfriend to let him take the wheel of her car as they drove fast along a freeway. The girl was caught up in his mood, both were laughing hysterically, and then he heard her clicking her cigarette lighter again and again, and he sensed the panic in the noise. He heard something else too, a sound he had not heard since he was four, his mother clicking the light switch off and on, desperately trying to persuade herself that Ved's vision was returning. Ved used to count the clicks, trying not to disappoint her. The click of the cigarette lighter and the click of the light switch, two sounds thousands of miles and more than miles apart, eerily merged the girl's panic with his mother's, and it induced a panic, I suspect in Ved Mehta too, the panic that his whole autobiography is designed to assuage.

More often, such connections are embarrassing. The Dadar School for the Blind catered for poor children. In all senses it was very far away from Ved Mehta's family house and his tennis-playing, bridge-playing father. But Ved Mehta is nothing if not adaptable. He soon made friends, one in particular, Deoji. One Christmas, when Ved had gone home for the holidays, Deoji wrote to him:

The boy's dormitory is to requesting you to bringing new toys. The sighted master is to asking your Daddy-Doctor for to sleep medicine. Everyone is to missing you and to counting the days for your to coming back to school. The boy's dormitory is to sending you good health and wishes. Mr Draughtswallah, who is to knowing English and to writing this letter for me, is to sending you his compliments. Your affectionate loving Big Brother, Deoji.

Ved stood, stiff with embarrassment, as his sister read him the letter, and then 'ran out of the room and pushed the letter as far back as I could under the shelf paper and clothes in my cupboard'.

In Little Rock, Ved, 16 now and perturbed by his adolescent urges, wrote rather prim letters to his father and sister which skirted uneasily around his problem. The school secretary called him into her office, and read out his father's reply:

From the physiological point of view, I may acquaint you with the fact that there are excretions in the body such as perspiration urine, and faeces which must be thrown out of the system to keep it in a healthy state, and there are secretions like saliva and semen which it is not necessary to throw out – in fact, they are reabsorbed into the system and are necessary to the development of various organs, particularly the brain. From this, please do not conclude that the loss of a little saliva or a little semen is harmful – not at all – but it is the habitual discarding of such valuable elements which is not very desirable.

The letter left Ved and Mrs Hankins at a loss for words, but after a few moments Mrs Hankins said, 'Your dad is a fine gentleman.' Ved nodded, and suddenly became aware of other people in the room, the school principal and one of the teachers. 'There is no privacy in this damn place', he thought. It is easy to understand how writing such things down might be important to Ved Mehta, his prose working like a cool compress on the prickly heat of his boyhood embarrassments.

These are incidents connected with Ved Mehta's blindness, and in the long sequence of disruptions that makes up his early life, all but one – partition – was also a direct consequence of his being blind. It is because of his blindness that Ved Mehta's experience is unique, but its uniqueness seems to me not the most interesting

thing about it. If blindness precipitated Ved Mehta's autobiography, it did so only by making more urgent the pressure that
impels all the autobiographies that I have discussed.

When Gandhi decided to write down the story of his life 'a God-
fearing friend' had his doubts:

> 'What has set you on this adventure?' he asked. 'Writing an
> autobiography is a practice peculiar to the West. I know of
> nobody in the East having written one, except amongst those
> who have come under Western influence.'

Had the God-fearing friend looked further East than India, he
would have found a tradition of autobiography that owes nothing
to Western influence, but for practical purposes his point remains a
just one. In India, autobiography is a form peculiar to those who
have come under Western influence, and this is evident in all the
autobiographies that I have discussed.

The first two volumes of Ved Mehta's autobiography are called
Daddyji and *Mamaji*. He does not just tell his own story, but the
story of his parents and grandparents. He has to do that, because
his need is not just to work out the continuity of his own
experience, but its continuity with the lives of his parents and his
parents' parents. Those two needs are not easily reconciled. One
impulse leads him to assert the uniqueness of his own identity, the
other to merge himself with the long line of his ancestors. A similar
conflict can be traced in all the other autobiographies. Gandhi may
claim consistently that his one goal throughout his life has been
'self-realization', but he uses the word in two utterly different
senses. It may mean the achievement of self-knowledge, but it
refers elsewhere to a union with God, the supreme self, in which
the individual is released from the burden of personal identity.
Chaudhuri ends his autobiography with the claim that he has won
independence from his environment, that he has become a 'free
man', and then adds immediately that he is 'in every atom of his
being' the product of the land in which he lives. Nehru ends his by
confronting the 'queer mixture' in himself of Western habits of
mind and 'subconscious racial memories' of the 'hundred, or
whatever the number may be, generations of Brahmans' who were
his ancestors.

We are sometimes apt to speak as if Indians have a choice of
whether to retain their Indian traditions or yield to Western

nfluence. This is true only up to a point. A person may choose what clothes to wear, what language to speak. Beyond that, there is no choice. For an Indian to become alert to himself and to the world around him is inevitably to become aware that he has two different ways of understanding himself and his world. The problem is not to choose between them – that is impossible – but to find some way of holding the two together.

Ved Mehta's father was a doctor, trained in England and America, dashingly handsome, most at his ease in his club, where he played an elegant baseline game of tennis, and was a good enough hand at bridge to rely on his skill to make valuable additions to the family income. He agreed to an arranged marriage, and felt cheated in his wife. She had been advertised to him as an educated girl, but he found, after he married her, that she did not know English, was unfamiliar with Western ways, and incapable of sharing his enjoyment of the club life that he loved. There were strains in the marriage. But by exercising a wise tolerance of each other, Ved Mehta's parents made the marriage work. They gave to Ved and to his brothers and sisters a home life that was ordered, serene and loving. Their marriage can stand as a metaphor for the goal that inspires all these autobiographies, for all these writers find themselves, through no choice of their own, married to two apparently ill-suited selves, and left with the problem of trying to make the marriage work.

Some marriages, like Yogananda's, work by husband and wife having as little to do with each other as possible. But Gandhi, Nehru, Chaudhuri, and Ved Mehta manage something much more than that. It is not a coincidence that amongst these names are the two heroic figures of the public life of modern India. Nor is it a coincidence that, in their different ways, all four of these men are remarkable for their courage. The task that they take on is the most difficult, the most daunting, that confronts any modern Indian, the task of somehow holding together what in them is Indian with what comes to them from the West. In modern India, autobiography, the attempt to make a complete and single picture of oneself, is a heroic enterprise.

Some Westerners, too, have written heroically about India – notably Kipling – but the quality of the heroism is different, it is always in danger of tumbling into heroics. What this points to is that the relations between India and the West are asymmetrical. Westerners encounter India out of choice or by accident, Indians

encounter the West because they cannot realise themselves as
Indians without doing so. Their encounters have a dignity born out
of necessity that Kipling cannot match. Another sign of this is that
Indians mark their meetings with the West most completely in
autobiography, a form in which the writing is subordinated to the
constraints of history: Westerners chart their meetings with the
East in novels, in the optional universe of fiction. In the final three
chapters I will turn to the novels about India written by Westerners.

10
Sex in the Indian Novel

'I may as well say straight off that many of these adventures were sexual.' This is the narrator of Ruth Jhabvala's story 'An Experience of India'[1] beginning her account of her travels through the country in third class railway carriages and in those old lumbering buses that go from one small dusty town to another', but she might as well be speaking on behalf of almost any of the Europeans who have written about India in the past 60 years. It all started innocently enough with a strap breaking on Adela Quested's binocular case. Miss Quested decides in the end that she only imagined that Dr Aziz assaulted her, but what happened to Daphne Manners in the Bibighar Gardens was real enough. She made love with Hari Kumar, and then she was raped by five or six Indians, 'Black shapes in white cotton clothing; stinking ragged clothing.' It is a theme that Ruth Jhabvala has made her own. From *Esmond in India* until *Heat and Dust* and beyond she has written novels and stories that return almost obsessively to the theme of a sexual encounter between an Indian and a European. This is odd, and it seems even odder if we recall that in Indian novelists' writing in the same period the possibility of inter-racial sex has aroused very little interest. Even those Indian writers whose main concern is to explore India's relations with the West have usually resisted the temptation to represent those relations so literally.[2]

It is not, on the face of it, an oddity difficult to explain. Europeans who think about the East have inherited a language to do their thinking in, a language that Edward Said, in the first and still the best investigation of this matter, calls orientalism. Orientalism is a poetic language; its communications are indirect, channelled through metaphor. Said suspects that its indirection is camouflage concealing hostile purposes. The vocabulary of orientalism is for him 'a mobile army of metaphors, metonyms, and anthropomorphisms'.[3] His suspicion may well be correct, but, in any case, he is surely right to direct our attention to the metaphors of the orientalists, and, as soon as we do so, one metaphor emerges as dominant. The West is a man, the East is a woman. As a woman

147

the East may appear in various guises. She may be a mother t
whom the Western child returns to renew his contact with hi
origins. She may be a daughter, whose chastity is to be protecte
from the blandishments of some idle seducer, who could be a riva
imperial power but could just as well be a nationalist agitator. O
the East may be a temptress, a whore, whose seductive charms ar
to be stoutly resisted or deliciously yielded to, depending on th
temperament of the man who happens to be wielding th
metaphor. But more often than not the East appears in on
feminine role, as a bride.

The East is sleeping, beautiful, mysterious, and can be awoke
only by a European kiss. The kiss may be hard, it may bruise th
lips, but a woman happily accepts such pain as evidence of he
lover's potency. She knows that in such a rough embrace he
barren life will be fertilised, just as the Orient accepts that it
barren culture can be fertilised only by a European seed, only b
suffering the short-lived pain of European penetration. The Eas
needs the West as a woman needs a man. In accepting the Wes
she finds a strong man to protect her weakness; a stern man wh
will impose on her the discipline she is too feckless to impose or
herself; a wise man who will understand the difference betweer
her needs and her caprices; and an articulate man who will speal
for her when she lacks the command of language to speak for
herself. This I take to be the central metaphor of orientalism. It i
not hard to guess how it came to be selected, and why it proved s
useful.

The secret project of orientalism, Said insists, is to justify th
imperial venture. This involves a tricky paradox . Military occupa
tion must be presented as equivalent to national liberation
Oppression must be represented as identical with benevolen
altruism. It is predictable that the men of the nineteenth century
whose task it was to accommodate this paradox should find
themselves thinking of their relationship with their womenfolk.

The history of an empire becomes the story of a marriage, bu
this notion enters the public language of imperialism only ir
ghostly form, as metaphor. Novelists are less circumspect thar
diplomats. In M.M. Kaye's *The Far Pavilions* Ashton Pelham
Martyn, Ash for short, the novel's hero, is out riding with Anjuli,
an Indian princess.[4] The two of them are overtaken by a sand
storm, and take shelter in a cave. There they consummate their
love:

For a moment only she knew a pang of fear, but it passed as quickly as it had come, and when he said: 'I'm going to hurt you', she tightened her arms about him , and did not cry out at the lovely cruelty that ended her girlhood.

The Far Pavilions is a novel without pretensions, an unashamed blockbuster, but it is literate. This curious lapse into the prose of Victorian sado-masochistic pornography – 'lovely cruelty', indeed – is surely not an indication of M.M. Kaye's personal tastes. All it shows is that she is unselfconscious. Ash and Anjuli are the hero and heroine of her Indian novel. Nothing is more natural than that when they first make love they should act out the central drama of imperialism, and so nothing more natural than that his promise to hurt her should only encourage her to tighten her arms around him. It is, after all, a prime article of imperialist faith that gentleness in a ruler is despised by the Oriental as weakness, that the more firmly one stamps one's authority on a subject race the better one secures oneself in their affections.

Ash is a reluctant, guilt-troubled servant of empire, but his qualms function in the novel only to appease the liberal conscience of M.M. Kaye's readers. Ash's guilt frees the reader to succumb without shame to the chief experience that the novel offers, nostalgia for a lost age of imperial confidence. It is this potent combination, a liberal commentary subordinated to a full-blooded imperialist plot, that has secured the novel's huge popularity, but it is also what makes it essentially frivolous. *The Far Pavilions* is set in the second half of the nineteenth century, but it was published in 1978, by which time Britain's power in the world had been declining for more than half a century, and India, once the richest jewel in the British crown, had been independent for more than 30 years. It works by distracting its British readers from the deflating actualities of history, and re-creating Kipling's India, an imperial vision now softened and blurred by nostalgia. No serious novelist can afford so blithely to disregard present realities, and there have been serious European novelists who have written about India in the past 50 years. They are the inheritors of the language of Orientalism. That is why they retain a reliance on sexual metaphors to adumbrate the relationship between India and the West. But in their work the traditional metaphors are subjected to the pressure of history, and they undergo some surprising transformations.

Ash is a gifted linguist, trilingual in Hindi, Pushtu, and English,

and able to master Gujarati in a matter of weeks. He has inherite
the gift from his father, Professor Hilary Pelham Martyn,
professional orientalist who specialises in the study of India
languages. His chief monument is a scholarly work in tw
volumes, *'Unfamiliar Dialects of Hindustan'*. His son goes to Sanc
hurst and becomes an officer in the Indian army. I doubt wheth
Said's central thesis, that knowledge confers power, that orienta
ism, the study of the East, prepared the way for the milita
subjection of the East by the West has ever been more entertai
ingly illustrated. There is an orientalist, too, in Ruth Jhabvala
Esmond in India, first published in 1958, and set in Delhi in the ear
1950s. Esmond Stillwood speaks Hindi fluently, though not in a
accent that his servant can understand, but his expertise is in th
field of Indian culture; classical poetry and Moghul architectur
He earns a living by offering tuition in these, mostly to the wives
European diplomats, and by offering himself as a 'very superio
tourist guide for visits to the Red Fort or the Taj Mahal.

What is immediately obvious if we compare the two novels is th
difference in the prestige of orientalism. Professor Hilary Pelha
Martyn is rich and well-born. Members of parliament pay eag
attention to his private reports on Indian affairs. His knowledg
confers power on him, and it begets power. The Professor has
warrior for a son. For Esmond Stillwood orientalism has become
trade: he earns his living by it. European power in independer
India is located in the embassies and in the offices of internation
corporations. Its representatives are diplomats and businessmer
whose dealings with Indians are confined to the Europeanise
upper middle class. Orientalist expertise, knowledge of India
languages, history, and culture is for them a redundant skill, an
like all redundant skills it is despised. It serves only as a harmles
hobby for under-occupied wives. 'Mister Esmond Stillwood', th
English businessmen call him with ill-concealed contempt. 'H
knows *every*thing there is to know about India', they tell a youn
Indian girl: 'he's come specially to India to teach you people a
about your own country'. The businessmen live in a male world
power, and Esmond, the Orientalist, has been relegated to
women's world of decorative accomplishments. He serves to kee
their wives happy, to lecture to the women's clubs, to visit th
women for afternoon tea, to offer them cultural diversions, an
even, from time to time, to serve them in bed.

Esmond has a British mistress, but he has an Indian wife. In hi

lat he imposes on his wife a strict adherence to British ways;
uncomfortable Western furniture, a notion of how their son should
be brought up derived from Western childcare manuals, and a
bland British diet, cheese salad and boiled vegetables. The power
of the orientalist that once stretched over half the world has
dwindled to the four walls of a tiny Delhi apartment. His wife's
eyes, 'Beautiful sad eyes, which once he had thought full of all the
wisdom and the sorrow of the East' now strike him as a 'mere
blank'. He shouts at her for leaving the flat without his permission.
As he stands over her, her 'pungent body smell' maddens him,
and he twists the flesh of her upper arm. She reacts passively, and
that enrages him more; it seems like the passivity of an animal:

> To his horror he found himself wanting to seize her again and
> tear at her flesh and even to bite into her, to let his teeth sink
> deep into her soft body; to hurt her till he got some human
> response from her, even if it was nothing more than a cry of
> pain.

'I'm going to hurt you', says Ash to Anjuli, and his threat is a
declaration of love. But Esmond no longer has a sexual relationship
with his wife. He cannot pretend that there is anything 'lovely' in
his cruelty. Neither can he claim that the pain he inflicts is only an
unavoidable accident of his essential male power. He knows it for
what it is, not an expression of his strength, but a betrayal of his
weakness, a proof of his impotence rather than his virile masculin-
ity. His cruelty leaves him sick with self-contempt.

Esmond believes that he loathes his wife because he wants in
marriage a 'companion' rather than a 'slave'. But he is mistaken.
His wife is obedient not to him but to her Indian ideal of how a wife
ought to behave. When a servant clumsily gropes at her breasts,
she is freed. Her husband has failed in the one duty a husband
owes a wife, the duty to protect her, and she leaves Esmond
without a misgiving. Esmond seduces a young schoolfriend of his
wife's, Shakuntala, seduces her out of boredom and because his
mistress had irritated him. 'Let me be your slave, please allow me,
let me humble myself before you', says Shakuntala. Esmond
believes her, and nervously worries how to extricate himself from
the relationship. But Shakuntala is no more his slave than his wife.
For her, even though she does not realise it, Esmond is only a
romantic interlude, an episode that she will be able to look back on

nostalgically after she has married the eminently suitable son of Professor Bhatnagar.

The Far Pavilions nostalgically summons back a nineteenth century in which orientalism was an expression of male power, a mark of imperial sovereignty. Esmond Stillwood in the 1950s is a post-imperialist expert on the East, and by the 1950s the orientalist is no longer an empire-builder, he is more like a gigolo; not a leader of men but a dependant of women. As the novel closes Esmond feels 'young' and 'sprightly'. Betty, his mistress, has taken pity on him, and promised to lend him the money for his passage home. In England he has an aunt and a sister. One of them will put him up. And Betty is 'well connected': she may be able to find him a job.

In *Esmond in India* Ruth Jhabvala transforms the man's man, the traditional hero of the Indian novel, into a lady's man. But she is still content to represent the encounter between East and West as a marriage between a European man and an Indian woman. More radical transformations are available. Kipling had entertained the possibility of West and East confronting each other in the guise of two strong men standing face to face. J.R. Ackerley does not insist on strength, and the two men rather than confronting each other stroll together hand in hand. It is night-time, and Ackerley holds a lantern as he walks with Sharma, the Maharajah's valet:

> After a moment Sharma took the lantern from me, without a word, and carried it himself, on his far side so that it should not knock against me. His near hand was in his coat pocket. I put my arm through his.
>
> Immediately he took his hand from his pocket, so that for a second I thought myself rebuffed: but instead he seized my hand in his and linked his fingers with mine.[5]

Ackerley was recommended to his post as private secretary to the Maharajah of Chhatarpur by E.M. Forster, and it is Forster who is chiefly responsible for transforming the metaphor for the relationship between Britain and India as a marriage between a British man and an Indian bride into a tender friendship between two men.

The friendship between Dr Aziz and Fielding is the central relationship in *A Passage to India*, and it can be charted in a sequence of unusually intimate encounters. Fielding first meets Aziz when he invites Aziz to tea. He is dressing in the bathroom when Aziz arrives, and calls Aziz in to hand him the collar stud that Aziz has offered to lend him. Fielding visits Aziz and sits by his bed, when Aziz imagines himself to be ill. The two walk together from the train arm in arm after Aziz has been arrested, and after his acquittal they lie side by side on the roof of the Nawab's house under the stars.

Theirs is not, of course, a homosexual relationship, and neither, for that matter, is Ackerley's with Sharma. But it is a relationship incompatible with the conventional heterosexuality of marriage. When Fielding and Aziz meet again in the novel's third section, the two men clear up a misunderstanding and renew their friendship, but they never recover their old intimacy. Fielding is no longer a teacher, he is an inspector of schools: he has become, that is, an officer of the Raj. And he has married. Forster suggests that the two events are related. Fielding 'had thrown in his lot with Anglo-India by marrying a countrywoman, and he was acquiring some of its limitations'. Fielding can still laugh with Aziz, and the two talk politics, but it is Ralph Moore, Fielding's unmarried brother-in-law, whose hand is taken, and who finds in touch a direct contact with Aziz's heart.

Harry, the English homosexual who serves as a retainer in the court of the Nawab of Khatm in Ruth Jhabvala's *Heat and Dust* is best seen as a composite parody of Forster and Ackerley. Through him Ruth Jhabvala registers her awareness of Forster's effort to imagine a relationship between East and West founded not on power but on friendship, and so best figured by a relationship between two people of the same sex, by Fielding arm in arm with Aziz, or by Ackerley walking hand in hand with Sharma.[6] A heterosexual embrace becomes the mark of a relationship founded on a perception of difference. The two men join hands in recognition that they are both alike.

Ronald Merrick seems to me the one interesting character in Paul Scott's huge and hugely overrated *Raj Quartet*. He rises to a high position in the Indian police service, and marries the younger daughter of General Layton. His wife grows accustomed to his habit of slipping out of the house at night dressed up as a Pathan, and not returning until early morning. This may seem eccentric behaviour, but it is conventional enough in the Indian novel. Kipling's hero, Strickland, is a master of disguise, and Ashton Pelham Martyn spends two years across the border in Afghanistan masquerading as a tribesman. It seems a crucial ingredient in the imperialist fantasy that the difference on which imperial prestige

insists is itself subject to the imperial will, and can be eradicated by
a cunning application of walnut juice.[7] But unlike Strickland and
Ash, Merrick does not confine his undercover activities to spying: he
goes cruising for bazaar boys. His homosexual career begins when
he smears Hari Kumar's genitals with blood, and ends when he is
murdered by a young Indian he has taken into his household service.

Merrick is a grammar-school boy: 'his origins,' he confesses,
'were humble'. But in India he can live on 'equal terms with people
who would snub him at home'. He is accepted by his social
superiors, but not quite:

> He could be in a room with a senior English official and a senior
> Indian official and he could catch the eye of the English official
> who at home would never give him a second thought, and
> between them there'd be a flash of compulsive understanding
> that the Indian was inferior to both of them, as a man. And then
> if the Indian left the room the understanding would subtly
> change. He was then the inferior man.

Merrick knows that all the various attitudes of Europeans towards
Indians rest on one emotion, contempt; and he understands that
because he too knows what it is to be the object of contempt. If we
think of Merrick as a psychological study, he is no more than a
grotesque, but the sexual insecurity that makes him a sadist is only
the badge of his social insecurity. His homosexual encounters
register his sense of his own kinship with Indians, but they can
express that kinship only perversely, because it is what he spends
all his daylight hours violently denying. His bisexuality is figura-
tive, a mark of his ambivalent position in the social hierarchy.

The last transformation is, I suppose, inevitable. The hot-
blooded European lover, after becoming (for a while) a homosexual, turns into a woman. He becomes Adela Quested, ingenu-
ously eager to see 'the real India', or Mrs Moore so alert to
the niceness underlying Aziz's prickly sensitivity. He becomes
Daphne Manners making love with Hari Kumar in the Bibighar
Gardens, and he is transformed at last into the constellation of
European women who people Ruth Jhabvala's novels and stories.

As a lover Hari Kumar is no more delicate than Ashton Pelham
Martyn:

> There was a moment when I was afraid, perhaps because he
> wanted me to be . . . There was nothing gentle in the way he took

me. He tore at my underclothes and pressed down on me with all his strength . . . Entering he made me cry out.

The experience is much the same, but the racial roles are reversed. We seem to have come full circle. *The Jewel in the Crown*, the first volume of *The Raj Quartet*, was published in 1966 when Britain had become just a small European country, with a capital city that Gore Vidal could compare with Oslo. It may be that the sexual reversal reflects Britain's post-war sense of itself, and an uneasy recognition that there are Indians who exercise their wealth and power more flagrantly than any Briton can aspire to. Ruth Jhabvala has a number of characters whose European weakness is exposed by Indian power. There is Etta, the ageing German blonde of *A Backward Place*. Like Esmond she is stranded in India without the money to go home; cast aside by her wealthy Punjabi lover, she is reduced to an elderly Parsee. To the end she remains effervescent, fashionable, but her social graces become ever more desperate. They are all that stand between her and starvation. Or there is Georgia, in the short story 'A Young man of Good Family',[8] who has followed her Sikh boyfriend to India only to find that, though prepared to sleep with her, he has no intention of lowering himself by marrying someone he does not consider his social equal. Or there is the balding unsuccessful academic in 'A Course of English Studies'.[9] He is seduced by Nalini, whose family have sent her to England to pursue her studies, but who has been unable to gain admission to any but a modern Midlands university. When she grows bored having an affair with her tutor, she confesses the relationship to his wife, and then flies back to India complaining that in England there is no 'genuine love of literature'. In the East such Westerners meet a hard carelessness born of utter self-assurance, and inhibited as they are by their Western post-war insecurities, they are helpless against it.

But this will not quite do. Hari Kumar is not remarkable for any modern Eastern self-confidence. He is himself a mass of insecurities. We must look elsewhere for an explanation of why the relationship between East and West has come more and more regularly to be represented as a sexual encounter between a European woman and an Indian man.

The central episode in *The Far Pavilions* describes Ash's adventures as he supervises a huge bridal procession travelling across India from one princely state to another. When he arrives to take up his duties Ash finds the bridal camp in disarray: it is running short of water; there is no food, and no fodder for the animals; the local tradesmen are in uproar at their unpaid bills; and the whole camp is 'in a state of near hysteria'. Equipped with a fluent command of the language, a deep knowledge of Indian custom, and his British habit of disciplined thinking, Ash is soon able to reduce this chaos to order. Ash has been brought up 'in the bazaars of an Indian city': he is familiar with the hubbub and the confusion, knowledgeable in the ways of the East. But his familiarity and knowledge is valuable only in so far as they help him in the supreme task, to bring order out of chaos. That is his mission, just as it is the mission of the British administration he serves.

Compare that with Ruth Jhabvala's description of a shopping street in Dehli:

Most of [the shoppers] were women – great, heavy Punjabi women who had eaten well for many years, sisters and sisters-in-law, with their children and adolescent daughters who had pigtails down their backs and dreamy eyes and breasts just budding. The mothers moved forward resolutely, in consolidated blocks, not caring where or whom they jostled and pushed, only intent on their own business, which was buying the best at the cheapest price possible. They peered suspiciously into each shop from which the shopkeeper – already busy serving several other parties of shoppers – cried hospitably, 'Please come, please come, please command me!' On the outside of the pavement stood the transitory tradesmen – men with little barrows on which were piled towels or children's red slacks or slices of water-melon, all offered at competitive prices. Hawkers and beggars pushed through the crowd, choosing their prospective clients and fastening onto them with perseverance. Progress in all that crowd was difficult, but no one was in much of a hurry. In the roadway traffic grew denser and denser, cyclists were now six abreast, and the cars hooted incessantly, and even the men who rode on top of the bullock-carts had wakened up. The swinging doors of the coffee-houses were constantly opening and shutting and one could see that inside all the tables were crowded.

This is from *Esmond in India*, but it could be from any Indian novel. It has become obligatory to include at least one description of the bustle, the crowd, and the confusion of an Indian city street. Ash is positioned outside the crowd, organising it; Esmond is enfolded within it. And it is that difference, that single transformation, that all the inflexions of the sexual metaphor that I have described are concerned to indicate. As an imperial possession India is a challenge to the British ability to organise. As an independent country it is a challenge to the Westerner's ability to experience. Ash has no sooner arrived in the bridal camp than he sets about organising it:

> By the time the tents were stored on the following morning and they were ready to move on, the townsmen's accounts had been paid, a majority of the disputes settled, and Ash had managed to meet and exchange courtesies with most of the bridal party.

The passive mood of the verbs marks the subordination of India to Ash's active intelligence. The camp yields to the strong syntax of empire. Ruth Jhabvala represents Indian streets in a loose, paratactic prose. Her task is not to impose her syntax on the streets, but to submit her syntax to them. Ash's success is marked by the completeness of the order he imposes, Ruth Jhabvala's by the fullness of the experience she records. The sexual transformations that I have noted are a sequence of metaphors charting this development. Within the Indian novel sexual stereotypes are alive and well. Men organise, women experience, homosexuals are betwixt and between. The role of the West in India is no longer organisation. When what is required is to submit oneself to the experience India offers, the European protagonist of Indian novels is transformed stage by stage from a man into a woman.

What remains stable throughout this process is that the relationship between East and West is represented most intensely by some sexual encounter between an Indian and a European. But as the pressure begins to be felt that will eventually transform the European man into a woman, as the impulse to organise gives way to the impulse to experience, something very odd begins to happen. The sexual encounters begin to assume one dominant pattern. A moment of erotic arousal is followed quickly by a spasm of sexual disgust. Even in *A Passage to India* such a sequence is very lightly indicated. Just before she enters the cave, Aziz arouses in Miss Quested a flash of erotic curiosity. She sees his 'beauty, thick hair, fine skin': 'What a handsome little Oriental he was.' Adela

can never recall what happened to her in the cave, but Mrs Moore
remembers her own experience: 'some vile naked thing struck her
face and settled on her mouth like a pad'. Here the pattern is so
lightly touched on that one could quarrel over whether it was
there. But there is nothing understated about what happens to
Daphne Manners in the Bibighar Gardens. She lies side by side
with Hari in a warm drowse of sexual fulfilment, his hand on her
breast, hers in his hair. Then: 'Five or six men. Suddenly. Climbing
over the platform. My nightmare faces. But not faces. Black shapes
in white clothing; stinking, ragged, clothing...' Then there is
Esmond whose sensitivity to his wife's beauty turns to disgust at
the fullness and softness of her body and its 'pungent body smell'.
Or Olivia in *Heat and Dust*, who is penetrated by the Nawab amidst
the cool verdure of a ruined garden, and then with a twig by the
old Indian lady who efficiently if crudely aborts her child. Or, most
violent of all, there is the narrator of 'An Experience of India', who
travels India sleeping with Indian men – all of them different, all of
them the same. As their love-making becomes more frenzied, they
begin to question her: 'How many men have you slept with? How
many? How many?'; and then as they climax, 'the last frenzy, the
final outrage, "Bitch!"'. 'An Experience of India' the story is
entitled. But Ruth Jhabvala in particular has come more and more
to represent it as if it were *the* experience of India, a moment of
frenzied coupling culminating always in insult, rejection, and
disgust.[10]

It seems unlikely that what is at issue here is some suspicion
common to Europeans who write about India that Europeans and
Indians are sexually incompatible. It is worth suggesting that the
explanation lies in the profound shock delivered to Western
writers by India's independence. By this I do not mean simply a
political rearrangment, though India's political independence is
associated with it. I mean the notion that India is independent of
any representation of it that can be offered by Europeans. Imperial
India is a country that came to exist only in the act of being
represented. Independent India is a country defined by its
resistence to Western attempts to represent it.

The echo in the Marabar caves is a representation of the unrepresentable, a signifier that cannot be attached to any signified. Mrs
Moore is the character most sensitive to the opacity of that sound,
and it is offered as a guarantee of her sensitivity to the East. In the
cave she achieves knowledge of her own incomprehension. But as

he ship taking her back to England pulls away from the quay, even that knowledge recedes from her: 'So you thought an echo was India: you took the Marabar caves as final?'; the palm trees laugh at her, 'What have we in common with them or they with Asigarh? Goodbye!' India for Forster is a country of infinite recession: 'Beyond the sky must not there be something that overarches all the skies, more important even than they? Beyond which again . . .' It is Mrs Moore who best understands that India recedes infinitely from any Western attempt to know it, and Mrs Moore becomes Esmiss Esmoor, the presiding deity of the European Indian novel: the proof of her wisdom her bewilderment, the only knowledge she achieves a knowledge of her own ignorance.

In independent India the business of the European novelist becomes impossibly paradoxical. India must be represented, but the only proof of authenticity is to represent it as unrepresentable. We can identify three modes in the European Indian novel, modes that correspond very approximately with the sexual transformations that I have noted. In the imperial Indian novel the novelist, like the novelist's central character, is a hero. The novel performs the heroic task: it gives order to the formless; it represents what before was unrepresented. In the writing of Forster and Ackerley an ironic mode displaces the heroic. There is the smug confidence of the British officials that they know India, and there is the novelist's secret knowledge that India is unknowable. The prose becomes ironic in an effort to mediate between the two, between the flat self-assurance of people like the Turtons, and the metaphysical vertigo that overcomes the visitor to the Marabar caves. The central character becomes a man like Fielding, ironically aware of himself and ironically aware of others.

But irony is an unstable mode. It threatens always to collapse, as Miss Quested in the cave collapses, into hysteria. Ruth Jhabvala is the chief exponent of the third mode of the European Indian novel, the hysterical. The stories shuttle between a cool Europeanised room, and the India outside, the India of heat, smells and crowds. The gap between the two is too wide to be bridged. The central character is not an ironist, but a hysteric.

In 'An Experience of India' the narrator is married to a foreign correspondent. She lives in a flat in Delhi, air-conditioned, and carefully decorated to look 'just like the apartment at home except for some delicate Indian touches'. It is from this flat that she makes her forays into India. Her travels are punctuated by sexual encounters, all the men are different, all the experiences are the same. Frantic urgency, then the questions: 'How many men have you slept with? How many? How many?'; and then the climax 'Bitch!' Every encounter ends in a violent gesture of contempt. It is always like that, and Ruth Jhabvala comes close at times to suggesting that there is no other way that it can be. Ruth Jhabvala's project, the attempt to represent India, has become a hysterical venture. She is trapped in the futile repetitive cycle of hysteria. Knowledge of India can be gained only by experience, but to experience India is to know that India is unrepresentable. It is only in rejecting her experience, in detaching herself from it, that the novelist becomes able to represent it. So it is that the brief moment of hysteria, the moment when acceptance and rejection follow each other so quickly as almost to coincide, the moment of orgasm and insult ('Bitch!'), becomes the last privileged moment available to her. It becomes the last fragile point of purchase that the European novelist has on a subcontinent.

11

The Hill of Devi and *Heat and Dust*

n *Heat and Dust* two stories alternate, the story of a young English girl who goes to India in search of her family history, and the story of her grandfather's first wife, Olivia. The two stories approach each other, and drift apart. They coincide just once, at Baba Firdaus's shrine, where both women conceive a child, Olivia by the Nawab of Khatm, the modern girl by Inder Lal, a clerk. After aborting the child Olivia retreats to the mountains, and lives out her life silently, brooding, one supposes, on the past. The other girl goes to the Himalayas too, but she goes there to bear her child. The two stories – one of them takes place in the months from February to September in 1923 – the other in those same months 50 years later, act as distorted reflections of each other. Through their likeness and their difference Jhabvala explores how independent India is connected with, and severed from, its imperial past. But modern India she knows, whereas the Nawab of Khatm, an Indian prince ruling his tiny state surrounded and dominated by British India, is a figure from a past that she has only read about. *Heat and Dust* is concerned not only with the relationship between two Indias, but with Ruth Jhabvala's relationship with her literary predecessors, the Englishmen who described life in Indian princely states in the 1920s. Behind Ruth Jhabvala's Khatm lies Chhatarpur as it is presented in J.R. Ackerley's *Hindoo Holiday*, and Dewas as it is described by Malcolm Darling and by E.M. Forster.[1]

The Nawab of Khatm, proud, vicious, an adept in palace intrigue, who once a year orchestrates a ritual massacre of Hindus, seems quite different from Tukoji Rao III, Forster's gentle Hindu prince, and yet there are suggestive similarities. Both princes succeeded to the throne young; Tukoji Rao at the age of 11, the Nawab when he was 15. Both married the daughter of a powerful neighbouring prince, and both marriages mysteriously broke down, alienating the bride's family. 'The Cabobpurs were absolutely furious with the Nawab', and Forster's Maharajah had

161

'made an implacable enemy of the leading Maratha power', the
Maharajah of Kohlapur. Both the Nawab and the Maharajah
ruined their states' finances and fell deeply into debt. But family
feuds, marriage difficulties, and financial maladministration might
be reckoned complications too general in the lives of the Indian
princes to suggest any peculiar bond between Jhabvala's Nawab
and Forster's Maharajah. A trivial detail represents stronger
evidence. Exploring the Nawab's palace, Olivia comes across the
detritus of the Nawab's mindless extravagance; an immense store
of rusting camera equipment, bathroom fitments still in their
packing cases, the kit for a hockey team, and 'not one piano but
two, a grand and an upright', both with their keys swollen and
stuck. Forster finds in the Maharajah's palace a similar collection
'£1,000 worth (figure accurate) of electric batteries, dozens of
clothes-horses, a cupboard full of tea pots, and two pianos, one a
grand', 'their notes sticking and their frames cracked by dryness'.
Both the Nawab and the Maharajah promise to summon a piano
tuner from Bombay.

But the most striking similarity is also the most obvious: the
Nawab and the Maharajah both retain in their service an English
homosexual. Harry, the Nawab's secretary, as some say, 'hanger
on', as the British prefer to have it, entered the Nawab's service in
1920, the year before Forster arrived at Dewas. He hates the British
in India: 'They're the sort of people who've made life hell for me
ever since I can remember. At school and everywhere.' He has
been three years in Khatm, trapped in a love for the Nawab that is
painfully entangled with self-contempt. He is worried about his
mother:

> She's on her own you see, in a little flat in South Ken. Of course
> she wants me to come home. But whenever I mention it, all he
> does is send her some marvellous present.

Only after Olivia runs away from her husband and the disgrace of
her abortion to join him, does the Nawab allow Harry to return to
England 'to lead his quiet life with his mother in their flat in
Kensington'. When his mother dies, his friend Ferdie moves in
with him. Forster, whose schooldays at Uppingham and Ton
bridge were the most wretched of his life, and whose pleasure in
travelling was alloyed until her death only by the worry of leaving
his mother alone, was, for all that, not much like Harry. For one

hing Harry is utterly without genius. He is a talentless Forster, an Ackerley without wit or social grace, but on that account, Ruth habvala suggests, he is the more trustworthy witness. *Heat and Dust* implies that Forster, Ackerley, and their like got India wrong: hey were deflected from it by their literary sophistication. The English girl whose diary entries make up the modern section of *Heat and Dust* – is Olivia's story a biographical novel written by her? – is the product of a meagre culture. But her gauche, unimaginative prose gropes, however clumsily, in an effort to reach out to her experience. Forster and Ackerley are never lumsy, never grope. Their experience never seems to lie outside he language in which they record it. Which is to say, of course, hat they are accomplished writers, but which may suggest also hat writers are not wholly to be trusted.

Forster was introduced to the Maharajah of Dewas by his friend, Malcolm Darling, who had served for two years as the Maharajah's utor and guardian. Forster and Darling had been undergraduates together at King's, and both were Apostles. Forster first met the Maharajah when he visited India in 1912–13, and, then, in 1921, he returned to take up a temporary appointment as his private secretary. *The Hill of Devi* is Forster's account of his relationship with the Maharajah.

Near the beginning of his book Forster quotes Darling's description of Dewas as 'the oddest corner in the world outside Alice in Wonderland': it has 'no parallel except in a Gilbert and Sullivan pera'. These are crucial literary references: they control the account of Dewas that follows. Lewis Carroll and Gilbert and Sullivan are at once fantastic and quintessentially English. By invoking them Forster contrives to present his liking for Dewas and its ruler as a properly English relish for eccentricity; and to impute to the English officials, who in 1933 stripped Tukoji Rao of ruling powers, and forced him to flee from Dewas and take refuge in French India, a humourless and self-righteous rectitude that Forster's readers would be happy to accept as a less congenial expression of the English national character. But it is a tactic that has consequences.

The fantastic and the eccentric are lovable only so long as they re not threatening. Tukoji Rao was an autocratic monarch who had power of life and death over his subjects. His wife left him, pleading that his behaviour towards her was intolerable; his son believed that his father had tried to murder him;[2] the citizens of

Dewas were impoverished by the taxation inflicted to pay for the
Maharajah's extravagances. This is the man whose behaviour
Forster consistently describes as something between that of a
playful puppy and a five-year-old child. He is a 'dear creature'.
After intimidating British guests had left, he 'sported like a kitten'.
His 'clever merry little face peeped out of a large turban'. When
Forster arrived, he was 'so sweet': he 'darted up from behind and
put his hands over my eyes'. He is given to 'capering'. When he
visits Delhi he has to make some official calls. Afterwards, he is
'like a boy loose from school': he 'bounced up and down among
the cushions' in his carriage.

The second consequence is more serious. Dewas comes to have a
necessary place not in the Indian subcontinent but in the English
imagination. Like nonsense, like comic operetta, it offers relaxation
from the pressures of moral and social responsibility. The British
administrators who destroyed the Maharajah are resented in much
the same way that Leavisite critics once were, as threats to the
harmless pleasures of unserious, immature, irresponsible imaginative play. Forster beautifully describes Indian music as 'like
Western music reflected in trembling water'. It supplements
Western music while remaining subordinate to it. The pleasure
Forster feels as he listens is available only to a man aware of how
the firm clarity of Western music is dissolved into lines of charming
elusiveness. The pleasure he takes in Indian music is a Western
pleasure, and so is the pleasure he takes in India.

Forster's first and greatest Indian friend once accused him of
measuring his emotions 'as if they were potatoes'.[3] The remark
struck Forster with the force of a revelation. It was the lesson that
England, and particularly its ruling classes, were in need of -
educated as they were in public schools that equipped them with
'well-developed bodies, fairly developed minds, and undeveloped
hearts'. Before he ever went to India he thought of it as pre-
eminently a school for the heart. In *The Hill of Devi* the Maharajah is
India, and so when Forster looks at him he sees what he heard
when he listened to Indian music, the rugged contours of British
character dissolved into a shifting, ungraspable play of emotion:
'the Maharajah was all moods. They played over his face, they
agitated his delicate feet and hands.' If he is 'shifty and cunning', it
is because shiftiness, a perpetual quivering, is of his essence, and
because it establishes him the more completely as the ideal anti-
type of the public school head boy.

India and Tukoji Rao, its representative, are not be be argued
with, they are only to be loved. 'Affection, all through his
chequered life, was the only force to which Bapu Sahib re-
ponded', writes Forster. It is a judgement that united Forster and
his friends. The great lesson that Malcolm Darling learned at
Dewas was that 'no people are more responsive to kindness than
the Indians',[4] and Ackerley begins his account of his stay with a
quite different Maharajah with the sentence – so casual, so
calculated, so English – 'He wanted someone to love him – His
Highness, I mean; that was his real need, I think.'
A conversation recorded by Darling with the commander of the
Dewas army helps to explain this surprising unanimity. The
Commander tells Darling that he suspects him of liking Indians
better than Europeans. Darling does not deny it:

'And Mr Goodall (another of us from King's whom he had met at
Dewas) likes Indians too. He is very nice gentleman, very nice.
How many more (he asked) are there in this country from the
same College?' I mentioned two more whom he had met.
E.M. Forster he had not yet met. "I don't know how it is," he
continued, "but you all like Indians. I wish I could understand
this." "We are very well educated there," I said. 'Ah, that is it;
and it must, I think, be (as he shrewdly added) some form of
the climate when you went there,' meaning no doubt the
atmosphere in the College.[5]

That was certainly shrewd. Forster, Darling and Ackerley are all of
them exponents of the cult of personal relations that dominated
Cambridge when they were undergraduates, and that centred on
King's. They went to India predisposed to find in another country
what they could not find in Britain, somewhere where understanding took second place to affection, judgement was subordinate to
sympathy, and people were bound to one another not by political
and economic interdependence but by bonds of love. As late as
1940 Forster, in a broadcast to India said: 'you cannot imagine how
much we over here are in need of inspiration, of spirituality, of
something which will deliver us from the tyranny of the body
politic'.[6] In 1940 Forster must have been one of a rather small elite
who recognised that the country's real need was to free itself from
the body politic rather than to preserve it, but, in any case, he is
confident that such freedom is to be found in India.

The Maharajah sent a message to Forster when he was back in England: 'tell him from me to follow his heart and his mind will see everything clear'. The advice is 'too facile; doors open into silliness at once', but, re-phrased by Forster in a more cautious, more sophisticated English, it becomes the lesson that India offers to the West: 'But to remember and respect and prefer the heart; to have the instinct which follows it whenever possible – what surer help than that could one have through life?' The better to liberate the heart, India assaults the intellect. Perfectly ordinary mistakes become symptomatic of the fallibility of the understanding. Walking with Darling, Forster comes across a shrine: 'A shrine of Durga, Malcolm thought, but he was wrong, it was Moslem; one was always going to be wrong.' A 'small dead tree' is mistaken for a snake, an 'exciting and typical adventure', so typical that Forster included it in *A Passage to India*. 'Everything that happens is said to be one thing and proves to be another', so that Forster lives 'in a haze'. His mind must become foggy so that he is forced to trust his heart, so that he may realise: 'It doesn't do to think. To follow the promptings of the eye and imagination is quite enough.' Presiding over all this, as its ideal embodiment, is the Maharajah, 'an unknown and possibly unknowable character'. With him Forster touches the full ecstasy of freedom from the intellect: 'Quite often did not understand him – he was too incalculable – but it was possible with him to reach a platform where calculations were unnecessary. It would not be possible with an Englishman.'

It is precisely because it is not possible with an Englishman that for Forster, Darling and Ackerley it must be possible with an Indian. They found in India what they needed to find. In the wake of Edward Said a good deal of fuss has been made about this sort of thing, rather too much fuss. It is not to be wondered at that Englishmen travelling in India should ask themselves what India means to them, and it is unsurprising that they should form an English view of India. What they may properly be held to account for is not whether their view of India is English, but whether it is intelligent.

Forster, Darling and Ackerley describe a personal relationship with a Maharajah. That their friend is a king adds piquancy to the narrative, but is not crucial to it. Darling once confessed to Tukoji Rao that when he first arrived in Dewas he 'instinctively' regarded the Maharajah as his 'inferior'.[7] The Maharajah responds charmingly, admitting to 'a feeling that the English in this country do not belong to the most aristocratic class', acknowledging that he regards himself as Darling's 'superior', but only 'on official occasions', 'Not when we are in a house like this.' What the English writers celebrate is the possibility of a friendship that can transcend barriers of race and class. Darling, as an Englishman, instinctively feels superior to a member of a race that England rules: the Maharajah, as a king, instinctively feels superior to a commoner. But the point is that friendship can survive these instincts. Political and social differences cannot separate men prepared to trust the instincts of the heart that draw them together. The failure of Forster, Darling and Ackerley to do more than note in passing their Maharajah's political circumstances is a deliberate omission, central to their whole endeavour.

The Indian princes ruled approximately one third of the Indian subcontinent. Their relationship with the British monarch was feudal. They acknowledged their loyalty to the crown, and, in return, their sovereignty within their own states was ratified. Effectively, they were allowed independent control of the internal affairs of their territories, but were prohibited from pursuing any foreign policy. Nevertheless, even within the native states, British interests were paramount, and an Indian prince who threatened those interests, by, for example, abusing his powers so grossly that he provoked popular unrest, might find his ruling powers suspended. British interests within the native states were looked after by political agents, whose role was uncomfortably between that of an adviser and that of a watchdog. Until about 1920 the policy of the Indian princes was clear. Their business was to preserve their power from further erosion by the British. After 1920 it became more complex, for by then their sovereignty was threatened not only by the Government of British India but by the Indian Congress party, which saw no place in an independent India for the princely states. In that they were now faced by two threats to their rule the position of the Indian princes after 1920 was more uncomfortable, but there were compensations. The princes became increasingly important to the British as allies in the struggle against Congress, and it was possible for them to use their new status to encourage the British to show them a greater respect.

Malcolm Darling was posted to Dewas in 1907. Forster records the event in a daringly naive sentence designed to mime the bursting of warm, loving emotion through dry political arrangements: 'The Government of India appointed Malcolm Darling,

I.C.S., to be his [the Maharajah's] tutor and guardian, and the great friendship of his life began.' The Maharajah was then 18. He had succeeded to the throne at the age of 11, but had yet to be granted ruling powers. A letter from the Government of India to Darling describes the role that was envisaged for him: 'The Raja has actually completed his literary education and the object of the Tutor would be to teach him the principles of administration preparatory to his being granted ruling powers which would probably be in about two years time.'[8] It seems safe to assume that Darling's appointment served two purposes. He was to teach the young man the principles of administration, and he was to acquire a knowledge of Tukoji Rao's character on which the Government might base its decision as to when, and if, to grant him ruling powers. Darling's arrival in Dewas could only have been a tense moment for the Maharajah. He could not but have suspected that Darling would have a decisive influence on the Indian Government's attitude towards him.

He responded to this tricky situation with a maturity beyond his years. He made Darling his friend, and he did this so successfully that even at the very end, when the Maharajah fled from his bankrupt state and took refuge in French India, taking with him, it seems, what was left of the crown jewels, Darling anxiously interceded with the Government on his behalf. It is hardly going too far to say that the Maharajah succeeded in instilling a loyalty in Darling that took precedence over Darling's loyalty to the Government.[9] He did so by using to the full what seem to have been great powers of personal charm, but his task was easier than it might have been. He was peculiarly fortunate that the Government appointed as his guardian a Kingsman, a man brought up in an atmosphere in which men prided themselves on holding the claims of personal friendship higher than those of mere political loyalty. I find this the easiest explanation of the curious naivety that overcomes Darling – clearly an able and intelligent man – when he describes his function in Dewas: 'I am really H.H.'s friend, and the friend of his friends. I have so little to get out of them, and they even less to get out of me. So our relationship is almost natural, which is most rare in India.'[10]

Others were not so trusting. Some of the Maharajah's fellow princes warned him against Darling: 'It was a shock to find myself regarded as a Government spy. Throughout my time at Dewas no attempt was made to use me in that way.' It seems never to have struck Darling that the Princes' suspicions might not have been aroused by his behaviour but by his function. He seems never to have accepted that in his role as the Maharajah's guardian a personal and a political relationship were inextricably entangled. He became the Maharajah's accomplice in allowing the personal to obscure the political.

By the time Forster arrived in Dewas, the Maharajah was an older, more experienced man, and his political situation, too, had changed. His marriage had broken up, enraging the bride's father, the powerful Maharajah of Kohlapur. On the other hand, Gandhi's emergence strengthened his position with the British as it did that of all the other Princes. Forster notes how followers of Gandhi were in the habit of alighting at the local railway station to 'shout subversive slogans over the border'. Such demonstrations were a lively reminder to the British of how useful the princely states were as a bulwark against the rise of nationalism. Forster was entering a complex political world, but he gives little impression of understanding it.

To begin with a simple incident. Forster's Maharajah paid elaborate court to a neighbouring prince, the Maharajah of Gwalior, a man that Forster considered a boor. Forster is nonplussed: 'What he wanted from a person so inferior to himself, I do not know. He had a craving to be liked, and perhaps the very inferiority of the other person stimulated it.' The Maharajahs of Gwalior and of Kohlapur were the two most powerful of the Maratha princes. In comparison with them Tukoji Rao was weak and vulnerable. Once he had alienated Kohlapur, it became a matter of great political importance to him to maintain good relations with Gwalior. Forster, apparently not understanding this, falls back on the preferred Cambridge diagnosis – the Maharajah 'had a craving to be liked'.

It is, I suppose, forgivable that Forster should be ignorant of the power relations that existed between the Indian princes. One would expect him to be better attuned to the relationships between the Indians and the British. Forster visited for a few days the Maharajah of Chhatarpur, who was later, on Forster's recommendation, to employ Ackerley. The Maharajah went to a picnic with the political agent and his party, and Forster went with him. The English people ate 'while the Maharajah sat apart and asked permission for his Dewan [his first minister] to sit down'. Forster comments, 'feeble and undignified move'. I cannot tell, but it seems to me much more likely that the Maharajah's humble petition was bitterly ironic, and designed to signify to the agent that he felt in some way slighted.[11] His behaviour afterwards would suggest so:

> when we reached the Guest House he made me walk up the slope to it instead of driving me to the door. This doesn't do in India, you know, it doesn't do!!! It would never have happened at Dewas. It has made me decide to go tomorrow unless warmly pressed, and I've written a note to that effect.

It is a cunning piece of prose. Forster mocks the pukka sahib's reaction to an affront from a native, but he feels it all the same. He responds with a righteous indignation that is at the same time a fit of feminine pique. His prose stylishly contains the insecurity of his response, but it is that insecurity, I suspect, that blunted his social antennae at the picnic.

While Forster was at Dewas the Maharajah was visited by the Agent to the Governor-General, a powerful British official. In recognition of his status the Maharajah had to call on the AGG at the Guest House before the AGG called at the palace. At the Guest House a ceremony was to be performed at which attar and pan (perfume and an edible leaf) would be distributed by the AGG's staff to their Indian guests. Forster's presence in the Maharajah's service raised a question of protocol. Should he be given his offering by the AGG's Chief of Staff, an Englishman, or by his attaché, an Indian. The Maharajah let it be known that he would prefer the former, but accept the latter. In the event Forster was not given his attar and pan at all. The Maharajah was furious, and took the matter up with the viceroy. Forster seems to understand the importance of the episode. The Maharajah 'grew livid with passion – partly, and I know largely, for my sake, but partly for his own, because the omission implied that the A.G.G. would not recognize his right to have Europeans under him.' Apart from the absurd suggestion that Tukoji Rao was likely to be more enraged by a trivial embarrassment to Forster than by a serious affront to his prestige as a monarch, Forster offers here a reasonable explanation of the event's significance. But he can do so only in passing, because his principal concern is to establish that the episode is nonsensical, a chapter from *Alice in Wonderland*: 'I have been *Insulted*, but you are not going to be as angry as you expect, for it was an official insult.' He fails to learn from it what he might have done – that his appointment as the Maharajah's temporary private secretary was a political act.

The appointment of Europeans to posts in native states could only be made with the permission of the Government of India. Forster's appointment had been approved, but it is unlikely even so that the Government would have been happy about it. There had been talk about Forster accepting an appointment in Dewas in 1916. The postal censor in Bombay, knowing of this, intercepted a letter from Forster to his friend Masood, and forwarded it to the political department with the comment that, on the evidence of this letter and another that the censor had intercepted a year before, Forster was 'a decadent coward and apparently a sexual pervert'. The letter and the censor's comments were then sent to the AGG who five years later officially insulted Forster with the suggestion that he give the Maharajah 'a hint that Forster is not altogether a suitable person'.[12] It seems likely that when Tukoji Rao renewed his invitation to Forster some years later, it was a calculated gesture of independence. In the changed political situation, the Maharajah felt strong enough to assert himself by deliberately flouting the advice of a senior British official. That the Government eventually approved Forster's appointment suggests that his judgement was right.

The Hill of Devi glows with an admiration for the Maharajah that Forster is never able to explain. This is, of course, his point: that affection can flourish independent of understanding. All the same it is disquieting to read that the Maharajah was 'certainly a genius and possibly a saint, and he had to be king', when, on the evidence Forster offers, the reader would scarcely be prepared to allow him ordinary common sense. Judgement of character comes to seem too much a matter of irrational intuition. But Forster has a better reason for his high opinion of the Maharajah than he is prepared to make public. It is implied in a manuscript not published until after Forster's death. The manuscript, titled 'Kanaya', contains Forster's account of his homosexual experiences at the Maharajah's court.[13] It is a strange and distressing story.

Two palace servants began to make homosexual advances towards Forster soon after he arrived at Dewas – one of them, a groom, none too subtly, by 'bunching up his garments to simulate an erection' when in Forster's presence. But Forster prefers the other, and makes an assignation with him. Ten minutes later

Forster overhears him telling some other servant what has happened. Forster 'melted with terror and shame'. That same day the Maharajah announced that he was determined to expel catamites from his court. This convinced Forster that his worst fears were confirmed, that the gossip had reached the Maharajah's ears. For four days Forster waited, feeling sure that he was mocked and despised by the whole court. Then he confessed the whole story to the Maharajah. 'You know about it,' Forster said, 'and if you agree I think I ought to resign.' The Maharajah replied, 'But Morgan – I know nothing about it – this is the first I've heard of it.' He advises Forster not to masturbate – 'that's awful' – and promises, if Forster gives the word, to find him a partner. This is how Forster came to meet 'Kanaya'. His services were arranged and paid for by the Maharajah. After some time the Maharajah warned Forster that Kanaya had been boasting of his relationship with the Sahib to Forster's assistant. The whole court soon become aware of Forster's habits, and he has to put up with 'a good deal of impertinence and ill-breeding': 'They weren't openly rude but there was an air of rollicking equality.' Then the Maharajah tells Forster that Kanaya has come to him begging a better position on the ground that 'Sahib goes to bed with me'. The Maharajah advised Forster against dismissing the boy, and their sexual relationship continued until Forster left Dewas, allowing Forster to learn something of himself that he would rather not have known: 'I resumed sexual intercourse with him, but it was now mixed with the desire to inflict pain.'

Forster's feeling of obligation to the Maharajah, his admiration of him, are surely founded very largely on the generosity and the delicacy with which the Maharajah received what Forster continued to think of as his betrayal of the Maharajah's trust. The Maharajah had to choose between a principle and a friend. He chose the friend, and Forster honoured him for it.

I find Forster's understanding of these events incredible. It seems wholly unlikely that so soon after Forster's arrival in Dewas two palace servants should make obvious or gross advances to him. The risk they ran, had Forster been offended, was too extreme. It is also improbable that the Maharajah would have remained ignorant for long of servants' gossip. Both Darling and Forster record as one of the Maharajah's foibles the maintenance of an elaborate spy system both within his own court and elsewhere.[14] The same evening that Forster made his assignation with the servant boy, the Maharajah introduced into the conversation his fierce objection to homosexuality. It is hard to accept this as coincidence. Forster's first reaction was surely right. The topic was raised because the Maharajah knew what had happened. The evidence seems to me to suggest that before Forster was appointed as his private secretary the Maharajah knew him to be a homosexual. That from his first arrival at Dewas the Maharajah orchestrated an elaborate series of manoeuvres designed to tempt Forster into active homosexual behaviour. I think it likely that Kanaya's indiscretions, if real, were also prompted by the Maharajah. I find it hard to believe that, in an Indian princely state, a menial servant, a barber, would have dared attempt to blackmail his ruler in the manner that the Maharajah describes Kanaya as doing. This is to say that throughout the six months that Forster spent in Dewas he was the victim of a very unpleasant game devised by an accomplished sadist.

If I am right, there remain two pressing question. First, why was Forster, who knew the circumstances better than I can do, not more suspicious? When the Maharajah insisted, after Forster's confession, that he had known nothing of the matter, Forster immediately asked himself, 'was he lying?', and admits, 'For a time I thought so'. Only later did he come to feel that this was 'complete illusion on my part', and that if the Maharajah had known, he could only have known 'subconsciously'. In a more normal mood he would not have preferred to invoke extra-sensory perception when a perfectly rational alternative was available. 'Pert and meagre word', Fielding thinks to himself when Miss Quested raises the possibility of telepathy. I can offer three possible explanations. Forster in India was predisposed to trust his heart rather than his head. Second, the decision whether or not to believe the Maharajah presented itself to him as a crucial act of faith, a test of his capacity for love and friendship, and a test he had to take at a time when he was at his most vulnerable, just after he had acted in a manner that seemed to him to betray the trust that the Maharajah had placed in him. Lastly, I think Forster believed Tukoji Rao because the alternative was too horrible for him to contemplate. Vicious behaviour in Forster's fiction results almost always from lack of imagination and lack of sympathy. In order to understand the Maharajah's behaviour in the way that I have suggested it ought to be understood, he would have been forced to contemplate something quite different, something that finds no place in his novels, and that he was perhaps temperamentally incapable of receiving, an idea of evil. For all that, I doubt whether Forster ever quite convinced himself that his suspicions were a 'complete illusion'. I suspect that they continued to reverberate deep in his mind, where they added something to that echo in a cave that Mrs Moore heard, and that threatened 'in some indescribable way to undermine her hold on life'.

The second question I cannot answer. Why did Tukoji Rao do it? But an answer may be indirectly suggested by returning at this point to *Heat and Dust*. Harry is the Nawab of Khatm's pet Englishman, alternately fondled and insulted, and Harry responds to his master with a dog-like devotion:

> I do want to do everything I can to make him – happier. Goodness knows I try. Not only because I like him very much but because he's been fantastically kind to me. You can have no idea of his generosity, Olivia. He wants his friends to have everything. Everything he can give them. It's his nature.

As he says this his face is full of pain, and Olivia comforts him. The Nawab is generous to Harry, she says, because he likes him:

> Who knows? With him you can't tell. One moment you think: Yes he cares – but next moment you might as well be some . . . object.

Forster's prose, unlike Harry's, is wittily self-aware: 'I think he was fond of me, though one can never be certain of saints.' But one can sometimes hear Harry's painful yearning peep through: 'I never feel certain what he likes, or even whether he likes me: consideration for others so often simulates affection in him. I only know that he is one of the sweetest and saintliest men I have ever known . . .' To move others while remaining oneself, if not as stone, then at any rate unreadable, is perhaps an activity that might appeal to a connoisseur of the more delicate stratagems of power.

Unlike Forster Harry cannot deny that there is another side to the Nawab. He witnesses it once a year at the festival known as the Husband's Wedding Day when Hindus go on pilgrimage into the Nawab's dominions, and the Nawab presides over a murderous communal riot. Then Harry sees him as strange. He becomes 'terribly excited', his eyes 'burn', he looks 'devastatingly handsome'. As for what goes on, Harry does not know. During the days of the festival he shuts himself in a room in the palace. He would rather remain ignorant of a side of the Nawab's character that would make his love for him unbearable.

Olivia's husband, Douglas, is a magistrate. He and his colleagues are perfect exemplars of slow-witted public school rectitude. They embody all that is best in the British Government of India, and hence all that is a threat to the Nawab's unrestrained enjoyment of his power. For this the Nawab hates them. He seeks to establish himself as the ideal antithesis to all that the British in India stand for, responding with cunning to their affectation of frankness, with style to their stolidity, with triumphant malice to their protestations of even-handed justice. He prizes Harry as a parody of all those English virtues from which he suffers. He looks at Harry, puffed out and recumbent after a short walk:

> The Nawab laughed: 'What a state he is in. He is a very weak person. Because he is so flabby in his body I think. He is not a proper Englishman at all. No – shall I tell you – I think he is a very *im*proper Englishman.'

The British officials, he knows, are made uncomfortable by Harry's presence under his roof. He retains as his court buffoon a homosexual Englishman of weak character, a living exemplar of all the possibilities of Englishness that the British in India would rather deny existed. His patronage of Harry is a delicate racial affront. Racial hatred is the motive of much of his behaviour.

Olivia becomes pregnant. It might be by the Nawab or by her husband, but both she and the Nawab are convinced that it is his child. The Nawab is under pressure from the Government who are threatening an enquiry into his administration. He 'sat up all night composing telegrams'. (The Maharajah of Dewas was famous, as both Darling and Forster note, for the extravagantly long telegrams in which he expressed his protests and appeals to British officials.) 'You should have heard him last night', Harry tells Olivia: 'Wait till my son is born, he said, then they'll laugh from the other side of their mouths.' The Nawab, like Forster's Maharajah, is the successor to a long line of warrior princes. But under British rule his word has become merely ceremonial. There remains to him only one weapon with which he can inflict pain on his enemies, his 'devastating' personal charm. Like Forster, Darling and Ackerley he is an exponent of 'personal relations', but for him they are the last available weapon of war.

The Hill of Devi is a warm and charming book. It tells how two men, if they will only trust their hearts, can set aside differences of race. It shows how a relationship based on power may be superseded by a relationship founded on love. Ruth Prawer Jhabvala responds with a picture of a princely state in which love, power and race are inextricably entwined, in which personal relations can never triumph because no relations are simply personal. She lived in India much longer than did Forster. It may be that she knows it better.

Or is it so? For after all the most significant product of Forster's Indian travels was not *The Hill of Devi*, but *A Passage to India*, and it may be that the full meaning of his Indian experience was unavailable to him in his Indian letters and journals, and could be approached only within the bewildering duplicities of fiction. I was a meaning that Forster could find only by assuming multiple disguises – as the bluff, almost parodically manly Fielding; as Mrs Moore, who responds to Aziz with an affection that is disinfected of sexuality by her age; as Adela Quested, who, just for a moment is struck by the contrast between Aziz's brown lissomness and her ruddy-cheeked stiff fiancé; and as Ralph Moore, so tremblingly sensitive to the pressure of the doctor's hands. In fiction the plot is at Forster's mercy. It is an Indian, not an Englishman, who is suspected of succumbing to physical desire and so betraying a position of trust, and no Indian – not the Nawab, not Aziz even in the Temple section where he is more self-confident and has lost his girlishness, and certainly not Godbole – is allowed to exercise the power that the Maharajah of Dewas wielded. Most remarkably, the hole in *The Hill of Devi*, the episode omitted because it was, as Gertrude Stein would have said, *inaccrochable*, could be transformed into a cave, and either consecrated as a mystery or shrugged off as a muddle. Perhaps it was only from behind such elaborate fictional defences that Forster found it possible to strain to breaking point his belief in the efficacy of personal relations. Mrs Moore takes ship for England, tired of a life spent caring for others, Adela returns to a life of unattached spinsterhood, and Fielding and Aziz meet again in an Indian princely state only to realise that an Englishman and an Indian could not be friends, at any rate 'not yet' and 'not there'.

12

A Passage to India

I chose two epigraphs for my book, but they have a single source. Both are taken from *A Passage to India*. 'How can the mind take hold of such a country?' It is the question of a young English lady, aware – because Adela Quested is a very honest young lady – that India has 'avoided her well-equipped mind'. But it is E.M. Forster's question, too, and most completely his in its mingling of wonder and irritation that a country can so evade the clutches of even a sympathetic intelligence. 'Half-closing his eyes he attempted to love India.' This is not Forster, but Dr Aziz, newly acquitted and transformed by mishap into a nationalist hero, trying somewhat feebly to flesh out 'the sage and bulky figure of a mother-land' for which he had 'no natural affection'. Forster smiles gently as he records Aziz's efforts. He seems in full command of his character's limitations. It is just that those limitations are also his own. If Aziz's knowledge of the land of his birth is partial and inadequate, if he can love India only by blurring much that seems to him foreign or incomprehensible or barbarous, then Forster's position is no different. His superiority over Aziz has at this point no real basis. It is just a trick of style.

When I first went to India in 1970 I knew nothing about the country, and there is a sense in which I know nothing more about it now, because, before I ever went there, India already existed for me, existed completely, perfectly, as only fictitious countries can exist. India had been given to me by E.M. Forster, and after all the time I have spent there and all the other books I have read, my India is still recognisably the India that E.M. Forster created in a single novel. It is inevitable that the gratitude I feel for such a gift is ambivalent.

Why Forster should still exercise such a hold over me, and, I suspect, many others, is hard to say, for Forster's is a minor literary achievement – just a handful of novels, two of them rather slight, and two rather silly, which leaves only *Howard's End* and *A Passage to India*. And yet Forster's is the most authoritative voice of twentieth-century English letters. It is an authority carried not so

177

much by a particular novel or story or article as by the voice that Forster invented. Forster is the last of the Victorian sages, he is the last of those writers whose moral stature is an achievement of their prose style. What most strikes, of course, is Forster's difference from his Victorian predecessors. He can make Dickens seem strident, George Eliot ponderous, and Thackeray spiteful. He looks past them to the eighteenth and early nineteenth centuries, to Fielding and to Jane Austen, to find models for a moral authority worn with sufficient ease and grace, but he adds a new quality all of his own, diffidence. In Forster, diffidence is not the antidote to the authority he exercises over his reader, it is its ground. When we yield to Forster's judgements we yield to them because of their unassumingness. He devised a prose style that made strength out of meekness, and it was a historic achievement.

Even in the novels written before the First World War Forster was fashioning a new rhetoric, a moral posture fully accommodated to his quick sense that England was no longer the centre of the world. He devised an English voice that commanded assent because it accepted at the outset that Englishness could no longer represent itself as a universal moral value. In doing so, one might say, he helped his countrymen to reconcile themselves to the impending loss of their empire by indicating how it was possible for prestige to outlive power, how the loss of power might become itself the foundation of a new kind of prestige. 'Englishmen like posing as Gods', Mrs Moore tells her son, irritated by his insistence that his job in India is not to be pleasant, but 'to do justice and keep the peace'. He is not, Heaslop replies, some 'vague sentimental sympathetic literary man', he has more important concerns. Forster's self-characterisation is a little coy, but it is carefully placed. Heaslop's kind of authority, substantial authority, is made to seem already antiquated, soon to become obsolete, and if a new authority is to be found, it will have to be different in character, more literary, more self-deprecatingly self-aware, more a matter of style.

At the bridge party Heaslop waves his hand towards the nervous line of Indians, each of them rendered comic by some incongruous article of Western clothing, a pince-nez or a shoe. Forster pauses to characterise Western dress as a disfiguring disease: 'Few had yielded entirely, but none were untouched.' Forster's prose falls naturally into antithesis. It is what gives his style its distinctively eighteenth-century balance. But almost always the antithesis is blurred, deprived of its sharp point. Here he admits a grammatical looseness – 'none were' – and his negligence is a sort of politeness, as reassuring as the spot of dried egg yolk on the impeccably dressed man's tie. It is eighteenth-century prose transformed by a twentieth-century feel for the democratic proprieties, and it gives Forster the means by which he preserves his authority without compromising his egalitarian principles.

Throughout the first section of *A Passage to India* India is presented to us neatly packaged in antitheses, formally posed in doublets. At the bridge party the Indian ladies occupy themselves with a dog, 'alternately fondling the terrier or shrinking from him'. Mrs Bhattacharya makes a gesture signifying that 'everything pleased her, nothing surprised'. When they come to Aziz the antitheses become more expansive. For some days before the bridge party he is 'very gay and full of details of operations', but on the day of the party he is suddenly pierced by grief for his dead wife: 'he mourned his wife the more sincerely because he mourned her seldom'. He gazes at his wife's photograph: 'It was unbearable, and he thought again, "How unhappy I am!" and became happier'. The antitheses are witty, but the wit is not sharp. It is wit that has been permeated by sympathy, and it places Aziz as the object at once of our amusement and our affection.

But Forster is not operating a system of stylistic apartheid: the English are treated similarly. There is the lady at the club, 'entirely stupid and friendly', and Ronny Heaslop feeling 'scratchy and dictatorial'. The Turtons live in 'the oldest and most uncomfortable bungalow in the Civil Station', and the station itself 'charms not, neither does it repel'. When she agrees to marry Ronny, Adela Quested feels the loss of her 'important and cultivated uncertainty'. Again, the effects can be more leisurely as with McBryde, the superintendent of police, who 'owing to a somewhat unhappy marriage had evolved a complete philosophy of life'. It is the clash of 'somewhat' against 'complete' that tightens the humour into wit, but the wit remains quite unobtrusive.

Forster's style has most often been noticed, by Cyril Connolly for example, as distinguished by its casual ease, but Forster's liking for doublets and antitheses reveals the Augustan musculature that underlies the relaxed colloquialism. Strength is at least as important to Forster as ease. It is what enables him to intersperse his narrative with passages of general reflection, passages marked by an old-fashioned eloquence, and it is what enables him to exercise over his readers an authority that is the less easily resisted because it is so nonchalantly assumed. But by the end of the second section of *A Passage to India* there is not much of this strength left. The ship carrying Miss Quested back to England docks at Port Said. She goes sightseeing to the Canal, and a fellow-passenger, an American missionary, points out the significance of the statue of Lesseps:

> 'He turns to the East, he re-turns to the West. You can see it from the cute position of his hands, one of which holds a string of sausages.' The missionary looked at her humorously, in order to cover the emptiness of his mind. He had no idea what he meant by 'turn' and 're-turn', but he often used words in pairs, for the sake of moral brightness.

The missionary is too vividly sketched for this, his sole appearance in the novel: he obtrudes too much for his role as simple bystander. He becomes another sly self-characterisation by a Forster who has come to recognise his own relish for using words in pairs not as a way of controlling his material and giving it point, but as meaningless jingling. It is a Forster prepared to recognise his comic gift as just a flimsy disguise for an empty mind, a foolish posture which is all that remains to him of the principles he once lived by. To turn or re-turn from this passage to one of Forster's sprightly sentences – 'Professor Godbole's conversations frequently culminated in a cow' – is to detect in the alliteration a false jauntiness, to hear in the neat opposition between the four syllables of 'culminated' and the single syllable of 'cow' only a feeble attempt to preserve 'moral brightness'. It is to experience something like what Mrs Moore experienced after a few minutes in a Marabar cave.

Summoned by Major Callendar, Aziz leaves the dinner party he is attending and cycles into Chandrapore's British section, the Civil Lines, and as he enters its 'arid tidiness, depression suddenly seized him': 'The roads, named after victorious generals and intersecting at right angles were symbolic of the net Great Britain had thrown over India. He felt caught in their meshes.' It is the true measure of Forster's sympathy for India and Indians that he repeats Aziz's experience. As he accompanies Miss Quested on her voyage back to England, and invents a missionary to say a few words and break up her journey, he too is seized by a sudden depression, and his own prose style seems to him a net, the words

all too neatly arranged to intersect at right angles, the effect
stifling. The click of word against word comes to seem an arid
stylistic formality, turning and re-turning and getting nowhere,
intent, like the planners of India's civil lines, only on creating a
cantonment safely enclosed against the India all around.
What remains is *A Passage to India*'s other style, a style in which
sentences do not close with a witty point, but overreach themselves and fade away as they address a reality that can never be
accommodated because it recedes infinitely from the grasp. The
novel's third paragraph turns from the city of Chandrapore to the
sky above it, from the town's Civil Lines with its buildings
'disposed along roads that intersect at right angles' to a sky in
which there are no firm outlines, where there are only tints
blending or melting into one another:

> The sky too has its changes, but they are less marked than those
> of the vegetation and the river. Clouds map it up at times, but it
> is normally a dome of blending tints, and the main tint blue. By
> day the blue will pale down into white where it touches the
> white of the land, after sunset it has a new circumference –
> orange, melting upwards into tenderest purple. But the core of
> blue persists, and so it is by night. Then the stars hang like lamps
> from the immense vault. The distance between the earth and
> them is as nothing to the distance behind them; and that further
> distance, though beyond colour, last freed itself from blue.

In the first section of the novel the two styles are harmoniously
blended. The section is entitled 'Mosque', and it is as he looks at
the mosque, where he is about to meet Mrs Moore, that Aziz sees
an emblem of such a harmony:

> The front – in full moonlight – had the appearance of marble,
> and the ninety-nine names of God on the frieze stood out black,
> as the frieze stood out white against the sky. The contrast
> between this dualism and the contention of shadows within
> pleased Aziz . . .

It pleases Forster too. It is a contrast that dominates the first section
of the novel, and it allows Forster to present India as at once
contained within his narrative and as what eludes his grasp. When
Aziz quotes poetry in Urdu, Persian, Arabic, his friends lose their

sense that they are intruders in an alien land: 'India – a hundred Indias – whispered outside beneath the indifferent moon, but for the time India seemed one and their own . . .' India is what forever recedes from them, and it is also fully present in the rich pathos of the verses that Aziz recites: it is both outside the window and enclosed within the room where they sit so comfortably together. But such moments achieve only a fragile harmony.

As the novel proceeds the prose changes its character. It loses its Augustan snap, and the moments of recession into fathomless mystery begin to dominate. The sky comes to seem more important than the earth. It is the sky rather than Mr Turton that presides over the bridge party:

> Some kites hovered overhead, impartial, over the kites passed the mass of a vulture, and, with an impartiality exceeding all, the sky, not deeply coloured but translucent, poured light from its whole circumference. It seemed unlikely that the series stopped here. Beyond the sky must not there be something that over-arches all the skies, more impartial even than they? Beyond which again.

It is a thought that threatens Mrs Moore's simple faith in the efficacy of her God: 'Outside the arch there seemed always another arch, beyond the remotest echo a silence.' Fielding, gazing at a star, fancies it a tunnel, 'and when this fancy was accepted all the other stars seemed tunnels too'. Even the dark night-time sky no longer encloses the earth, but tempts the watcher into a giddy contemplation of infinitely receding distances. Not only space but time plunges giddily away into unimaginable depths:

> Bland and bald rose the precipices; solid and white a Brahmany kite flapped between the rocks with a clumsiness that seemed intentional. Before man, with his itch for the seemly, had been born, the planet must have looked thus. The kite flapped away . . . Before birds, perhaps . . .'

In the West time and space are finite, but in India they slip forever from the grasp and tumble ever further away until the mind can no longer track them.

People too recede until they drift beyond the reach of even the most generous sympathy. Outside the law courts sit clients waiting for pleaders. These people have not been invited to the bridge party:

And there were circles even beyond these – people who wore nothing but a loincloth, people who wore not even that, and spent their lives knocking two sticks together before a scarlet doll – humanity grading and drifting from the educated vision, until no earthly invitation can embrace it.

Novels create closed spaces, finite worlds within which the novelist can exercise a divine omnipresence, but in *A Passage to India* an awareness of all the things that the novel cannot include begins to press on the narrative. When Hamidullah and Fielding briefly discuss the death of Mrs Moore, they are not much affected:

If for a moment the sense of communion in sorrow came to them, it passed. How indeed is it possible for one human being to be sorry for all the sadness that meets him on the face of the earth, for the pain that is endured not only by men, but by animals and plants, and perhaps by the stones? The soul is tired in a moment, and in fear of losing the little she does understand she retreats to the permanent lines which habit or chance have dictated, and suffers there.

The limits that the novelist must place around his world are no longer felt as necessary or inevitable, but put there by chance or habit, a line of defence within which the human imagination can shelter its meagreness. The novelist is in the same predicament as the missionary, Mr Sorley, when he is mischievously badgered about the capaciousness of God's love. Mr Sorley is prepared to allow that there may be a place in Heaven for monkeys, even, to push a point, jackals, but he becomes uneasy when the case of wasps is mentioned, and when he is asked to consider oranges, cactuses, crystals, mud and bacteria, he throws up his hands in despair: 'No, no, this is going too far. We must exclude something from our gathering, or we shall be left with nothing.' Heaven becomes like a club or a party, defined not by what it admits but by what it excludes, and so does the novel. The novel is no longer a tribute to the inclusiveness of the novelist's imagination, but a confession of its limitedness.

As the novel proceeds everything seems to cooperate towards

one end, Aziz's arrest and his trial. This will be, it seems, the emblematic incident, the event that will elucidate and assess the relationship between two nations. But when the acquittal comes, it is messy, chaotic, nothing resolved and nothing proved, the only reconciliation that odd, edgy respect that Fielding acquires for Miss Quested. The two of them talk 'at the height of their powers – sensible, honest, even subtle', and yet all their words 'were followed by a curious backwash as though the universe had displaced itself to fill up a tiny void, or as though they had seen their own gestures from an immense height – dwarfs talking, shaking hands, and assuring each other that they stood on the same footing of insight'. The novel begins in an assured ironic mode. For all the narrator's friendliness, the characters are looked at from a height, their moments of emptiness exposed by the fullness of the narrator's presence. But by this point, if there is still irony, it is a cosmic, impersonal irony, and the novelist is its victim as much as his characters. He shares their sense of their own dwarfishness, and if they are conscious of their own words as empty, as voids momentarily disturbing the indifferent fullness of the universe, then the novel that records their words inhabits the same emptiness.

'Visions are supposed to entail some profundity, but – wait till you get one, dear reader.' So Forster comments when an echo in a cave obliterates Mrs Moore's faith that human life has value. He addresses the reader suavely, with a commanding intimacy, but his tone has been emptied of significance, it has become parody. Forster may say 'dear reader', but Mrs Moore has lost her belief that other people matter. She is no longer interested in whether they behave well or badly – 'boum, it amounts to the same'. She has lost her faith in the values that sustained her life, the Christian and humane values that made possible her unselfishness, her kindliness, and her clear-sighted judgement of others. It is not her loss alone, because these are also the values that have sustained Forster's novel. Adela Quested cannot get the echo in the caves out of her ears, and neither can Forster. The echo sounds all the way through Aziz's arrest, and his trial, and his acquittal, and it works subversively to undermine our sense that these events are impor- tant, and that we should concern ourselves much about them.

Novels have always made great play with trials, and this is hardly surprising for the novel is itself a kind of trial in which each of the characters stands at the bar and the novelist dispenses justice. If the novel includes a court of law then its judgement may speak in unison with the judgement of the novelist, but much more often the injustice of that verdict will be contrasted with the novelist's true grasp of things, or the limited, partial justice that emerges will be supplanted by the divinely unerring justice administered by the novelist. In Forster's trial justice is done, it is right that it should be done, but the reader does not much care. Fielding acts for us as he busies himself about his friend's defence, but so does Mrs Moore, who feels tired, refuses to offer herself as a witness, and wants only to be left alone.

When Aziz is arrested, Fielding hurries to see McBryde, the police superintendent, and then Hamidullah, the town's leading barrister. Then he goes back to his school. Professor Godbole is waiting for him. 'I hope the expedition was a successful one', he says. Fielding assumes that the news has not reached him, but Godbole admits that the whole college is talking about it. Godbole is a parody here of infuriating Oriental imperturbability, serene in a carelessness of others that Mrs Moore at least has the Western grace to suffer. Godbole talks on, eloquent, nonsensical: 'When evil occurs, it expresses the whole of the universe. Similarly when good occurs.' His voice remains infuriating, but it becomes insidious:

> Suffering is merely a matter for the individual. If a young lady has sunstroke, that is a matter of no significance to the universe. Oh no, not the least. It is an isolated matter, it only concerns herself. If she thought her head did not ache, she would not be ill, and that would end it. But it is far otherwise in the case of good and evil. They are not what we think them, they are what they are, and each of us has contributed to both.

Individuals experience pleasure and suffering, but these are matters that concern only themselves. Good and evil, on the other hand, are not attributes of the individual but dispositions of the universe, contrary aspects of God. Godbole blandly severs the connection between experience and value on which all Western thought and all Western art is founded. He denies, as it were, any logical connection between the evidence heard by a court, and its verdict. In doing so he repudiates the novel. The echo of that repudiation sounds all through A *Passage to India* disrupting the well-made novel, the satirical comedy of manners, that Forster seems to have set out intending to write. It is as if every one of the novel's events is accompanied by a hollow ring. But Forster is not haunted simply by a sense of the futility of his enterprise, he is haunted too by a dim, scarcely articulable sense of the kind of novel that Godbole makes possible, a novel in which individual experience and personal relations are somehow subsidiary and unimportant.

After escaping from the amateur performance of *Cousin Kate*, Adela and Mrs Moore are chatting idly in the billiard room of the club. Mrs Moore is tired, her mind a blur: 'Let me think – we don't see the other side of the moon out here, no.' She is answered by a pleasant voice: 'Come, India's not as bad as all that. Other side of the earth, if you like, but we stick to the same old moon.' The voice belongs to a man she has not met, and will never meet again: 'He passed with his friendly word through red-brick pillars into the darkness.' It is not an original technique, this intrusion into the novel of an unnamed man who speaks once, and then fades into the darkness. Realist novelists use such devices to create the illusion of life stretching out around the characters whose fortunes the novel traces. But in *A Passage to India* that is not, I think, quite the effect. The passers-by in the novel, the bit players, are consistently too vividly rendered for their function. When, for example, the American missionary speaks to Miss Quested in Egypt, his words and mannerisms are weighted by a lifetime's experience, but it is an experience that the novel has no room for. The same is true of a more important character like McBryde. His glum tolerance born of a large cynicism invites an interest that the novel does not satisfy. To think about McBryde is to be aware of him passing, like the man at the club, into darkness. Forster trains his spotlight on Aziz, Miss Quested, Heaslop and Fielding, but he reminds us from time to time that outside this light there is only shadow. At the bridge party Miss Quested and Mrs Moore take their leave of the Indian ladies they have been talking to, and as they do so 'three ladies, who had hitherto taken no part in the reception, suddenly shot out of the summer-house like exquisitely coloured swallows, and salaamed them'. The three ladies dart into the novel and out of it, from the darkness into the light and once more into the darkness. All they are is a brief flash of colour, but it is vivid colour, and the effect of such moments is to permeate the novel with Miss Quested's anxiety that 'the true India' is sliding by 'unnoticed' or scarcely noticed, that the novel's real subject cannot be focused on and is glimpsed only for brief moments out of the corner of the eye. The effect is at its most intense during the trial. It is Aziz whose fate is to be decided, but we see him only through Miss Quested's eyes, and he seems to her now just a 'strong neat little Indian with very black hair, and pliant hands'. He seems 'negligible, devoid of significance'. The scene is dominated by the almost naked figure of 'a person who had no bearing officially upon the trial', the punka-wallah. It is he who 'seemed to control the proceedings', but they are proceedings to which he is utterly indifferent:

Something in his aloofness impressed the girl from middle-class England, and rebuked the narrowness of her sufferings. In virtue of what had she called this roomful of people together? Her particular brand of opinions, and the suburban Jehovah who sanctified them – by what right did they claim so much importance in the world, and assume the title of civilization?

It is the climactic scene of the novel, and even before it is enacted it is dwarfed, made to seem insignificant. All the machinations of Forster's plot have culminated in this scene, and before it begins Miss Quested wonders, and Forster wonders with her, why this roomful of people have been collected together.

As a social and political novel *A Passage to India* collapses at the trial. It suffers the same fate as McBryde's case against Aziz. 'Right, I withdraw', says McBryde nonchalantly, and 'the flimsy framework of the court broke up'. So, whether it is flimsy or not, does the framework of the novel. But perhaps one ought to say that with the collapse of the courtroom proceedings the novel's true framework is revealed. It was after all Forster himself who claimed that the novel was 'not really about politics', that 'it is – or rather desires to be – philosophic and poetic . . .'[1] Perhaps what happens at the trial is that the social novel, the novel of character, is sloughed off to reveal a poetic novel that finds its coherence not in a play of character but in a pattern of symbolism. This, or something like it, is the case that has been well argued by Malcolm Bradbury, who reads *A Passage to India* as a Victorian novel subjected to the pressures of modernism, as a symbolic novel subverting a novel of character.[2] Aziz's trial may be the climax of the social novel, but it is just as obvious that the climax of the symbolist novel is the visit to the caves.

From the novel's very first sentence that visit has been elaborately prepared: 'Except for the Marabar caves – and they are twenty miles off – the city of Chandrapore presents nothing extraordinary.' The cave is a potent symbol in the Western mind, a place of revelation, whether erotic as for Dido, or religious as for St John. It is in the caves that one expects the novel's truth, the 'true India' that Miss Quested finds so elusive, to be revealed. All four of the novel's central characters enter a cave. Aziz lights a cigarette, Fielding is unimpressed, but Mrs Moore and Miss Quested have visions. Miss Quested's vision is erotic, and Mrs Moore's is religious, but they have a peculiarity in common. They are not so much moments of revelation as its opposite. Miss Quested has a vision of a sexual encounter failing to take place. Mrs Moore's vision is religious only in the sense that it negates religion. Symbols are objects so full of meaning that they overflow and flood with meaning all the world around them. The caves in Forster's novel are the reverse of this: they empty the world of the meaning it once had. They are not so much symbols as the antithesis of symbols.

Gillian Beer has noted how the word 'nothing' sounds all through the text of Forster's novel,[3] and all these references are compacted here, in the caves, which act as an embodiment of nothingness: 'Nothing, nothing attaches to them.' She argues that somehow the novel converts this negative into a positive. 'Nothing embraces the whole of India, nothing, nothing . . .' says Aziz, and Gillian Beer suggests that Forster finds a way of persuading us to read such a remark as an affirmation. But her argument at this point becomes too mystical for me to follow. The caves reveal a world emptied of meaning and emptied of value, and to find in this grounds for satisfaction is to surpass Professor Godbole in visionary indifference. Even he admits that 'the difference between presence and absence is great, as great as my feeble mind can grasp', and will claim for absence only that it 'implies presence' and is not 'non-existence'. The visit to the Marabar caves marks the climax of *A Passage to India* as a symbolist novel just as obviously as the trial marks its climax as a social novel. But in both cases the climax is identical with anticlimax. As a symbolist novel *A Passage to India* is like the boulder that swings on the summit of the highest of the Marabar Hills and is rumoured to contain a sealed cave: 'If the boulder falls and smashes, the cave will smash too – empty as an Easter egg.' In the caves the novel's symbolic patterns converge and yield a meaning that turns out to be no meaning at all.

By the end of the second section the novel has finished, but there is no sense of finality. It has not ended so much as lapsed. The dominant impression is of weariness; Mrs Moore weary of life, Adela Quested weary of seeing India, Aziz and Fielding weary of living more heroically than it is natural for them to live. 'So it petered out', writes Forster of a conversation between Fielding and Miss Quested, but he might just as well be writing of his novel. Fielding's sudden sense of freedom when he takes home leave and goes sightseeing in Venice before taking the train northwards to gaze on the buttercups and daisies of a temperate English June is like the surge of relief felt by the novelist who has at last decided to abandon the novel that he cannot write, to give up wrestling with material that has resisted all his attempts to impose on it a satisfactory shape.

But Fielding, like Forster himself, returns to India. The novel has a third section in which Aziz and Fielding meet again. It is much the shortest of the book's three sections, just a thin sheaf of pages, some twelve thousand words, and scarcely anything happens in it, and yet somehow, in these few pages, the novel is redeemed. The characters, Aziz, Fielding, Ralph – Mrs Moore's saintly idiot of a son – and his sister – Fielding's bride, are pushed to the margins. At the centre is a religious ceremony, the festival of the birth of Krishna. The plot of the novel ends in its final sentences as Fielding and Aziz recognise that their attempt to be friends with one another cannot succeed, but that recognition is by now both true and peripheral. What has become crucial is something else, something so odd, so nearly silly, that there is only one character who could possibly articulate it, Professor Godbole.

Godbole chants a hymn to God, and as they sing the singers allow themselves to surrender to love:

They loved all men, the whole universe, and scraps of their past, tiny splinters of detail, emerged for a moment to melt into the universal warmth. Thus Godbole, though she was not important to him, remembered an old woman he had met in Chandrapore days. Chance brought her into his mind while it was in this heated state, he did not select her, she happened to occur among the throng of soliciting images, a tiny splinter, and he impelled her by his spiritual force to that place where completeness can be found. Completeness, not reconstruction. His senses grew thinner, he remembered a wasp seen he forgot where, perhaps on a stone. He loved the wasp equally, he impelled it likewise, he was imitating God. And the stone where the wasp clung – could he ... No, he had been wrong to attempt the stone.

'One old Englishwoman and one little, little wasp', Godbole thinks to himself afterwards: 'It does not seem much, still it is more than I am myself.' As Godbole impels Mrs Moore and the wasp to 'that place where completeness can be found' the novel too is completed. As he thinks of a dead woman and a wasp, Godbole for a brief moment brings Mrs Moore back to life, reincarnates her as she looked at a wasp clinging to the tip of a clothes peg and murmured, 'Pretty dear', and as he does so *A Passage to India* at last finds its shape, not a shape born of personal relations or conferred by symbolism, but a pattern momentarily glimpsed in apparently random, seemingly meaningless connections. Life, the novel is always telling us, is a 'muddle', but in these brief moments muddle is transfigured, it becomes mystery.

One such moment occurs when Ronny tells Mrs Moore about the car accident:

Mrs Moore shivered, 'A ghost!' But the idea of a ghost scarcely passed her lips. The young people did not take it up, being occupied with their own outlooks, and deprived of support it perished, or was reabsorbed into the part of the mind that seldom speaks.

There is another such moment when Adela climbs with Aziz on her way to another Marabar cave: 'The rock was nicked by a double row of footholds, and somehow the question was suggested by them. Where had she seen footholds before? Oh yes, they were the pattern traced in the dust by the wheels of the Nawab Bahadur's car.' There was an accident, and the Nawab Bahadur believes it to be the work of the ghost of a man accidently run over long ago. There is an accident and a ghost, a muddle and a mystery, and the third section of *A Passage to India* is dominated by Forster's sense that mystery, that elusive and baffling power that confers meaning and completeness on experience, is only to be found within muddle.

It is to be found above all in the muddle of Gokul Ashtami, the ceremony of the birth of Krishna. Krishna, 'a silver image the size of a teaspoon', is the focus of the ceremony, but he is 'indistinguishable in the jumble of his own altar, huddled out of sight amidst images of inferior descent, smothered under rose leaves, overhung by oleographs, outblazed by golden tablets representing the Rajah's ancestors, and entirely obscured, when the wind blew, by the tattered foliage of a banana'. The thumping of a generator clashes with the rhythm of the drums, the sacred hymn is sung against the waltz being played by the military band outside. Inscriptions in various languages are hung everywhere, some positioned where they cannot be read, some fallen from the wall. There are games with butter and messes of rice, and bits of food are pashed into the carpet. But it is from within the chaos of this ceremony that Godbole contemplates the 'place where completeness can be found'. It is the fragmentedness of the ceremony, its refusal of all Western order and dignity, that allows those who participate in it to share a vision of wholeness. 'No definite image survived', but it is through the refusal of definite images, the rejection of single meanings, that the ceremony arrives at its truth. Meaning is passed from one thing to another, from Mrs Moore to a wasp to a stone, and these 'imitations', these 'substitutions' continued 'to flicker through the assembly for many hours'. What is achieved at the ceremony is a new kind of meaning, a meaning that is the more complete the more completely it is deferred. It is meaning that melts away in a dizzying, ecstatic recession, and it alone can embrace a country where humanity is forever 'grading and drifting beyond the educated vision'. It is a kind of meaning that requires a new kind of novelist.

The Rajah of Mau attends the ceremony of the birth of Krishna, but he is dying, and before the festival is completed he is dead. The King dies and Krishna is born: it is a coincidence but a moving one, as if Forster were somehow aware that *A Passage to India* could be completed only by accepting his own death as a novelist. As Aziz rows Ralph across the lake, Ralph sees something flash between the trees: 'Floating in the darkness was a king, who sat under a canopy, in shining royal robes.' It is the statue of the Rajah's father 'made to imitate life at enormous expense'. It is a striking image, but it is only an image, and it is the image of a man who is dead. Life is no longer to be represented but absorbed as a random play of images, whatever happens to occur, and if somehow the result is completeness then this is not a triumph won by the artist's skill, but a gift to be received humbly.

That is the kind of novel that Forster gestures towards in the

final section of *A Passage to India*. It is not, of course, the kind of
novel he wrote. The ceremony was 'not an orgy of the body; the
tradition of that shrine forbade it'. 'But the human spirit had tried
by a desperate contortion to ravish the unknown, flinging down
science and history in the struggle, yes, beauty herself. Did it
succeed? Books written afterwards say "Yes".' Books written
afterwards: his own book says 'No', or at least it ends saying 'No':

> But the horses didn't want it – they swerved apart; the earth
> didn't want it, sending up rocks through which riders must pass
> single-file; the temples, the tank, the jail, the palace, the birds,
> the carrion, the Guest House, that came into view as they issued
> from the gap and saw Mau beneath: they didn't want it, they
> said in their hundred voices, 'No, not yet,' and the sky said, 'No,
> not there.'

If there is a 'Yes' it can only be whispered or silently intimated, for
the 'Yes' is contained in a religious experience that cannot be
'expressed in anything but itself', in a vision of completeness
found by an art that does not struggle against but accepts the
random, chaotic fragmentation of human experience.

When he went to India, Forster, like Stella, Fielding's young
bride, was 'after something', but what that something is is never
articulated. Fielding suggests that Aziz ask Ralph, who is 'a wise
boy, really', but he is also a simpleton, and Stella, remarkably,
makes only one physical appearance in the novel, and remains
quite silent. Fielding himself admits that it is something that
cannot be explained 'because it isn't in words at all'. The novel
ends when it arrives at a truth that can remain intact only by being
unspoken, which is to say that it is a truth that is grasped only in
the moment when one fails to apprehend it. 'Absence implies
presence,' Professor Godbole remarks, 'absence is not non-
existence', and India, by the end of the novel, is deprived of any
but this most shadowy of existences, present only in so far as its
presence is implied by its absence. And we are therefore entitled
to repeat, 'Come, come, come, come', Godbole continues. It is an
invitation like the invitation that Mrs Bhattacharya extends to Miss
Quested and Mrs Moore, an invitation without a sequel, an
invitation that is an end in itself:

> How can the mind take hold of such a country? Generations of
> invaders have tried, but they remain in exile. The important

towns they build are only retreats, their quarrels the malaise of men who cannot find their way home. India knows of their trouble. She knows of the whole world's trouble, to its uttermost depth. She calls 'Come' through her hundred mouths, through objects ridiculous and august. But come to what? She has never defined, she is not a promise, only an appeal.

India is unfathomable, and that this is so, that the mind in contemplating it swoons away into endlessly receding depths, confers on the country its special value. Forster can meditate on it with the same portentously edifying vagueness with which Pater regarded the 'Mona Lisa'. Professor Godbole explains to Mrs Moore the hymn to Krishna that he has just sung: 'I say to him, Come, come, come, come, come, come. He neglects to come.' In that neglect he preserves his divine mystery, and it is with India as it is with India's most popular God. India's place in the Western imagination is secured only by its refusal to manifest itself.

When Aziz hears that Fielding has come to Mau, and bitterly reviews their shared past, he thinks, 'This pose of "seeing India" which had seduced him to Miss Quested at Chandrapore was only a form of ruling India.' But Forster anticipates a time when the British will no longer rule India, a time when the obligations of sovereignty will no longer require the British to look at India closely, and tabulate their knowledge of it in those bulky volumes that are in their own way as impressive a monument to the Raj as the Indian railways. India will continue to exercise its appeal, it will continue to say 'come', but those who come will not know what they have come for, and they will develop a new kind of expertise, which is to be measured only by the degree of their bafflement. India becomes necessary to Westerners as a focus for their modest self-awareness that their way of life and ways of thinking are limited. It can fill the inner emptiness, the cave in the heart that has come increasingly to define the Westerner's experience, but it can do so only for so long as it remains inexplicable. The visit to Mau has been a success for Fielding's wife: 'She found something, some solution of her queer troubles here.' India offers something, but what it offers is effective only so long as one cannot tell what the something is.

Stella, of course, need not bother about that. It is enough for her if India has made her feel better. But the case is different with Aziz,

who is an Indian. Aziz continues to write poems after he has come
to Mau, 'all on one topic – oriental womanhood':

> Bulbuls and roses would still persist, the pathos of defeated
> Islam remained in his blood and could not be expelled by
> modernities. Illogical poems – like their writer. Yet they struck a
> true note: there cannot be a mother-land without new homes.

It is a patronising, pertly offensive paragraph, but it serves at any
rate to show one thing. Indian and Western writers on India have
more in common than it is fashionable to admit. The task,
imagining India, is one that they share, and so are its difficulties.
But there remains a crucial difference. For Western writers the
failure to imagine India, the realisation that India is unfathomable,
can be presented as an imaginative triumph. Indian writers have
no such easy recourse. An absence, even if it does imply a
presence, is not a place one can comfortably live in. After Aziz's
acquittal, he is asked by Mr Das to write a poem, a poem not for
Hindus or Muslims but for 'Indians generally'. Aziz objects, 'There
is no such person in existence as the general Indian', and Mr Das
replies, 'There was not, but there may be when you have written a
poem.' Aziz's poem never gets written, and Aziz's somewhat
feeble attempts to write it are subordinated by Forster to his
Western need to find in India a solution for his own 'queer
troubles', but Aziz's project, his attempt to imagine 'the vague and
bulky figure of a mother-land', to clarify its vagueness and to
comprehend its bulk without lapsing into the limply general, is in
the end a more important project than Forster's. It is only the
Indian writer who can say with Mr Das, 'India does not exist, but it
may when I have written a poem.'

Notes and References

1. THE ENGLISH INDIAN NOVEL: *KIM* AND *MIDNIGHT'S CHILDREN*

1. The absolute number of Indians who have a good command of English is very large, around 13 million, but this represents only 2 per cent of the population.
2. This is, I am aware, a tactless thing to say: India is a secular state. But – whether we blame it on Jinnah and the creation of Pakistan, or see Jinnah responding to what he recognised as an inevitable historical logic, or whether we prefer to blame the British and their perverse desire to fragment the country that they were about to abandon – I find it impossible to doubt that India is a Hindu country, a country in which Hindus are in a huge majority, and in which they monopolise all real power. This is at any rate the view forcefully argued by Nirad Chaudhuri in his *The Continent of Circe* (Chatto and Windus, 1965).
3. Angus Wilson brilliantly observes as a recurrent feature in Kipling's work 'that transformation of a small space into a whole world which comes from the intense absorption of a child'. See his *The Strange Ride of Rudyard Kipling* (Secker and Warburg, 1977), p. 1.
4. Bengal, the Indian province in which education was most widespread, was also the first province in which nationalist politics took root.

2. THE INDIAN ENGLISH NOVEL: *NATION OF FOOLS* AND *THE MAN-EATER OF MALGUDI*

1. See V.S. Naipaul, *An Area of Darkness* (Andre Deutsch, 1964), p. 232.
2. It is Nataraj's assistant Sastri who identifies Vasu as showing 'all the definitions of a rakshasha'. He goes on to define a rakshasha as 'a demoniac creature who possessed enormous strength, strange powers, and genius, but recognized no sort of restraints of man or God'. But such a creature only 'thinks he is invincible, beyond every law . . . sooner or later something or other will destroy him.' Sastri recalls several examples to prove his point. The case closest to Vasu's is that of Brahmasura 'who acquired a special boon that everything he touched should be scorched, while nothing could ever destroy him'. In the end he was deceived by Vishnu into touching his own head, and was 'reduced to ashes that very second'.
3. See Graham Greene's introduction to R.K. Narayan *The Bachelor of Arts* (Heinemann, 1978).

195

3. RIDING THE BEAST: RUTH PRAWER JHABVALA IN INDIA

1. All quotations in which Ruth Prawer Jhabvala speaks in her own
    person are from her autobiographical essay 'Myself in India' in *How
    I Became a Holy Mother and Other Stories*' (Penguin, 1981). 'Rose
    Petals', 'The Housewife', 'In a Great Man's House' and 'Suffering
    Women' are also included in this volume. 'A Young Man of Good
    Family' is one of the collection of stories entitled *A Stronger Climate*
    (Granada, 1983).

4. THE QUIET AND THE LOUD: ANITA DESAI'S INDIA

1. Victoria Glendinning, *The Sunday Times*, 31 August 1980, p. 32.

5. THE POLITICS OF R.K. NARAYAN

1. See V.S. Naipaul, *India: A Wounded Civilization* (Penguin, 1979),
    pp. 18–27 and 37–43.
2. Srinivas does work. He edits a paper. But it is journalism of
    a peculiar kind, for Srinivas never finds time to leave his office.
    He offers his readers a kind of extended meditation rather
    than reporting. By all accounts Narayan's own efforts as editor
    of the short-lived *Indian Truth* had something in common with
    Srinivas's.
3. *The Painter of Signs* was serialised in the *Illustrated Weekly of India*
    before its publication in book form in 1976, so that Naipaul could
    have read it, at least in part, during his visit to India. It is probable,
    of course, that the whole or a large part of the novel was written
    before the formal Declaration of Emergency in June 1975, but the
    declaration was little more than a name-giving ceremony for a state
    of affairs that had already been in existence for two years.
4. A point also made by Salman Rushdie. In *Midnight's Children*
    (Jonathan Cape, 1981) the son of the child of midnight is born at the
    moment of the Declaration of Emergency.
5. See, for example, Gandhi's advice to Bharati on how to spend her
    time in prison: 'Wherever you may be with a copy of *Ramayana* and
    Gita, and a spinning wheel, there you are rightly employed.'
6. The Indian National Army, largely recruited from Indian prisoners
    of war. Chandra Bose believed the Germans and the Japanese to be
    India's natural allies in their struggle against the British. He planned
    to invade India with the cooperation of the Japanese, oust the
    British, and establish an independent government.
7. I do not claim that Narayan misrepresents Gandhi here or else-
    where. It would be possible, I believe, to document each of the
    utterances Narayan ascribes to Gandhi from Gandhi's own writings.

It is just that Narayan consistently resolves or minimises the paradoxes that lie at the centre both of Gandhi's character and his achievement. Compare, for example, the brief appearance of Gandhi in Mulk Raj Anand's *Untouchable* (Wishart Books, 1935). It seems to me clear that the less talented novelist has a firmer and truer grasp of these paradoxes than does Narayan.

8. The funeral of Sriram's aunt, during which she wakes up, seems a delightful comic interlude unrelated to the novel's main development, but, if I am correct, it offers in miniature a version of the novel's major theme, the miraculous triumph of continuity over the threat of sudden, abrupt change.

9. A technique noticed by William Walsh: *R.K. Narayan A Critical Appreciation* (Heinemann, 1982), p. 156.

0. Compare Rosie in R.K. Narayan, *The Guide* (Heinemann, 1980): 'Why did she call herself Rosie? ... She looked just the orthodox dancer that she was.' Rosie implicates Raju in her vocation, just as Daisy implicates Raman in hers, with similar disruptive results.

1. An exactly similar bag is carried by Raju's uncle in *The Guide*.

2. At the beginning of the novel Raman prides himself on being a rationalist, a mocker of superstitious credulity. He reads promiscuously in Indian and Western literature. His contact with Daisy forces him to accept that his boast of rationalism is a mere posture. By the end of the novel he has given up the attempt to lay himself open both to Indian and Western culture, and has retreated into his Indianness. In other words, his new sense of the sublimity of minding one's own business is implicated with a larger cultural isolationism.

3. Shiva Naipaul, 'The Emergency and the Meteor', *The Observer*, 11 January 1981, pp. 25–6.

4. Despite occasional liberal disclaimers, Naipaul seems on the whole to approve of the Emergency, largely because he understands it as a belated governmental recognition of the cultural crisis that his book is concerned to diagnose. The means by which he seeks to undermine his Western readers' prejudice against the exercise of totalitarian power are sometimes outrageous. The bulldozing of squatter settlements in Delhi is described as an example of urban renewal. Its opponents are represented by a middle-class woman who complains that domestic servants in Delhi are now hard to come by. Censorship of the Indian press is said to have improved its quality – by diverting its attention from trivial political quarrels to important social issues.

5. Walsh, *R.K. Narayan A Critical Appreciation*, p. 88.

6. Naipaul characteristically presents himself as a moral rather than a political commentator, but the stance from which he looks at the world is rational, utilitarian, individualist, an attitude now associated with radical Toryism, but which in the nineteenth century was thought to be typical of liberalism. Naipaul and Narayan might, then, both be described as conservatives, but, if so, they are conservatives of very different, indeed incompatible, kinds.

6. INDIAN TRAINS

1. Karl Marx, *Selected Writings,* ed. David McLellan (Oxford University Press, 1977), p. 335.
2. *The Cambridge History of India,* ed. H.H. Dodwell vol. VI, (Cambridge University Press, Cambridge, 1932), p. 344.
3. Colonel Robert J. Blackham, *Incomparable India Tradition; Superstition Truth* (Sampson Low, Marston, 1949), p 292.

7. INDIAN FUGUES

1. V.S. Naipaul, *India: A Wounded Civilization* (Penguin, 1979) pp. 102–4.
2. See V.S. Naipaul, *An Area of Darkness* (Andre Deutsch, 1964) pp. 205 and 209–16.

8. AN AREA OF DARKNESS

1. V.S. Naipaul, *Finding the Centre* (Penguin, 1985), p. 70.
2. Ibid, p. 69.
3. Naipaul, as one might expect, has a sympathetic understanding o the difficulty of autobiography for those who have been radically separated by a Westernised education from the culture into which they were born. See, for example, his account of the difficulties experienced by the Indonesian poet, Sitor, in his attempt to write an autobiography in *Among the Believers* (Penguin, 1982), pp. 286–96.

9. INDIAN AUTOBIOGRAPHY

1. See Robert Payne: *The Life and Death of Mahatma Gandhi* (The Bodley Head, 1969), p. 234.
2. See V.S. Naipaul, *An Area of Darkness* (Andre Deutsch, 1964) pp. 76–81.
3. A Royal Commission headed by Sir John Simon was appointed by the British Parliament in 1927 to investigate the workings of the 1920 Constitution for India, but its true purpose was, it was believed by the Indian Congress, to furnish evidence that could be used to justify the continuance of the Raj.
4. The five are *Daddyji* (1972), *Mamaji* (1979), *Vedi* (1982), *The Ledge Between the Streams* (1984), and *Sound-Shadows of the New World* (1986).

10. SEX IN THE INDIAN NOVEL

1. In Ruth Prawer Jhabvala, *How I Became a Holy Mother and Other Stories* (Penguin, 1981).
2. In the work of R.K. Narayan I can think of only one example of an inter-racial sexual relationship. In *The Vendor of Sweets* Jagan's son Mali returns from America with a Korean girlfriend. Jagan sees the two sitting together in the back seat of a car, their legs pressed together. He averts his eyes. So does Narayan. He has no interest in their relationship beyond a general sense of its unseemliness. Anita Desai is a friend of Ruth Jhabvala's, and has clearly been influenced by her, but this, Ruth Jhabvala's central theme, rarely catches her attention. Nayantara Sahgal is at least as interested in the relationship between the East and the West as any of the European novelists that I discuss. In *Rich Like Us*, Rosie, a rather unconvincingly imagined Cockney, becomes the second wife of Ram, an Indian businessman. But Nayantara Sahgal is uninterested in their sexual relationship. Her most recent novel, *Plans for Departure*, concerns the experience of a young Danish girl, Anna Hansen, in the months she spends in a small Indian hill station. For the European reader the most remarkable aspect of her experience of India is that she remains throughout this time entirely chaste.
3. Edward Said, *Orientalism*, (Penguin, 1985), p. 203. Said is quoting Nietzsche.
4. In fact, and significantly, only half-Indian.
5. J.R. Ackerley, *Hindoo Holiday An Indian Journal* (Penguin, 1983), p. 273.
6. Forster's convention survives. In Andrew Harvey's *One Last Mirror* (Jonathan Cape, 1985), which is set in Ceylon, the English protagonist is a homosexual. Christopher Isherwood seems to think that the convention is firmly enough established to be played with. *A Meeting by the River* (Methuen, 1967), concerns an encounter in Bengal between two English brothers, one a film producer, the other about to become a Hindu monk. It is the film producer who has had an affair with an American called Peter. But the point is that his claims to take a sympathetic interest in his brother's religious beliefs and to be deeply in love with Peter are equally fraudulent. When his plane takes off from Calcutta, he retreats at once from Indian spirituality to Hollywood wheeler-dealing, and from Peter to the safe heterosexuality of his marriage.
7. The least expected exponent of this craft is Forster's Superintendent McBryde who is at one point reported by Mrs Callendar to be patrolling the bazaars of Chandrapore 'disguised as a Holy Man'.
8. In Ruth Prawer Jhabvala, *A Stronger Climate* (Granada, 1983).
9. In Ruth Prawer Jhabvala, *How I Became a Holy Mother and Other Stories* (Penguin, 1981).
10. There are, of course, even in Ruth Jhabvala's novels, exceptions to

this rule; notably the marriage between Judy and Bal in *A Backwar*
Place (Penguin, 1980), and the relationship between the narrato
and Inder Lal in *Heat and Dust* (Futura, 1976).

11. THE HILL OF DEVI AND HEAT AND DUST

1. Ackerley discreetly alters the name of the state and its ruler t
    Chhokrapur.
2. On 21 December 1927, the Maharajah's son fled from Dewas an
    sought the protection of the Assistant Governor-General. H
    claimed that his father had been trying to poison him. Forste
    disbelieves the story, but there were bullet holes in the car in whic
    the young man made his escape.
3. Forster recounts the anecdote in 'Notes on the English Character' i
    Abinger Harvest (Edward Arnold, 1936).
4. Malcolm Darling, *Apprentice to Power India 1904–1908* (The Hogart
    Press, 1966), p. 180.
5. Ibid, p. 242.
6. The text of the broadcast is given in *The Hill of Devi and other India*
    writings, ed. Elizabeth Heine (Edward Arnold, 1983), pp. 237–40.
7. Darling, *Apprentice to Power India 1904–1908*, p. 253.
8. Ibid, p. 131.
9. I find it significant that not long after Darling came to Dewas h
    wrote letters to the *Times of India* and the *Tribune* of Lahor
    protesting against the deportation to Burma of two anti-Britis
    agitators. The letters are honourable, but could only have bee
    understood by Darling's fellow civil servants as a betrayal. Hi
    comment on the political agent responsible for Dewas is als
    illuminating: 'neither I nor H.H. had any doubts about Spence: w
    both felt at home with him from the start'. He seems to assume tha
    he and the Maharajah had exactly the same requirements of
    political agent.
10. Darling, *Apprentice to Power India 1904–1908*, p. 183.
11. In *Heat and Dust* the Nawab sometimes treats the English peopl
    that he despises with 'that exaggerated courtesy that Olivia ha
    learned to recognize as his way of expressing contempt'.
12. The story is told by P.N. Furbank, *E.M. Forster A Life*, vol. 2 (Secke
    and Warburg, 1978), pp. 28–9. Furbank's conclusion is mor
    cautious than my own: 'Whether a word was spoken to th
    Maharajah is not clear; if it was, it had no effect.'
13. The manuscript is published in Forster, *The Hill of Devi and othe*
    Indian writings, pp. 310–14.
14. Typical, it seems, of Indian princes. Ackerley, speaking to th
    Maharajah of Chhatarpur's prime minister is told, 'You may b
    sure, for instance, that he knows very well that you are walkin
    with Babaji Rao and me at this moment.'

12.   A PASSAGE TO INDIA

1.   In Forster's broadcast 'Three Countries'. See Forster, *The Hill of Devi and other Indian writings*, p. 298.
2.   See Malcolm Bradbury, 'Two Passages to India: Forster as Victorian and Modern' in *Aspects of E.M. Forster*, ed. Oliver Stallybrass (Edward Arnold, 1969), pp. 123–42
3.   See Gillian Beer, 'Negation in *A Passage to India*', *Essays in Criticism*, vol. XXX (1969), pp. 44–58

Index